Dearest Phylabe

Dearest Phylabe

Letters From Wartime England
by Edith Base

Edited by
Benjamin F. Byerly and
Catherine Ridder Byerly

Introduction by
Stephen T. Powers

University Press of Colorado

© 1996 by the University Press of Colorado

Published by the University Press of Colorado
P. O. Box 849
Niwot, Colorado 80544
Tel. 303-530-5337

The University Press of Colorado is a cooperative publishing enterprise supported, in part, by Adams State College, Colorado State University, Fort Lewis College, Mesa State College, Metropolitan State College of Denver, University of Colorado, University of Northern Colorado, University of Southern Colorado, and Western State College of Colorado.

Library of Congress Cataloging-in-Publication Data

Base, Edith, 1903-
    Dearest Phylabe : letters from wartime England / Edith Base ;
    edited by Benjamin F. Byerly and Catherine Ridder Byerly ;
    introduction by Stephen T. Powers.
          p.   cm.
    ISBN 0-87081-421-4 (alk. paper)
        1. Base, Edith, 1903–   —Correspondence.   2. Houston, Phylabe,
    1910–   —Correspondence.   3. World War, 1939–1945—Personal
    narratives, British.   4. World War, 1939–1945—Great Britain.
    5. Women—Great Britain—Correspondence.   I. Byerly, Benjamin F.
    II. Byerly, Catherine Ridder.   III. Title.
    D811.5.B2618   1996
    940.54'8141–dc20   95-50196
                                                                    CIP

This book was set in ITC New Baskerville and ITC American Typewriter.

The paper used in this publication meets the minimum requirements of the American National Standard for Information Sciences—Permanence of Paper for Printed Library Materials. ANSI Z39.48–1948
∞

10   9   8   7   6   5   4   3   2   1

Contents

Acknowledgments   vii

Introduction   1
Benjamin F. Byerly, Catherine Ridder Byerly,
and *Stephen T. Powers*

August 4, 1941–December 10, 1941   35

January 17, 1942–December 10, 1942   44

May 8, 1943–November 19, 1943   82

January 26, 1944–December 28, 1944   95

January 27, 1945–December 14, 1945   131

January 14, 1946–December 29, 1946   162

January 20, 1947–September 2, 1947   188

Acknowledgments

The editors wish to express their indebtedness to Dr. Marvin Ernst, the former associate dean of the Graduate School at the University of Northern Colorado, and to Mrs. Geri Harding, who typed the manuscript. Thanks are also extended to friends and colleagues of the University of Northern Colorado Department of History and Michener Library, who encouraged us in the completion of this project. Finally, we are especially grateful to Phylabe Houston, who preserved the letters and constantly encouraged the editorial work, and Edith Base Bacon, who placed her World War II diary at our disposal, critically read the introduction and the edited letters, wrote a short biographical sketch, and unselfishly gave of her time, literary skills, and journalistic experience.

B.F.B.
C.R.B.
S.T.P.

Dearest Phylabe

Introduction

The correspondence in this volume provides a very intimate and individualized account of everyday life in wartime London at the hand of a highly literate and acute observer. Sometimes written while bombs were falling and the author, Edith Base, was in a shelter or on duty as an air-raid warden, the letters were, in many instances, a form of therapeutic exercise. Through them Edith sought psychological relief and escape from the drudgery, the endless boredom, the bone-numbing fatigue, and the inescapable fear in a city besieged.

In addition to the vivid picture presented of life on the home front, the letters dating from the postwar period reveal the frustration and impatience of the English people who had suffered through the war years but saw no appreciable improvement in their condition and prospects. The rationing, the interminable shortages, and the endless queues continued long after the victory in Europe.

But Edith's letters are more than a report on conditions and events in London and England. They express her hopes and aspirations both for the cessation of hostilities and for a better world after the war. They reveal the very personal conflict concerning the fundamental principles of human decency and the condition of mankind. Like the "confessions" and "apologiae" of every age, her letters bear evidence of a deeply troubled mind. Her Christian humanism, with its unbounded faith in education and the capacity for human improvement, was sorely tried by the revival of anti-Semitism, the rabid nationalism of the "patriotic Hampsteadians," and the thinly veiled fascism of those advocating capital punishment for the striking apprentices. Her social conscience was seriously disturbed by the dilemma of being employed by a "rampant Tory," whose policies ran counter to her own humanistic principles and those of the Socialist government she supported. Her intense concern for the status of women was subordinated during the war to

1

the greater cause, but her letters reveal a sharp sensitivity to the chauvinism and social injustice of the times. It was bitterly frustrating for her to be saddled with the "Martha chores," a heavy editorial obligation—often with insufficient help—and to be constantly reminded by smug employers that women do not have the creative ability of men and are actually poorer workers because they are distracted by domestic problems and should, therefore, be paid less.

After the war ended, Edith was only slightly less outraged by the defacing of the English countryside by industrial capitalism than she had been by the destruction of Hitler's bombers. She was quick to point out that the artistic and architectural sacrileges wrought by the seventeenth-century dictator and religious fanatic Oliver Cromwell were no less an abomination than those committed by his twentieth-century counterparts. But in spite of the soul-searching and the occasional note of pessimism, there is no doubt about Edith's ultimate faith in the inherent goodness of humankind. She found this faith confirmed aesthetically and spiritually in the parish churches and great Gothic cathedrals; poetically, in the words of John Donne and his vision of the unity of mankind; and musically, proclaimed in the oratorio of Sir Michael Tippett. This then is the spirit expressed in Edith's letters that found such a receptive reader in Phylabe Houston and formed the basis of their deep and enduring friendship.

The letters of Edith Base to Phylabe Houston of Greeley, Colorado, span the years 1941 to 1987, but only those written before September 1947, when Edith became Mrs. Cecil Bacon, have been included in this volume. The letters that emanated from London were generally typed, whereas those written during holidays or at odd moments of the day were penned in ink or, less frequently, in pencil. They are, in all cases, quite legible except for the occasional one or two that were carelessly censored with resulting lacunas on both sides of the page. Censored materials are indicated by ellipses, as are those that have been deleted because of redundancies or for personal reasons. By great good fortune no letters were lost in transit during the war, but unhappily several loaned by the recipient were never recovered.

The material in this introduction has been drawn from a variety of sources: an autobiographical sketch written by Edith in 1985; a journal kept by her for the first month of the war, which includes clippings of articles she wrote for the Newcastle papers; personal interviews with the subjects; Edith's wartime letters; and numerous contemporary newspapers, periodicals, and books on World War II.

In the summer of 1936 Phylabe Houston accompanied a friend on a coastal cruise to Alaska. On their return, they stopped at Victoria, British Columbia, for some sightseeing. While discussing at breakfast what to see in Victoria, they were overheard by a young Canadian woman, Bessie Crowther, who offered to map out an itinerary for their visit. The women exchanged names and addresses and, after Phylabe arrived home, she wrote to thank Bessie and invite her to visit in Colorado.

Bessie Crowther accepted this invitation in 1939 on her return from England where she had been visiting relatives. Like many foreigners caught abroad in the months preceding the outbreak of the war, Bessie made the decision to leave England very suddenly. According to the story often told by Phylabe Houston, Bessie embarked for home on the last ship to sail before the start of hostilities. She had been scheduled to leave on an earlier crossing, but at the last minute had relinquished her place to a man who was desperate to accompany his family, already on board. Bessie had no time to retrieve her luggage and it was all lost when that ship, the *Athenia*, was sunk on its voyage to America.

Bessie, in later years, remembered a somewhat different sequence of events. She had booked passage on the *Athenia* but sailed a week earlier on the *Antonia*, a ship that had been held over to take on passengers from Southampton. Because she changed her plans so abruptly, some of her luggage was loaded on the *Athenia* and was lost when that ship went down.

The SS *Athenia*, the first British passenger liner of the war sunk by a German U-boat, was attacked by mistake. After war broke out in September 1939, Adolf Hitler, hoping to avoid another *Lusitania* incident, issued specific orders that his submarines were not to attack British passenger ships. His orders were disobeyed by Captain Fritz-Julius Lemp of the *U–30*, much to the Führer's displeasure. The Germans could not hide the fact that the *Athenia* had been sunk by a submarine and, a few months later, they lifted the ban against attacks on passenger ships. All British shipping became fair game.

On her arrival at Phylabe's home, Bessie was full of news of the developing crisis in England and very enthusiastic about a cousin, Edith Base, whom she had met for the first time. Her English cousin had been to the United States and Canada as a representative of the Soroptimists and was at the time on the staff of the *Newcastle Journal*. Bessie suggested that Phylabe might like to correspond with Edith and later sent some of her cousin's letters from wartime England to Phylabe. This casual suggestion was to produce a pen-pal relationship that would span more than forty years, surviving the disruptions of a world war, the strain of international upheavals following the war, and drastic changes in the personal lives of the two women involved.

Phylabe Houston first wrote to Edith Base in 1941 and, after some delay, Edith answered. The letters continued at more or less regular intervals and soon between the two women "there grew to be a wonderful empathy," as Edith described the relationship.

> We shared our thoughts, opinions, experiences and Atlantic-crossing friends. We let down our hair on matters ethical, political, social, literary and personal. I think we reached an intimacy quite unusually close.
>
> But we have never met.
>
> Of course I have often wished we could. But my freedom to travel was limited by staffwork and a need to watch expenditures; and Phylabe, though I imagine she could have come to England without hindrance, never did. Was it possibly just as well? Pen-friendships have been known to founder when the participants personally met. And for writing people especially, perhaps,—for they may easily be temperamentally solitary and shy—it is easier to "open up" on paper than face to face. Phylabe and I did not suffer many barriers of hesitance or reserve in our letters, but on the occasions when we talked on the telephone, I tended to get tensed up and tongue-tied.

Two more different women are difficult to visualize—one English, the other a western American; one an urban career woman, the other, having turned her back on a teaching position, a family-oriented woman living close to the land; one thriving on travel and activity, the other, partly due to health problems and partly from choice, a homebody bent on shaping her small corner of the world.

Perhaps the sharpest contrast in the lives of the two women stems from their markedly different backgrounds. Edith was born and raised in the north of England, steeped in tradition and custom. Her surroundings were lush green fields and wooded areas; her world is full of flowers and foliage. Phylabe's, in contrast, is a new land, open prairie, an area at one time called the Great American Desert. The very existence of settlements depended on irrigation. The trees surrounding her home and shading the town were barely a half-century old, many having been planted since the turn of the century.

Phylabe Houston was born 15 September 1910 in Greeley, Colorado, a city incorporated only twenty-six years before. Greeley had its roots in a semi-communal enterprise fostered in 1870 by Nathan Meeker, one-time agricultural editor of the *New York Tribune*, with the enthusiastic support of Horace Greeley, in whose honor the town was named. Phylabe's grandfather, Burton Sanborn, had joined the Union Colony in its first year and had become a very influential man in the community. He has, in fact, been credited with much of the colony's success, having had the foresight to see that the future depended on an adequate water supply. He envisioned, developed, and owned Boyd Lake, the largest local reservoir not developed by a city or government agency.

Phylabe's father, George M. Houston, moved to Greeley from Otis, a farming community on the eastern Colorado plains, in 1890 to attend the recently founded normal school. He first worked as a gardener and handyman for Nathan Meeker's widow, Arvilla, and her daughter, Rosene Skewes. When the Meekers could no longer afford to keep him, George Houston offered his services to the Sanborns. After graduation from the normal school and a year's teaching at Otis, Houston returned to Greeley, where he became a partner in the Sanborn real estate business. He later married Gladys Sanborn and they lived on a large farm to the west of town.

George Houston quickly became a respected figure in Greeley, serving both on the board of trustees of the school he had attended and as mayor of his adopted city, a position he held at the time of Phylabe's birth. He also served as director of the board of the Greeley and Loveland Irrigation Company (1923–1935) and as secretary of the Mountain States Beet Growers' Association. In 1935, he was elected to the upper house of the Colorado Legislature.

Phylabe's early years were passed in this atmosphere of community service. She attended the public schools, and the summer heat and monotony were broken by visits to Estes Park, the popular mountain resort. On one of these outings Phylabe met the family of the noted Kansas newspaper editor, William Allen White, and went climbing with his daughter, Mary. This idyllic life ended shortly after Phylabe's twelfth birthday, when her mother, only thirty-eight years old, died; four years later George Houston remarried.

The Great Depression that began in 1929 had affected agricultural communities such as Greeley somewhat earlier, and, about the time Phylabe was to graduate from high school, bank foreclosures began in earnest throughout Weld County. In the resulting slump, the Houstons lost their home and the greater part of their land. They were left with some forty acres of mostly rocky soil that the bank considered worthless. Mr. Houston rented a small home in town and purchased some acres of dryland east of Greeley, which he farmed throughout most of the war years.

Phylabe was able to continue her education at the normal school, then called Colorado State Teacher's College, thanks to an advance on a legacy received from her maternal grandmother. She graduated in four years with a degree in English and accepted a position in a rural school district. She stayed five years, part of the time in a house with no electricity or running water, then returned to Greeley to begin work on a master's degree. Two years later she again tried her hand at teaching, but this situation proved even less satisfying than the earlier experience. Disillusioned with the profession, Phylabe returned to Greeley to care for her sick stepmother.

Greeley by the 1940s had grown to a population of 15,995, the fourth largest city in Colorado, and was noted for a compact business district, wide streets, and well-groomed residential areas. The economy was still agriculturally based, a fact that assumed greater importance with the approach of the war. Beans became a prime commodity for export, especially to England under the Lend-Lease agreement. The early disruption of the sugar cane industry in the islands emphasized the need for vigorous sugar beet production for home consumption, as well as for export. To meet the manpower shortage that developed after the United States entry into the war, the Weld County farmers turned to the women of the community, and by 1942 half of the 7,500 beet workers in the county were women. The Japanese internment camps and a German POW camp west of town also supplied labor for planting and harvesting.

During the war years, Phylabe worked for a time at the Army Air Force Technical Training School that operated under the auspices of the teacher's college, and later at the POW camp. For most of the war years, though, she was farming with her father on the dryland east of Greeley. It was from these colorless, somewhat isolated, fields that she often walked miles to the mailbox in hopes of a letter from Edith.

Edith's letters fascinated Phylabe with their descriptions of a world so different from hers; they became her more immediate contact with the war and her response in letters and packages was her personal contribution to the war effort. But early in their correspondence Phylabe realized that Edith's letters deserved a wider audience. She shared them with friends in Greeley, and, more important, she kept them very carefully preserved, always with a hope of their being published.

Edith Base was born in Gateshead-on-Tyne, near the Scottish border and not far from the sea, on 29 July 1903. When she was five years old, her father gave up work as a guard with the North Eastern Railway and the family moved to Whickham in County Durham, where Mr. Base formed a partnership with a brother-in-law in a small building venture. The business, however, "was shattered one night when a terrace of new houses they built subsided into an unsuspected worked-out coal mine!" The Bases lived in one of the houses and Edith, six or seven at the time, remembers "the excitement of climbing out of the slipped and sliding bedroom and seeing our neighbors in their bedroom through the cracks in the wall." The 1914–1918 war and the Great Depression brought further setbacks in the family's economic fortunes.

The young Edith always pictured herself as an author, usually of great novels "like *Heart of Midlothian* and *Middlemarch*—deep human stuff. . . . But I had to earn my living, right from school." And so in the autumn of 1919, at age sixteen, Edith started training on the broadly conservative *Newcastle Journal,* a morning daily that dated from 1702. The *Journal*'s editor, Mr. F. T. Souden, greatly influenced Edith's views that a newspaper should be a responsible voice in a community and present news objectively and fairly. She spent twenty years (in two periods) on the *Journal,* working as a reporter, sub-editor, columnist, critic, and specialist on women's issues and editor of the daily women's page.

The First World War had just ended when Edith started to work for the *Newcastle Journal*. As she writes:

> I remember that I reneged on having grown up and went back for a day to being a schoolgirl so as to walk in the Victory Parade in our village ... and claim a china mug and a free (child's) tea at the Celebration. These benefits realized, however, I had to pin up my long plaits in a grown-up bun for good and all and, as it happened, cross the line "where womanhood and childhood meet" right into a prime expansionist period in English women's history. The first lot of women had just, in 1918, got the vote and achieved a small step towards equality—having rather forcefully demanded it through the Suffragist movement, and then shown how they merited it by doing war-work. Now they were organizing themselves into active and varied associations, clubs and societies, and young Miss Base of the *Journal* found herself as a reporter involved in many of these.

She joined or was an honorary member of the League of Nations Union, the Housewives' Union, the National Council of Women, the International Council of Women, the Guild of Empire, the Women's Freedom League, and many others. She was a founder member of the Newcastle chapters of the Soroptimists and the Business and Professional Women, and was later elected Founder President of the Soroptimists. In 1938 Edith traveled to the United States to attend the international convention of the Soroptimist movement in Atlantic City, and with the English delegation visited New York, Washington, Philadelphia, and Toronto, Canada.

On two occasions Edith left Newcastle and the *Journal*.

> For a few years I roamed away from Newcastle "to widen my experience" and, having advertised myself in that early feminist organ *Time and Tide*, accepted an invitation to "help with her literary work" (for which read "ghost," but I hadn't heard of that form of literary activity then) that Socialist Countess of Warwick, Frances, who had been a favourite of the Prince of Wales (later Edward VII) and later tried to blackmail the Crown into paying her a lot of money for his love-letters. (She was rather cleverly stymied by a matter of copyright, and it was all kept very secret, though it nearly got out in the United States, which didn't then, in 1914, subscribe to international copyright law). I knew nothing about such colourful strands

in her life, of course; my deep reason for joining her was that I was still expecting to become a novelist, and as novels at that time tended to be set in aristocratic circles, I thought a little first-hand knowledge of high life would authenticate my backgrounds!

I enjoyed a very interesting stay with Lady Warwick, her fourteen lap-dogs, her vicious old parrot and her monkeys (not to mention the mice that used to come out of the parlour wainscot to join us for afternoon tea); but the work was not what I wanted, and I was not what she needed, so I did not stay long. She very kindly put me in touch with Mr. J.W. Robertson Scott, who was in the early days of building up his quarterly magazine, *The Countryman*—so to *The Countryman*, produced from a mellow old manor-house in delectable Cotswold country, I went, and working for that demonic tyrant of an editor (but in a team of delightful, starry-eyed and most variously talented girls) was an education in much more than literary journalism! . . . I left him after a more than usually fierce disagreement, but we made it up later, and I used to visit him when he was very old and had become touchingly gentle. He left me (and others who had worked with him at that time) a remembrance in his will.

Edith left the Cotswold country with deep regret and returned to Newcastle and newspaper work. Her years on the *Journal* furnished her with many interesting assignments. One of her earliest interviews was with Lady Astor, Britain's first woman Member of Parliament.

A decade or more later, Edith Base interviewed Lillian Gish, then playing at the Theatre Royal; Alfaretta Hallam, an early expositor of auto-suggestion or "applied psychology"; and Aimee Semple McPherson, the flamboyant Christian evangelist.

Then there was Eddie Cantor. I have the happiest recollection of that great little man. He was on a whirlwind tour raising money to settle Jewish orphans in the new State of Palestine, and when I went to his hotel to see him he called out from somewhere in his suite "Come right in here." Only just in the nick of time did I realize that "here" was the bathroom and Eddie was right there in the tub! He emerged, in a bath-robe, in due course to be properly interviewed, and later that evening, in the Grand Assembly Rooms, where he was charming huge donations out of a quite pyxilated audience (enthusing dozens of them to "adopt" or sponsor a child), he spotted me in the front row with my notebook and called "Why, hello, there," with apparent delight, and proceeded to tell the world about our not-quite encounter in the bathroom.

THEN, with everybody laughing and happy, he spurred them on to a whole new riot of giving by telling them (and Me!) that "this charming lady reporter" had done so much to help him that he was going to sponsor a little girl for adoption in my name. . . .

Edith stayed in Newcastle on the *Journal* till the paper was sold and its policies were substantially changed. She then applied for and received a position as Women's Press Liaison Officer at the Ministry of Labour headquarters in London, where Mr. Ernest Bevin then held a powerful post as Minister. It was from London that all but one of the wartime letters to Greeley were addressed.

Coming as it did toward the end of the summer of 1939, the outbreak of war in Europe caught many Britons on holiday. Edith Base was one of a group of English people enjoying a welcome August heat-wave on the coast of Brittany. The news of Germany's pact with Russia and the subsequent invasion of Poland filled them with consternation and uncertainty as to what course to take. As Edith tells us in a diary she kept of those early months of war:

> . . . there was a conference of English holiday-makers in the Vieux Moulin as to whether we should go home. Several people decided to leave next morning, Friday [25 August]; we decided to wait a while.
>
> Friday was a troubled sort of day—in spite of glorious sunshine and a happy time on the beach—waiting for news. After the 6 o'clock English news, we decided to stay at any rate till Monday. . . . Then in the 9 o'clock news, English people abroad were advised to get home, so sadly we decided to pack up and travel home by the Saturday night boat.
>
> Saturday morning, we had a last sunbathe and a last shopping expedition to the bourg, and after lunch packed our bags. Just as we finished . . . other people staying in the hotel, came back from Dinard to say Cook's advised them (and us) to stay till Tuesday. They said the boats were intolerably crowded—500 [people] left on the quay on Saturday morning. So joyfully we unpacked again and dashed down to the beach for a bathe—snatched right out of Hitler's hands, we felt, drat the man! We lay rapturously on the beach till dinnertime, and only listened to the news as a matter of duty.

It was easy to forget Hitler on the beach on Sunday. It was simply heaven there. We lay all day in the sun, and my skin turned golden. I'd never spent that kind of holiday before, and gosh! how I enjoyed it. We felt frantically anxious to stay. But on Monday . . . Cook's . . . advised getting home as quickly as possible. Our hearts slumped with a bang right to the bottom of our boots.

We traveled home on the Tuesday night boat, but spent an afternoon in St. Malo first. . . .

The boat was misery—literally not room to stand chairs on deck. We clung to places on the wooden deck seats even though the heaters under them scorched our sunburnt legs. An American family clinging to the opposite seat were having a marvelous European trip cut miserably short—couldn't get to Paris at all. The most stupendous thunderstorm took place while we were waiting to leave St. Malo (we were 3 hours on the boat before she left), all the time sitting on this hot seat, not daring to leave her in case we were left without a seat at all. When the boat sailed, however, we were lucky and got two berths among [four of] us. . . . Not that berths were any great picnic! The ship was traveling without lights, so all the ports were shut and the heat was enough to roast you. Still, we got our legs stretched and all slept a little.

While the blackout provisions may seem excessive for a Channel boat, remember that the *Athenia* was torpedoed west of Scotland on 3 September with the loss of 118 lives and Bessie Crowther's luggage. Arriving in London safely and hoping to finish their holiday there, Edith and a friend had a day at the zoo and a movie and planned on staying till Friday night, but:

the evening papers announced that all evacuation-area children were to be evacuated the next day. Joyce wanted to get home before her sister Rosemary left, so we dashed for King's Cross. The 7.25 train North was running in triplicate, and there wasn't a seat to spare on our part. Also, the train was traveling without lights. We had one dim blue bulb in our compartment—a dismal journey. . . . Much of the country was blacked-out though not all places.

Edith's mention of the evacuation of children from specified areas and the blacked-out countryside indicates the speed with which the British government implemented policies for civilian life under conditions of total war. The removal of children, mothers of infants, and invalids from major population centers was carried out with amazing efficiency. More than 600,000 were evacuated from

London and thousands more from other metropolitan areas. The problems encountered in this process involved more than just the physical aspects of locating housing and means of transportation. Edith describes the more personal side in an article she wrote for the *Newcastle Journal:*

> Evacuation's no easy matter! I felt yesterday that to be a house-holder having three or four strange children let loose upon you and perhaps a teething baby or a rampageous lad among them, must be the most trying thing in the world. Then I felt that to be an evacuee, thrust into a strange new world, full of doubts about your future, must be even harder to endure. Then it seemed to me that nobody on earth could have a more difficult job than the local authorities and the teachers, trying to reconcile these two sets of people and satisfy so many individual wants and tastes.

The luckiest children, according to another of Edith's articles in the *Newcastle Journal and North Mail,* were those from St. Lawrence's Roman Catholic School, Byker, who found themselves in a Y.M.C.A. seaside holiday camp.

> Instead of Byker's chimney pots, when they wake up in the morn-ing they see the sea, just a stone's throw away from them; instead of trolley buses they hear seagulls and waves, and instead of fishing for tiddlers in the nearest park lake (not so very near, either), they now catch crabs on the beach.
> "What are you going to do with that, sonny?" inquired a Camp Commandant of the urchin clambering proudly up to camp with a crab.
> "Why, boil the beggor," he replied.

Despite the government's good intentions and Edith's first impres-sions, the evacuation was not an unqualified success.

The temporary blackout measures that Edith had witnessed on her return from London soon gave way to all-out procedures. Orders were posted on 3 September for a complete blackout that night. Because dark fabric was already at a premium, Edith bought some thick brown paper from a street vendor for 3s. a sheet. Not until mid-September was she able to purchase some black Italian cloth, part of a consignment of 8,000 yards that the shopkeeper sold between the time of its arrival on Friday afternoon and 1:30 the next day.

The early temporary methods that people used to shut in the light were not completely successful and the wardens were often high-handed in their methods of enforcing the precautions. Many threatened to confiscate bulbs or ordered offices shut, if even the faintest light was showing. Edith vented her exasperation:

> These small people invested with a little brief authority! What would a bomber 5 miles up see of these faint suggestions of light.
>
> Besides, this utter blackness is dangerous. Going home tonight I was astonished to *hear* tramcars and not be able to see them! They carry one faint blue light on the front and one on the back. Otherwise they have *no* shape in the blackness . . . and crossing the street is terrifying. What driving must be like, heaven knows.

Driving was, in fact, very hazardous, particularly in London, where deaths from road accidents for the month of September jumped to 1,130 from 554 the previous year. During the first six months of the war, more fatalities were registered for civilians than among the combatants in France. To curtail the rising number of accidents, pedestrians were urged to pause before going from a lighted room into a dark street in order to accustom their eyes to the darkness. They were further advised to wear light-colored clothing and accessories and to carry a newspaper—advice scarcely needed in London at any time. Enterprising tailors and dressmakers were soon offering white belts and hat bands, together with white trouser stripes and umbrella bands. Women were encouraged to wear white stockings, but their reaction to this suggestion was less than enthusiastic.

Yet another sartorial change was prompted by the mandatory gas mask. Fashionable shops and street hawkers were soon offering attractive, appropriately colored covers for gas mask containers. Edith bought a white oilcloth cover, cost 3s., which had the added merit of standing out at night. Predictably, Londoners placed a nuisance value on the gas masks and often left them behind in public places, especially on buses and trains.

The earliest air-raid alert Edith experienced caused a near-panic in her parent's household at Whickham. At 11 A.M., the very day the war was announced, while her father was out on Air Raid Precaution duty, the sirens wailed:

Mother began to cry. The poor little soul. It was a good job in a way, for it gave Chrissie and me something to do. Mother had never tried her gas mask on, so Chrissie—who is a trained A.R.P. warden—persuaded her to try it. She got panicky inside it, but Chrissie was awfully good with her. In the meantime I got on with sweeping up the room. Father, in warden's tin hat and long boots blew in to say "Get your gas masks ready, and if you hear bombing get up there among the apple trees. But it may not be anything much." He looked a bit troubled to me, all the same.

Very soon after, the all-clear sounded. Later we learned the warning had been given all over the country on account of one doubtful-looking aircraft seen over the Channel! Comforting to think communication is so instant; nevertheless, several cases were reported of deaths from shock.

A little over a month later, however, a much calmer attitude is expressed in regard to a possible raid. On 17 October Edith wrote in her journal:

> Yesterday the Germans caught us napping and made an air raid on the Forth, and since Mr. Chamberlain rejected Hitler's peace terms and we have begun to feel that this shadow war ought now really to have begun, all of us have been expecting a raid here.
>
> This afternoon the warbling note of the warning went. I had just finished lunch at the flat. With Mrs. Collins, my char, Miss Mac-Fadzean, just recovering from quinsy, and half a dozen of the other tenants, I went down to our basement shelter. Semi-basement, rather, thank goodness. The sun streamed in at the window on the south side. Nothing else happened! Miss Sevenoaks brought us tea, Mrs. Park brought a hot water bottle for Miss Mac-Fadzean and tucked her up in a rug, Mrs. Collins read the *Express* (which bore a banner head I could read across the room, Air Raid on Scotland Completely Fails. What a lie! They got right over— 300 ft. above a destroyer in the Forth, without a warning being sounded or a shot fired, they dropped bombs, sank a couple of pinnaces, damaged a warship and killed and wounded 35 people), and I did my week's darning.
>
> Every now and again I popped up to the street. Each time the same pair of lovers sat peacefully in the park (beside the air-raid trenches!), two nuns from the convent next door were quietly facing the street, and the dustman was sitting smoking on the handle of his barrow. May all the air raids be like it!

Here, Edith's information was not entirely accurate. The attack on shipping in the Firth of Forth on 16 October was the first air raid on Britain. The cruisers *Southampton* and *Edinburgh* and the destroyer *Mohawk* were damaged. Two Junker 88s from Stab I/KG30 were shot down by Spitfires and a third was damaged. The Luftwaffe raided Scapa Flow twice on the 17th and reports of enemy air activity elsewhere triggered several false alerts, one of which Edith experienced in Newcastle.

The war brought grave financial repercussions to Britons of all classes. Before the end of September 1939, the Chancellor of the Exchequer presented his first war budget to the nation. Old taxes had to be increased astronomically and new taxes devised. The income tax was to be raised the first year from 27.5 percent to 35 percent and for the second year of the war an increment of 37 percent was projected. Exemptions were severely cut. Unmarried men earning only £2. 10s. ($10) per week were taxed and a surtax was placed on incomes of more than £2,000 ($8,000). For the very wealthy, the taxes were virtually confiscatory—a capitalist earning £100,000 ($400,000) per annum paid 80 percent in taxes. An excess profits tax of 60 percent, previously assessed against war industries only, was now levied on all businesses and the death duties also increased by as much as 20 percent.

Perhaps the most unpopular of the new taxes were those on everyday items—certain foods, notably sugar, wine, whiskey, and tobacco. Edith noted in her journal: "The Budget tonight! Income Tax up to 7s. 6d.!! Comical in the office to hear everybody as he came in say 'What's the Budget like?' and be told 'penney a pint on beer!'"

But of all the adjustments made necessary by the war, the average Briton was soon to become most impatient with the mounting red tape. A wartime bureaucracy was a legacy of the Great War, when professional experts were found necessary to supervise an increasingly complex war economy and mobilization. By the end of the war these officials exercised almost autonomous authority. Though this bureaucracy was dismantled after the armistice, in the months before Hitler's invasion of Poland the government made plans for reviving it, with all the red tape and restrictions that accompany such an administration. By October 1939 the authoritarian regime was firmly established and was to exert some influence over the life of every Briton. Edith's reaction was typical:

Friday Sept. 29

National Register Day. Everybody to fill in a sort of census paper today, and ration cards and goodness knows what depend on it. Now they've got us taped. Got Identity Card in return—terribly precious. All it has on it is one's name at one side; at the other a place for one's name and address, but marked in large capitals DO NOTHING WITH THIS PART TILL YOU ARE TOLD. Huh!

To combat the shortages of food that were sure to develop with the disruption of shipping, the government issued ration cards by November 1939, to be put into use in January 1940. The first items to be rationed were sugar, ham, butter, and bacon. Sugar was restricted to three-quarters of a pound per person each week and ham and butter were allocated at the rate of three to four ounces per person for the same period. By March 1940 mutton was added to the list of rationed foods, along with beef. Under the new regulations, all Britons over the age of six were limited to fresh meat—including bone and fat—not to exceed 1s. 10p. (37 cents) per week. Children under that age were allowed half rations. Edith was dismayed, however, when the weekly milk ration was set at a half-pint. Life in England was spartan, but not nearly so grim as the German propagandists chose to paint. Several times in her correspondence with Phylabe, Edith insisted that there was no need for her to send food, as supplies in England were adequate. One suspects that she did protest too much, for the packages kept coming, and Edith could barely hide her delight at their contents.

As the war dragged on, clothing as well as food came to be rationed. Adults were allowed sixty-six clothing coupons a year, which proved to be woefully inadequate. A black market soon developed in which a single coupon commanded up to 2s. To compensate for the shortages in ready-to-wear, domestic knitting and sewing were encouraged, but the home seamstress was then faced with the difficulty of finding fabrics that did not require coupons. There was no simple substitute for silk stockings, though for three pence a leg, a woman could have artificial stockings, which were rainproof, sprayed on.

The shortage of manpower and material affected every area of British life. The press was seriously jeopardized by curtailments in staff and the short supply of newsprint. With the blockade, Scandinavian wood pulp was no longer available. Paper drives were launched and conservation measures were introduced, but the results were never completely adequate and inevitably reduced publications were necessary. Advertising space was extremely limited and changes in format were forced on the papers. The *Daily Mail*, for example, for the first time printed news on the front page.

The *Newcastle Journal* was running an eight-page paper in which there was no space for a women's page. But Edith, as the page's editor, was determined to keep some small space daily for women's news. So when her editor sent her out to "see what women are doing in this here war," she did up her findings "in Women's Page type. Now more than ever we must keep women's work in the news. They are the ones who are doing all the ameliorative work, and most of the unpaid work; but they are not the ones who will get the glory." The notices concerning women were eventually limited to half of a mainly news column, under the heading "Women in Wartime."

In addition to its traditional function, the press was also expected to play a role in the propaganda efforts of the British government, but the heaviest burden the journalists had to endure was censorship. Wartime censorship dated from the spring of 1939, when the Ministry of Information was established under the supervision of Lord Perth. The Ministry exercised control over both press censorship and propaganda. Later Harold MacMillan replaced Lord Perth and the censorship functions were assigned to another department under Sir Walter Monckton. In her journal Edith expressed the general dissatisfaction with the set-up of the Ministry: "Anyway, the new Ministry of Information has had a quick end. 999 officers in it and only 42 of them journalists!"

Of the three offices that emerged after reorganization, the first, the Division of Home Publicity, produced propaganda for home consumption. The public was bombarded with posters warning that the "walls have ears" and admonishing the citizenry that "your cheerfulness, your courage, your resolution will bring us victory." Several motion pictures reinforcing the latter message were produced under the direction of Sir Kenneth Clark. Much of the agency's time, however, was occupied with the numerous pamphlets that kept the public informed on all new regulations.

The second division—that of Foreign Publicity—prepared the leaflets that were dropped on Germany during the early weeks of the war and was also responsible for the propaganda circulated in neutral countries, including the United States.

Yet another division of the Ministry of Information, with head-quarters in the senate building of the University of London, was that of News and Censorship. The staff in this office controlled news releases and exercised their much-maligned blue pencils, often with greater vigor than acumen. The censors were scarcely ever trained newspapermen. Rather, they were civil servants who had obtained their positions through traditional bureaucratic channels.

Although the shortages and restrictions created inconveniences for the English population, by far the most serious hardship they experienced was the disruption of family life. Not only were husbands, fathers, and brothers going off to fight, but also many women were separated from their children. As early as 30 September 1939, Edith wrote in her journal:

> Many people think the whole evacuation scheme will be called off, too. Evacuees, mothers especially[,] are trickling back in a steady dribble. The scheme that worked so beautifully on paper, and really was put into operation with remarkable smoothness at the beginning, is crumbling down simply because evacuees happen to be human beings, with human feelings about family ties and human weaknesses about putting up with desperate inconvenience and discomfort. Especially as there have been no air raids. (God grant there never will be). Mrs. Collins, as sensible as most, borrowed £1 from me today because she'd run herself short going over to Windermere to see how her little girl is getting on. Naturally she wanted to see for herself. And if the war lasts the three years the Government talks about, she and every other mother will have got tired of being separated from her children, even if they know the children are in good hands. It's a fantastic scheme for any long period. It's been too long already.

The first Christmas season was a particularly traumatic time. There was practically a national clamor to bring the children home for the holidays. National, county, and municipal authorities, however, discouraged such action. The cheap railway tickets issued to parents for monthly visits with their children were declared invalid for the Christmas to New Year's week. As a compensation for the children not being allowed to return home, the London County Council sponsored a Christmas Treat Fund which promised them the best Christmas ever. In spite of these efforts, and much to the chagrin of the responsible authorities, large numbers of children found a way to return to London. The stand taken by the government became more unpopular when it was discovered that the Princesses had returned from Scotland for the holidays. Officials explained that they were to remain only two days and then the royal family would retire to the country, presumably to Sandringham House in Norfolk.

In later life, many of the children who were evacuated did not look back on their experiences with fondness. One can only wonder at the psychological damage done to children who were orphaned while living in foster homes.

By the spring of 1940, the English people were becoming increasingly impatient with the war. Some were asking if the war would ever end; others wondered when it would begin. Edith expressed the frustration in her diary: "Can't believe today, some-how, in the reality of this war. No news comes from France, the workers wait here with nothing to do—it's all so shadowy. Just this farcical blackout. It's the 'precautions' that make it seem so unreal—just a bad dream."

The bureaucracy with its endless muddling and the pervasive "controlitis" were grating on the nerves of the Britons. The boarded-up windows were taking on a look of normalcy. A rock garden was built around an unattractive corrugated iron bomb shelter. Grass was growing out of the sandbags, giving them a "detestable air of permanence." But the period of the phony war was nearing an end, and the English people were soon to be called upon to meet the challenges of the Blitz, a bombing campaign that had no precedent in the history of warfare.

Perhaps nothing brought the immediacy of the war home to the British like the fall of France and the ensuing disaster at Dunkirk. After successful strikes against Denmark and Norway in April, Hitler unleashed the Wehrmacht against France and the Low Countries on 10 May 1940. Unable to check the German armored thrust through the Ardennes, the British Expeditionary Force (and various French Army units) soon retreated to the Channel coast at Dunkirk, where they faced capture or annihilation if they were not rescued. In an incredible operation, ships of the Royal Navy and private vessels of all shapes and sizes undertook the evacuation. In the words of England's poet laureate, John Masefield, "broken ships clotted the harbor and dark masses of men stretched the length and breadth of the shore." While euphoric Germans were wagering that London would be occupied within two weeks, a somber Winston S. Churchill, named Prime Minister to replace the discredited Neville

Chamberlain, broke the news of the disaster to a stunned Parliament. Special services at Westminister Abbey were attended by the King and Queen, in the company of the exiled Queen Wilhelmina of Holland. While the royalty devoutly prayed, many in congregations throughout the country openly wept.

After this brief moment of tears and prayers, however, resolution and strength of purpose reasserted themselves and the government began preparations for the expected invasion. A defense zone from five to twenty miles wide was established along the Channel and North Sea coasts. Beaches, golf links, and vacation facilities were expropriated and holiday makers were ordered home. Road markers and traffic signs were removed and the militarized zone soon bristled with artillery and machine-gun emplacements. Tank traps, land mines, and barricades were installed and obstacles were placed in open fields where German planes might attempt to land. Kite flying was strictly prohibited in these areas, as the kites might be used by spies to signal the enemy. The ports and harbor areas in Britain were divided into four groups, and the dock workers were readied for rapid transfer from one zone to another in the event of bombing or invasion.

Preparations were also made to resist a possible assault by parachute troops. On 14 May, Anthony Eden, the newly appointed War Minister, issued a call for men between the ages of seventeen and sixty-five to constitute a volunteer Home Guard. Within twenty-four hours, a quarter of a million men had responded to the appeal. Nicknamed the "parashootists" and immortalized later in the cherished and endless TV series as "Dad's Army," the force consisted of a motley contingent of teenagers and elderly men, armed with sporting rifles, antique weapons, and shotguns. They did, however, wear uniforms so that invaders would not confuse them with unauthorized civilian insurgents, spies, or guerrillas.

The Ministry of Information, in collaboration with the War Office and the Ministry of Home Security, issued careful instructions on what to do "If the Invader Comes." The civilian population was told to "stay put" and resist both the heeding and spreading of rumors. Civilians were cautioned to make sure any order was genuine before acting on it and if in doubt to consult a known local authority such as a policeman or an air-raid warden. Above all else, the population was enjoined to use common sense.

On the same day that Parliament passed the Emergency Defense Act, another bill was enacted making treason, sabotage, and espionage capital offenses. This measure was deemed necessary in part because of the influx of refugees from the Low Countries and France. The Home Secretary instituted a general crackdown on both uninterned aliens and Britons with fascist sympathies. In one swoop, three thousand Germans and Austrians (many of them women engaged in domestic service) were taken into custody. The majority of those arrested were shipped away to the Isle of Man, where they were interned for the duration of the war under conditions that were soon to be protested by civil rights activists. Perhaps the most celebrated arrest of a sympathizer was that of Sir Oswald Mosley, the British Fascist leader, together with one of his subordinates, an official from the Ministry of Health.

Friendly aliens, including Americans, were also subjected to close scrutiny and restrictions. A curfew was imposed requiring them to remain indoors between 8:00 P.M. and 6:00 A.M. They were to report to the police daily and were forbidden to use private cars, bicycles, or any transportation other than public conveyances. Correspondents, entertainers, and others with night jobs could get special passes exempting them from the curfew.

The Minister of Labour and National Services, Ernest Bevin, exercised control over the work force in Britain through local employment exchanges, which were to oversee all hiring for vital industries. As of May 1940, all women aged eighteen through thirty-one had to register with the exchanges and could not leave essential work without official permission or because of serious misconduct. The same guidelines applied to firings.

Women had, in fact, been mobilized from the beginning of the war, and eventually some three millions from all classes—between the ages of eighteen and fifty—were to be engaged in essential employment. The early involvement of women in the war effort was on a voluntary basis, as thousands of women enrolled in the Women's Voluntary Service, a national organization headed by the Dowager Marchioness of Reading. The members did all manner of work, helped with the evacuation of children, found shelter and food for the homeless, transported patients, staffed canteens, and acted as practical nurses.

Even the many women who joined the Auxiliary Territorial Service (ATS) worked as volunteers for a year before they were accorded "soldier's pay" of a shilling a day for a twelve-plus-hour day, seven days a week. This amount was supplemented by various allowances for food and other needs. The ATS, the Women's Auxiliary Air Force (WAAF), and the Women's Royal Naval Service (WRNS, commonly called Wrens), all had Queen Elizabeth (now the Queen Mother) as Commandant in Chief. Queen Elizabeth II was still young enough at the beginning of the war to be a Girl Guide, but later was to see service in the ATS, where she became an expert motor mechanic and driver.

The servicewomen lived in barracks and camps and were subject to the same discipline as the men. No one minded if they used lipstick and powder (though these were not government issue!) and they could opt for short cut or pinned-up long hair. They fraternized in the canteens and messes and had their clubs in London, but their salaries and rations, even while with the British Expeditionary Force in France, were about four-fifths of those their male counterparts enjoyed. Army regulations prohibited wives in restricted military zones overseas, but in England servicewomen could marry and remain in the Service unless they became pregnant. They served as clerks, typists, radio and telephone operators, cooks, and drivers, and in many more highly skilled and professional jobs, some of them highly confidential. Beginning in 1941, a number of women in the ATS saw combat service with antiaircraft units in Britain. Mary Churchill, the Prime Minister's daughter, served in one such unit. Interestingly, in view of today's standards, these women were allowed to perform every duty connected with their batteries except that of actually firing the guns.

The popularity of the uniformed Services may be judged by the fact that the "Wrens" soon had a waiting list of applicants! By January 1940, Wrens were working at one hundred Naval Stations, the strength of the Service was about 3,500, and the number was increasing by about 500 every month.

By April 1941, women aged twenty to thirty-one were subject to conscription. When called up, they could choose the Services, Civil Defense, the Women's Land Army, nursing, or a variety of war-supporting industrial occupations. Married women with children under the age of fourteen were exempt, and if they had a resident husband they were not moved away from their home district.

As the number of air raids increased and the fear of invasion grew, the role of women in civil defense became increasingly important. Even when engaged in full-time "war-work," they were required to undertake, or voluntarily undertook, additional part-time duties. Edith herself was drafted into this duty later in the war. Women did invaluable work as sentinels, spotting and tracking enemy planes, and, in the thousands, worked as drivers, nurses, air-raid wardens, fire-watchers, telephone operators, and canteen cooks.

In the early months of the war, many of the paid air-raid war-dens had been women, but they had been replaced by men when the feared raids did not immediately materialize. This decision affected some sixty women in the Newcastle area and Edith sought their reaction to the change. When confronted with the seeming inequity of the action, a civil defense spokesman told her that "[t]he men are the wage earners, the women have their homes to keep." Edith was outraged at the response and wrote in her journal:

> As if all men were their families' sole support or all women were married to wage-earners. It makes my blood boil, but women have *no power* to stop these things. There are always men in the high posts. So, in spite of the thousands of women enrolled for *volun-tary* service, the few who had paid jobs are kicked out.
>
> One of these women protested that she had given up a job to do this work, so they found her a paid job as a canteen cook. *All the other 59 agreed to continue as wardens on an unpaid basis.*

This was not the only aspect of the treatment of women that angered Edith and other like-minded liberal thinkers. In October she wrote in her diary:

> Started out to do a special about women doctors in the Army and stirred up a mare's nest. Women doctors are boiling with rage because once more the Army Office, though it *does* acknowledge them this time (last war, the women staffed and financed hospitals of their own in London, Russia, Dardanelles, Serbia and one in France), they are not to be allowed commissioned rank. Dr. Mona MacNaughton leading them in revolt. She happens to be the only woman on the local B.M.A. Emergency Committee, and so discov-ered in time that the otherwise male committee was proposing to send up to h.q. a requisitioned list of available medicals which *did not include any women at all.*

The next day she wrote in the same vein:

Another mare's nest today. At N.C.W. civic committee meeting heard of the Council's call for women special constables to be appointed for moral patrol work in the areas where young mothers are evacuated near to military camps. Margaret Darnell, social worker, told me that Hexham, where she lives, is a "sink of immorality." When I rang up the police to see if they were doing anything about the Home Office recommendation that women should be appointed, they were scathing and angry.

So was I, but silently.

The government action that angered her the most, though, was the "decision to pay compensation for civilians killed or hurt in air raids, *but not housewives!* Paid housekeepers, yes; *but not housewives.* Women are up in arms, but a Prayer to Parliament about it was turned down."

As the war intensified, the bitterness and resentment of the women were temporarily suppressed as all became immersed in a common war effort. The demand for workers in many areas led to new opportunities for women. They became bus drivers; they took jobs in factories; and they assumed government positions. Edith noted in an article that a style show in London was short mannequins because many models had left to become ambulance drivers and nurses. About 35,000 women were enrolled in the Women's Land Army; consistent with their slogan, "Make the home fields your battle field," they helped keep the farms productive and the much-needed food flowing to the population centers. Another 29,000 women held full-time jobs in the National Fire Service (an additional 41,000 served part-time). When called to active duty in the NFS's predecessor, the Auxiliary Fire Service, in September 1939, women had been paid £2 a week; male volunteers received £3.

A select few "educated women of character and keenness" were invited to apply for positions in the Criminal Investigation Department. After careful screening and training, the inductees might engage in police and counterespionage work. Some were used against IRA activists, who, after a brief cessation of terrorism in 1939, resumed overt opposition in 1940. Others were found useful in apprehending spies among the large numbers of aliens. Still others frequented bars and clubs where celebrating servicemen and bureaucrats might talk too freely. But as of April 1940, only 8 of the 143 candidates had been inducted into the CID.

The many measures taken by the government and the instructions and advice issued to the civilian population were tested in the late summer of 1940, when the German bombing raids on England began in earnest. The first major attack on the greater London area, in mid-August, was weathered well. In spite of sirens and alarms, theaters, restaurants, and bars remained open. Transportation was not seriously disrupted and an almost festive spirit was in evidence in Hyde Park, where large numbers congregated hoping to see a "dogfight" in the sky above.

The holiday spirit was short-lived, however, as August gave way to September and an intensification and diversification of the air war. The purpose was not just to destroy military targets and personnel. Progressively the attack was directed against civilians, and for the massed population of London it was the beginning of a long ordeal. Incendiary and high-explosive bombs rained down at random on city and countryside alike. Occasionally no bombs were dropped, but the planes skimmed the rooftops, strafing streets and residential districts. Empty parachutes, sometimes with dummies attached, were dropped; fictitious radio messages were sent to faked Fifth Columnists; and a white powder, later proven to be harmless, was dropped over the city and counties.

The first major night raid on London occurred about midnight on 24 August, as the theater and cinema crowds were going home. When the alarm sounded, some dispersed to shelters, but many stood in the doorways watching the searchlights probe the night skies for the bombers. The attackers penetrated the outer defenses of the city, dropping bombs randomly through the East End, especially the area around St. Giles Cripplegate (now the Barbican complex), where a block of multistoried buildings on Fore Street was destroyed. In all, nine Londoners were killed and another fifty-eight injured during the various raids that night. The raids continued the next day, when three bombs fell a few hundred yards from the country residence of the U.S. Ambassador near Windsor. Churchill promptly retaliated by ordering the bombing of Berlin the following night. But, because of heavy cloud cover, the fifty RAF bombers dropped most of their bombs in the open countryside. The air war had begun in earnest.

After a brief respite because of intermittent rain and cloudiness, September skies cleared to provide ideal conditions for bombing throughout Britain. Three or four raids a day were commonplace and for the first time Londoners were able to watch dogfights in the clear autumn skies. Throughout these raids the populace was reluctant to alter daily and nightly routines. From the fashionable Mayfair district to the East End slums, the air-raid shelters were consistently underutilized. When an official suspended play at a football match because of an air-raid alert, disgruntled fans shouted their disapproval, and many refused to leave their seats. But as the bombings increased in number and intensity, many business firms required their workers to find shelter whenever the alarms sounded and numerous restaurants stopped serving during the raids.

The nights were equally disturbed. On several occasions the alarms sounded continuously for six or seven hours; the next day, irritation, fretting, and edginess adversely affected worker performance and efficiency. On occasion the Germans would send a single plane over London for the sole purpose of triggering the alarms and disrupting sleep. As the war of nerves dragged on, the enemy developed new bombs that had psychological as well as physical effects. The most alarming of these were delayed-action devices that might detonate minutes, hours, or days after impact. Undeniably the day and night raids were seriously affecting the war effort.

The magnitude of the raids—eventually fifteen hundred planes were said to have been involved—and the resulting destruction were of unprecedented severity. In human terms, losses were high and suffering was extreme. An estimated twenty-five thousand people, mostly from the East End, had to be relocated and provided with the basic necessities. Some of the homes and apartment houses requisitioned were the properties of the interned and jailed fascists. Lord Redesdale's thirty-room townhouse in Knightsbridge was made available to the homeless, and his daughter's house was also used.

The Communist *Daily Worker* and other liberal papers launched a campaign for suitable and secure bomb shelters for the poor. The government had provided Anderson Shelters, named after the Home Secretary, which gave some protection from falling debris and bomb fragments. These backyard shelters, crudely constructed of corrugated iron sheets, were very uncomfortable and generally unsatisfactory. Better public shelters and a variety that could be used indoors were developed at a later date, but, in the meantime, the public was allowed to use the private facilities furnished by hotels and apartment house owners for their clientele. In addition, the subways were opened for air-raid protection. The line between

Aldwych and Holborn in Central London was one of the first to provide shelter for the thousands of apartment dwellers in that area.

An inspection of the shelters by the new Home Secretary, Her-
bert Morrison, and Sir Edward Evans, the famous World War I admiral, appointed "dictator" of the Underground, led to the opening of
additional Underground stations for the needy. A million season
tickets were issued to guarantee access to the designated areas,
which were to be heated during the winter. Hammocks and bunks
were furnished, along with sanitary facilities and other basic amenities. Rubber earplugs were distributed as a safeguard against the
almost constant din of high explosives. Metal helmets were in short
supply, but a plastic substitute was developed to provide much-
needed protection from shrapnel and splinters.

Two hundred emergency food centers were to be constructed to
provide inexpensive and nutritious meals for the homeless. But by
October fewer than half that number had been completed, and the
Minister of Food encouraged street vendors and sandwich shops to
help out in the crisis. A typical meal at the Peckham Center consisted of minced beef, cabbage, potatoes, spaghetti, and apple charlotte. The price was six pence (about ten cents) for adults and four
pence for children.

As winter approached, public health authorities became seriously concerned over the possibility of disease in the crowded shelters. There had already been an alarming increase in cerebral-spinal
meningitis, or "camp fever" as the World War I nemesis had been
called. Although the recently developed sulfa drugs proved especially helpful in the campaign against this disease, the cases soared
from fifteen hundred in 1939 to more than twelve thousand in
1940. The medical profession also feared a flu or typhoid epidemic
that might further deplete a London population already weakened
by loss of sleep and poor diet. Twenty-five London hospitals had
been bombed, and though most had reopened, their efficiency and
capacity had been affected. Thus the program chosen was one of
preventive medicine. Even though there was a shortage of doctors
and nurses, a trained medical professional was to be on call for
every shelter. The ailing were to be segregated from the others to
control the spread of communicable diseases, and inoculations
were mandatory.

Another war-zone malady that afflicted the home front was the
equivalent of "shell shock." This phenomenon was a result of the

combat-like conditions the London population was subjected to during the air raids. The doctors used the same conditioning treatment for civilians as prescribed by their military counterparts. Recordings of the sounds of gunfire, exploding bombs and shells, sirens, and diving planes were frequently replayed for the patients, who, with constant reassurances from and encouragement by the doctors, gradually lost their fears and anxieties.

To combat their lagging morale and to escape the grim realities of war, Londoners sought out all available forms of entertainment. Films were, of course, popular and the radio offered a variety of programs. An effort was made to keep zoos and circuses open, as they were great favorites of the masses, but the raids and blackouts upset travel and performance schedules and made the animals nervous and unpredictable. Shortages of food, gasoline, and labor forced the Sanger family, owners of a circus since 1821, to put it on the auction block in September 1941.

The theaters were disrupted sporadically during the Blitz, but the war-depleted London Symphony Orchestra continued the much-loved Promenade concerts that Sir Henry Wood had made popular. England's premier conductor, Sir Thomas Beecham, came out of retirement to conduct the London Philharmonic Orchestra, which remained intact thanks to fund-raising campaigns. The BBC orchestra, in contrast, had lost so many musicians to the draft that the group was limited mostly to chamber music. Ballet and opera were continued at Sadler's Wells, and musical programs were initiated at the National Gallery, where for a shilling (25 cents) an audience might enjoy a piano concert by Myra Hess, while having lunch. Many times in her correspondence with Phylabe, Edith mentioned attending a theater or concert performance.

The National Gallery was available for concerts because the art works had been removed to places of security within hours after the war was declared. Three to four thousand canvases from the Tate Gallery were coated with preservatives and shipped to various destinations in the country. Several large pieces of statuary, such as Rodin's *The Kiss,* were left behind, but they could scarcely be appreciated, buried as they were under sandbags. The British Museum was closed, its priceless possessions under heavy guard in places of safety far from public view and the Luftwaffe's bombs. The medieval manuscripts and other irreplaceable documents of the Public Record Office, the English national archives, received like treatment. A copy of the Magna Carta, however, was on tour in the United States when the war broke out and the English Ambassador in Washington arranged for its safekeeping until the war ended.

Throughout the bombing raids, civilian morale in England remained at a high level, although it came very near cracking at times, such as in Liverpool after a devastating raid on 7 May. But, after the United States entered the war in December, it was widely believed that Hitler's defeat was only a matter of time. Of course, the bombing would continue, and new weapons would be developed for use against the resilient British population, but with the expansion of the war into the Balkans, the Mediterranean, North Africa, and Russia in 1941, fears of invasion subsided in Britain, along with the worst of the air raids.

Between the fall of France in June 1940 and the Japanese attack on Pearl Harbor in December 1941, President Franklin D. Roosevelt and Congress had essentially committed the United States industrial and military might, if not personnel, to the European conflict. In spite of the die-hard opposition of isolationist senators, a significant portion of the press, prominent pro-Germans such as Charles Lindbergh, many in the American military establishment, and even the grave doubts of Ambassador Joseph P. Kennedy, aid to Britain was stepped up. On 11 March 1941, President Roosevelt approved Lend-Lease, that "most unsordid act" that allowed Britain and the Allies to buy, exchange, or lease arms and other equipment and supplies from the United States. The flow of military supplies across the Atlantic thus continued despite the bankruptcy of the British government and the unrelenting attacks of Admiral Karl Donitz's U-boats.

In the late summer of 1941, Edith gave up her job in Newcastle and moved to London to take a job with the Ministry of Labour and National Service. She was fortunate to have missed the worst of the 1940–1941 London Blitz. Although Newcastle and the nearby towns of Sunderland and Tyneside had been bombed regularly, they had not suffered to the extent that London had. After the bombing raid over London on the night of 10/11 May, the attacks decreased and shortly the Luftwaffe began redeploying its forces eastward in preparation for Operation Barbarossa, the invasion of Russia. Edith found the mood in London decidedly upbeat after Russia entered the war. Anyway, in London there was "lots to eat and plenty of clothes. . . ." But life in London had changed. Theater performances began at 5:15, and everyone was off the street by 10:00 P.M. She felt that Londoners had held up well under German attack and that no gloom was evident.

In late 1942, Edith began to notice the increasing number of Americans in London. The Allied invasion of North Africa (Operation Torch) put everyone in "high spirits . . . if only I could tell you how everybody over here was just aching for the Allied Nations to ACT, to go in and WIN something for a change." But her enthusiasm was dampened a month later when she reported on an air raid that had killed nearly fifty children. The incident she spoke of was the bombing of the south London Sandhurst Road School by a German fighter-bomber, which resulted in the deaths of thirty-eight children and six teachers. Londoners, she added, were again sleeping in the tube stations. However, even that expediency did not ensure personal safety. On the night of 3 March 1943, 173 people died in the Bethnal Green Underground station after they panicked at the sound of antiaircraft rockets being fired outside.

The raids on London continued in varying intensity throughout the war. Edith was one of the majority of Londoners who rarely used the shelters, preferring instead to sleep in her own bed or in a flat a few floors down when the noise became too great. On one occasion in February 1944, her flat was ringed by eight fires caused by Luftwaffe attacks. The din from British antiaircraft guns was "terrific," but "the sound of bombs falling is just sickening." Shortly thereafter her office was bombed and the two old houses used by her section completely gutted. She began her letter of 14 March 1944 while in her cellar bomb shelter. The flats of three of her friends had been hit by incendiaries, and another friend's home had recently been destroyed by a bomb.

The cross-Channel attack on 6 June 1944 raised everyone's expectations that the war would soon be over and that the bombing would at last come to an end. But that was not to be. On 13 June, the Germans launched the first V–1 jet-propelled bomb against England, the first of some eight thousand. Approximately 2,300 hit London, causing more than 21,400 casualties and damaging more than 1.1 million houses and buildings.

Edith tried to make light of the arrival of the German V-weapons in the summer of 1944, referring to the V–1 by its nicknames "doodlebomb" and "buzz bomb." She thought the V–1s were worse that the V–2s (ballistic rockets), although she wrote those words long before the extent of the attacks was understood. Little did she know that before that terror campaign had concluded the Germans would launch 1,115 V–2s against Britain, with by far the largest concentration falling on London. Again, she tried to make light of the "exploding gas mains," which was the first official explanation of the completely random explosions of the one-ton warheads. In January 1945, she was jumpy from the unexpected explosions and wrote: "Oh, Phylabe, will it *never* end!" Both V–weapons and piloted aircraft bombardments finally ceased at the end of March 1945, only a month before the German surrender. The five-year Blitz had taken the lives of 60,595 civilians and seriously injured another 86,182. Of that number, some 8,938 civilians were killed and another 24,504 seriously injured in the 1944–1945 V–weapons attacks.

In May 1943, Edith was called to part-time Air Raid warden service; she delightedly informed Phylabe that her new job entitled her to a free pair of trousers. But the work involved patrolling at night, even when the bombs fell miles away. Worse yet was the shopping for scarce goods, a chore that had become "the very dickens." London, she thought, was becoming very drab, not only the houses, but also the women, whose dress was "always simple and quiet and *practical*." In late 1944, Edith described the clothing shortage as serious. She found the quality of the clothing provided under the Utility scheme quite poor, but non-Utility clothes were beyond her means, as they were taxed at 100 percent. Many women, Edith included, sewed and mended with a vengeance—Edith even admitted to darning her handkerchiefs! And, of course, the greatest shortage was stockings.

In early 1945, Edith became editor of a monthly trade magazine, *The Corsetry and Underwear Journal,* which gave her great pleasure and a sense of accomplishment. Although frustration with her boss, Mr. Smedley, and the incessant deadlines plagued her at times, she continued to work in this area of the trade press for the remainder of her professional career. Her close friend, Thirza West, had found employment with the same press, so it was only natural that the two friends would celebrate the German capitulation on 7 May by mingling with the crowds in central London. In fact, they then repeated the escapade the next night, the officially proclaimed V-E Day.

The euphoria brought on by the end of the war was not long lived. Many Britons had been dismayed at the death of President Franklin D. Roosevelt on 12 April . The American president had been widely revered and respected in wartime England. Probably few Britons had taken note of the vote in Congress, a month before, that had extended Lend-Lease for another year but prohibited its use for "postwar relief, rehabilitation or reconstruction." Thus, it came as a shock to most when President Harry S Truman ordered the suspension of Lend-Lease shipments on 23 August, an act that provoked Edith to her only anti-American outburst. Fortunately for Anglo-American relations and for the history of the postwar world, the United States, although deeply suspicious of Britain's postwar policies, first extended loans to that beleaguered nation and then instituted the Marshall Plan in 1947. With that influx of American dollars, the economic recovery of Britain and Western Europe could begin.

The quality and drabness of food, if not its actual shortage, had been a fact of life in wartime Britain. In early 1942, Edith mentioned that she had not had much experience with Lend-Lease food because she was not cooking (she had a room in the Central YMCA), but that she had tried the spiced ham several times in restaurants and found it "excellent." She had not yet tried Spam—when we hear of that commodity again a year later, she said it had become a national joke. She did miss milk, which was rationed to four half-pints a week, and eggs, which had apparently disappeared from the London market. But she was especially indignant at the rumors that sparrows and seagulls were for sale in the markets. At the end of 1944, Edith had high praise for the Ministry of Food. The food might be "dull," but there had been no real shortages. On the whole, she believed that rationing had been "a masterpiece of good management."

Unfortunately for the British people, who had suffered the indignity of Lend-Lease Spam during the war, food rationing did not end with the peace. During the severe winter of 1947–1948, fuel and food—even bread and beer—were rationed. The rationing of clothing did not end until 1949. Shortages of milk and eggs continued until 1950. Meat rationing finally ended in 1954.

As with food rationing, clothing shortages did not immediately end after V-E Day; shoes especially were in short supply. Cloth, except for parachute cloth, was still scarce at the end of 1946. Housing was also a problem in postwar Britain, as some seventy-six thousand evacuees found that they had no homes to return to. On a late 1945 trip, Edith was dismayed to discover that much of the old part of Bristol had been destroyed and that Bath had been badly damaged. Years would pass before the physical damage to Britain's cities would no longer be so immediately visible.

But now Britain's fate was in the hands of the Labour Party. In a political turnabout that caught many Americans unaware, Churchill's conservative government was replaced by a Labour government in an unprecedented landslide in July 1945. The erection of the British welfare state then began in earnest.

These matters, undoubtedly important to someone as politically aware as Edith, took a back seat, in her correspondence with Phylabe, to such matters as her excitement over her impending marriage to Cecil Bacon, the fitting of her wedding gown, and the move to a new house and job. The war and the drabness of postwar life were all but forgotten.

⟫⧫⟪

In spite of Edith's protests that she would write long letters when she was a housewife and had more time, her correspondence with Phylabe fell off considerably after her marriage. In fact, a housewife does not have more time, and Edith found herself almost overwhelmed by domesticity. A large house that needed a great deal of repair and refurbishing, along with a large garden, with its upkeep and produce to be processed, left Edith little time for anything else.

When she was invited to join the staff of English Rose Corsetry Ltd., she accepted. "I wasn't enjoying housework and because we were embarking so late in life on buying and setting up a house we were needful of further income." Edith stayed with English Rose for sixteen years and continued to do free-lance work after leaving the firm. She became involved in every aspect of corsetry— manufacturing and fitting undergarments, making arrangements for style shows, and writing texts for the fitting and selling of foundation wear. She even helped to establish a school of corset design at Leicester College of Art. After retirement Edith pursued a degree in literature at the University of London. She remained active in her charitable organizations and indulged her great love of travel.

In 1954, Edith's mother died; her father died two years later. The home in Whickham was sold and her sister Chrissie moved to Beckenham, where she lived with Cecil and Edith for four years. She then moved to a retirement home where she died in 1979. Cecil and Edith had both retired by 1966 when they moved to an apartment in

Beckenham. Edith stayed active in journalism, preparing press releases for the Methodist Church she attended, and gathering material for her parish church's 1987 centenary booklet, which she hoped to "have a hand" in writing. But in 1986 Edith and Cecil entered a retirement home in Wallington, Surrey; three years later, Cecil, then ninety years old, died on Christmas Eve. Edith now lives in Yorkshire.

The postwar boom in population and economy in the United States caused a growth spurt in Greeley, and the Houston property was right in the path of the city's westward expansion. Phylabe's father gradually sold off much of his land as building sites for new homes and for an elementary school; Phylabe later donated land for the local Boys' Club to build a recreation center and playing field.

George Houston lived to be an old man and died only in 1968. Although Phylabe never made the trip to England, her father did in 1959 and stayed for a while with the Bacons. Phylabe devoted most of her later life to developing an old rock quarry into a garden area as a memorial to her father. The garden was designed to reflect the natural plant life at the different altitudes in Colorado. The walkways and bridges are laid out with special attention to the needs of the blind and handicapped. Still another part of the original farm has been divided into community garden plots. As Edith wrote in one of her more recent letters, "The garden will, of course, become a memorial to Phylabe herself as well as to her Dad." Phylabe Houston died of cancer on 1 November 1987.

Of the many other people mentioned in Edith's letters, Bessie Crowther remained in Vancouver, British Columbia; her husband Charley died in 1969. Virginia Fowlkes taught for twenty-seven years in the American school system in Europe for dependent military children. She had retired and returned to the United States before she died in 1978. Thirza West retired to Scotland after many years in exhibition and promotional work in London. Marjorie Redfern married and lives in a London suburb; she and Edith are still close friends.

Greeley, Colorado   Stephen T. Powers

Editor's Note: Benjamin Byerly died before this book reached publication.

1941
August 4, 1941–December 10, 1941

✉ **1**

3 Summerhill Grove
Newcastle-on-Tyne 4
August 4, 1941

My dear Phylabe

I don't know how long it is since I began to think of writing to
the Colorado girl who, through the good offices of Bessie Crowther,
had become quite a real friend; but I do know that if Bessie passed
on my promise of a letter, you must have given me up long ago as a
bad egg. However, here I come, at last!

It was most awfully nice of you to write to me. I wish I could tell
you just how touched we English people are at gestures of friendship from across the Atlantic just now, and though I know you feel
more of a personal friend to me than just to any Englander, I
expect, too, you were partly "being nice" to my country in writing;
so on behalf of my country I was delighted to hear from you, just as
I was delighted entirely on behalf of this child herself.

This is Bank Holiday Monday—is the first Monday in August a
public holiday with you? It is usually a very popular one here—the
sort that runs to roundabouts and bottles of pop on open spaces, to
great picnics (but picnics in this climate aren't the unmixed pleasures they probably are with you!) and to a sort of general autumn-
Pancake-Tuesday orgy of pleasure-seeking before the long fast till
Christmas. In fact, it's always the last holiday of the year, and we
make the most of it.

This year, the Government said it didn't want us to waste a day on playing. But as it didn't say we MUSTn't, and as we cling to our old rights whenever we can, it's a sort of hit-and-miss holiday, with some working (including me—but newspaper offices always did, anyway) and others not. But what the Government failed to achieve, the weather managed! It has been pouring nearly all day, so picnics and fetes out-of-doors are definitely NOT being held.

Of course, newspapers aren't allowed to mention weather conditions till a fortnight after they are over, so I had to write a "holiday story" for this evening's paper without mentioning the rain. We were also requested to refrain from mentioning any large crowds at rail or bus stations—so imagine what fun I had trying to think of something noncommittal to say!

Journalism is full of that sort of fun these days. Last week we had a terrific freak thunderstorm which struck our most notable town monument—a figure of Lord Grey of Reform Bill fame on a pillar 160 feet high—and knocked the old gentleman's head off. In our story of the event, we could only say his head FELL off—as if nobody knew how!

But indeed, newspaper work is exceedingly dull (except for the war correspondents, who must be having the time of their lives). I spend a great deal of my time doing nothing, which is just the most unsatisfactory use of life that I can think of. So we'll say no more about it.

England is a very happy place to be in just now. Especially since Russia showed herself such a lionheart—we're all convinced the war is nearly over now, and are planning victory celebrations even; but for far longer than that, ever since the fall of France, I think, when we really felt it all depended on us, there has been such a grand atmosphere of stimulation and energy and enthusiasm about. So different from the miserable year or two before the war, when nobody had a clear mind about it—felt we ought to be in it yet wanted to keep out if we could—oh, you've no idea how dismal and depressing those years were! Now it is as different as things could be. There just aren't any doleful folk any more! Argumentative— yes. You should just hear us putting the world (especially our own Government!) right. But it doesn't mean disagreement; just live- mindedness. In spite of all the horrors of air war, all the anxiety about friends in danger, all the vicissitudes of shopping (which are considerable!) I don't think there are many people who don't feel it's a grand time to be alive in, because once this tyranny is overpast, the rebuilding and growing will be glorious.

August 5

I'll continue with pen now, as I'm spending the morning in a County Court. The Judge is hearing judgement summonses, so I have nothing to do but listen with half one ear. His Honour is a curmudgeonly old soul, but he has a nice small boy, probably a grandson, beside him, so perhaps he is human after all!

Last night we had the grandest fun. A friend took me to the theatre to see a first-class London Company in a new comedy-thriller, *Cottage to Let.* It was all about spies and U-boats and the R.A.F., and at one point a surprise "bombing" took place with such realistic noises off-stage that before we realized it was part of the play, everybody had well and truly sat up to take notice! You should have heard the laughter when the excitement died down. It was a crowded holiday audience, full of high spirits, and they made such a lively atmosphere. There was a party of R.A.F. V[olunteer] R[eserve] flight sergeants having a party in one box, with two very handsome Canadian R.A.F. guests. There were plenty of lines in the play about the Air Force, and they did enjoy themselves! When the villain looked like getting the upper hand, one of them called out to the hero—"Hurry up, sock him!" and the whole house rocked with glee. I wish you could have been there—I've never had such fun in an ordinary theatre.

Bessie sent on your Colorado travel folder and we pored over it for hours, getting out atlas and encyclopedia and everything possible to augment our little knowledge. Now I am quite sure it is Colorado and not Arizona I want to be in—so don't be surprised if one day a knock comes at your door and when you answer it, it's me! The thing that flabbergasts us, of course, is your distances. You say blithely in your letter to me that you are 1,600 miles from Victoria. I should have to run up and down England *five times* before I'd gone so far! We think 100 miles is just about far enough for any journey! I wish there was an adequate pictorial guide to Northumberland which I could send you. So far as I know there has never been, and, these days, there isn't even an inadequate one to be had. It's a lovely corner of England, with friendly little hills, wide sweeping moors, beautiful fertile valleys, lovely peaty streams, and golden beaches down the coast. It has scores of Norman castles, miles of Roman

Hadrian's Wall (ask Bessie about that!) and tranquil old villages in which every stone is marked and lichened with history. It also has filthy little pit villages and lots of ugly pit heaps, but they're mostly in the southeast corner, and it is easy to get away from them. Or *was* easy! Nowadays hardly anybody runs a car, as the petrol ration is so meagre, so we mostly stay home.

In case you wonder, we get lots to eat and plenty of clothes, and most people are not suffering (in those ways) from the war *at all,* though we may have had to adapt our menus to the market. There are plenty of small annoyances for us to use up our grumbles on, but in the main we realize that things are being managed not too badly. Anyhow, we who survive will have lots of grand memories, and one especially is the way the war has made everybody so much more friendly. *Such* friendliness as there is in the world! It's marvelous to see it.

The court has risen now and I'm going out to lunch with a cheerful member of the staff. It's been nice to write to you, Phylabe, and it's nice to think we *may* one day meet. Do you know what I look like? I'll enclose a snap I've just had from my young colleague Marjorie. She's the smiling one with the dog and I'm what the staff calls the "sheep's-eyed one" on the right.
Lots of good thoughts to you

Sincerely,
Edith Base

✉ **2**
Central YWCA Club
Great Russell Street
London, WC1
Dec. 10. 1941

My dear Phylabe
When your long letter of Sept. 10 reached me about a fortnight ago, I wanted to sit down and reply straight away, but . . . because I was just new in London and in my job, all sorts of other things intervened, so that the letter I was longing to write to you had to be shelved from day to day.

But now here is your second letter, with its news of the parcel of goodies on its way to me, and although all my week's washing is waiting to be done, and I just can't go to work tomorrow unless I darn some stockings, I am going to do nothing more until I've written to you. More particularly, because within the last two days your country too has been dragged into this beastly war, and you must be feeling very sad and perhaps alarmed and certainly very much upset by the tragic news of your losses and ours in the Pacific.[1]

I am so awfully sorry America has had to start fighting too. While all your great land was free of the bloodshed and misery and terror, one could feel the sanity of the world still stood more or less secure. But now there is hardly a part of the globe where people can be carefree and rejoice in the sun and the moon—the moon, poor lovely goddess, brings her own peculiar terrors these days—and for all our thankfulness that we have so great and noble a country as our ally, some of us feel that that blessing is perhaps outweighed by the great spread of darkness over the globe. However, some of our speakers are putting the right side of the picture foremost—how good it is at last to have got all the villains clearly in front of us—no more skulking shadows in the background; and, distressing as the news of these first few days is, nobody can feel that the Japs stand an earthly chance of final victory. So before this reaches you, Phylabe my dear, I hope the scale of the battle in the Pacific has tipped well over to the other side, and the losses are on the enemy's list and not on ours.

Are you near enough to danger to come under these awful blackout restrictions? I do hope not. This Stygian blackness puts such a blight on life! At any rate you are not likely to suffer any shortage of food, are you? Wartime conditions will no doubt affect internal transport and so perhaps limit you locally to some extent; but at any rate you don't have to bring any of your essential foods over thousands of miles of ocean. One immediate reaction here to the new state of things is that everybody expects we may be a little less cosily supplied with food. Your lease-lend exports to us have made such a lot of difference to us—have made our wartime dietary quite sumptuous, indeed. So much so that I feel guilty at the

---

1. Pearl Harbor had been bombed 7 December 1941, and next day the United States declared war on Japan. Great Britain followed suit. The U.S. fleet was severely crippled in the attack; the British navy lost the *Prince of Wales* and the *Repulse* shortly afterward and was left with no capital ships in the Indian Ocean or the Pacific.

thought of receiving an EXTRA supply from you! How kind of you it is to think of us and go to all the trouble of sending us this parcel! I can't tell you how much it touches us to think of your loving and generous care, and I think the sum of all the kindly thoughts coming from your people to us and from us back again during the past year or two must have been of immeasurable value. In swelling the total of love and outweighing the hate in the world, I mean. It only makes us all the more grieved to think that now you are "in it" as well—not just because the flow of your gifts may cease; but because we have grown to love you so much and would have had you spared this war if we could.

So thank you, thank you, Phylabe, for your parcel which is not just a parcel of beans, sweeties, jam and such exciting *et ceteras* as chili sauce and BUTTONS, but a symbol—of a friendship that I trust not this war "nor any other creature" will ever be able to destroy. Please thank your Mom for her contribution of jam and your Dad for giving up the candies out of his dish. Yes, the sweet things will certainly be appreciated. I don't know whether the English as a nation is sweet-toothed more than most, but we certainly like our jam for tea, and we are certainly missing our sweeties. I think the biggest queues you ever see are at the sweetie shops which do once in a while have supplies to sell. I must add that most of the people who stand in queues to buy sweeties are buying them to send to their lads in the Forces!

Tell me, have you given up teaching for good? I would not be a teacher if I could be a farmer! The longer I live, the more I think mankind is MAD to make most of its occupations indoor, sedentary and generally UNnatural. How I long for a job in the sun and fresh air these winter days, when it is all I can do to manage a ten-minute walk in DAYLIGHT even each day!

And that reminds me, I ought to tell you about my new job, because I don't suppose you will have heard that from Bessie yet. It all happened so suddenly that a month ago I hardly knew a thing about it! Now I am in my third week as an officer of the Ministry of Labour and National Service—a wartime appointment, though I expect this particular Ministry will have so much still to arrange AFTER the war that I may count on a much longer period of service, if not a permanent post.

I am still listed as a "journalist," though so far I have only done journalistic work in a sort of reverse direction. One of my principal duties is (or will be when I've got into my stride; so far I'm still very much of a learner) to see members of the Press (women mostly) who come to the Ministry for information about this and that aspect of the war effort, and it gave me a very queer feeling when I read the first article which said "So and so and so and so, *said an official of the Ministry of Labour and National Service today*"—meaning ME! I also write articles for papers and magazines that don't want to write their own; I may have to speak at women's meetings where information about women's war work is desired; and I get lots of enquiries, sent in letters to women editors and radio-speakers, to find authentic answers for. It's all very interesting, and beautifully varied, thank heaven—for I'm a poor one at sitting put at any one job!—and when I've got over feeling like the new girl at school, who doesn't know ANY of the answers, I fancy I'm going to get a great kick out of doing it.

One funny thing about this Public Relations Department is that it's shown me something I didn't believe existed outside of American screen newspaper offices—frantically busy people answering three or four telephones all at the same time! It really made me laugh the first day—it didn't belong to ordinary well-behaved English life at all, but to a film! But it proved to be quite true—the phones just do not ever stop ringing, and the way the other officers in the Press Office keep three or four lines of thought quite separate in their heads at the same moment fills me with intense admiration! Don't know that *I* shall ever rise to it—first time I tried with TWO phones at once, heaven knows what I did with the lines of THOUGHT, but with the lines of telephone flex I got beautifully entangled and got the wrong receivers back on the phones. Result—chaos!

Poor old London is showing a lot of scars, and living in the big City is hardly the gay business it was in the days pre-1939! Theatres begin at 5:15 p.m. instead of 8:30, and it seems to me that everybody is in bed (some of them in the tube stations in case of air raids!) by 10 p.m. Now in the old days, London only reached its peak of gaiety AFTER 10 p.m., and from 10 till midnight the streets were BRILLIANT with lights and lovely women and LIFE. Most of the exciting little dress shops (which to my mind used to put Paris completely in the shade—though not New York, which surely is unmatched for its fashion shop displays!) are shut up—or if not completely gone, are shuttered and boarded round for protection's sake, and show little but "utility" clothes. The jewel shops, the art shops, the curio shops, all ditto. It's very, very sad.

The people, of course, are exactly the same as ever—or perhaps even more alert and lively. England is a grand place to live in, war or no war! Only yesterday, a woman in this Club was telling me with great gusto how her family had got on through the period of blitz in London last year. "Oh, we were all right," she said—but "all right" included not having slept a whole night through in their beds for FOUR MONTHS, having a bomb hit the building and carry away the complete top floor, and a land-mine drop in the street outside, demolishing numerous buildings and killing a number of their neighbours. But—"oh, we were all right."

I will tell you, too, about my friend Mary Houstoun (nearly your name but not quite). I wrote to tell her I had got this new job and to ask her to visit me. She wrote me the most lovely letter back. The first page was all given up to congratulations and good wishes to me, and then she added "But listen, dear—I've had rather a shock today—the news of the *Ark Royal*.[2] As you know our beloved Lindsey (her "baby" son of 19) is on board. I am sure he is all right— but if he has gone, I shan't go to Whitby on Monday, or, if he *is* all right, he is sure to come home—so I will come and see you as you suggest on Wednesday. But if I hear that he is all right and Not coming home immediately, then I shall go to Whitby and so shan't be able to see you. Forgive this badly expressed letter—I am rather shaken—I heard the news-boys shout the news and—you know— the sky turned black. But I am all right, and ready for whatever news may come." Then she comes back to *my* good fortune and her good wishes for *me*, with not another word about her own anxiety—for we had not heard then that all but one of *Ark Royal*'s men had been saved.

I don't know whether Mary's letter is typical—perhaps not, as she is a most rare person—a Christian of invulnerable faith and radiant joy. Her letter made me weep—not for Lindsey's danger but for *her* sublime courage, and if England has just a few of her spirit,

---

2. The aircraft carrier *Ark Royal* was hit by a single torpedo 13 November at 3:41 P.M. twenty-five miles off Gibraltar. It stayed afloat long enough for a destroyer to come alongside and evacuate 1,487 men. The single casualty occurred in the attack. The captain and a hundred men tried to save the ship, but were taken off next morning when the ship sank at 6:13 A.M.

then nothing can vanquish us. Please don't think I'm being boastful, Phylabe—I'm just trying to show you a picture of what it is like over here, and what I'm trying to make clear is—there's *no gloom.*

Not that we shouldn't rejoice to have the whole beastly business behind us, and life opening out sweetly again!

There's so much more I want to say—you are easy to talk to; I'm not so garrulous with everybody. But it's past my bedtime, and if I don't finish this letter off tonight, it may hang on for a week or even more[, b]ecause I work rather long hours and find myself with extremely little time in the evenings. I wish this could reach you by Christmas, but I fear that's hardly possible. It might manage to arrive by New Year, though—I hope so, and I do wish you a very happy and thankful 1942, and as tranquil as may be in the circumstances.

No more now—though I shall think of dozens of things I wanted most urgently to say as soon as I seal up the envelope!

Lots of good wishes to you—and I'm keeping my calendar marked with that 1943 "date" with you in the Colorado Rockies!

Edith

1942
January 17, 1942–December 10, 1942

✉ **3**
Central YWCA Club
Great Russell St.
London WC 1
Jan 17, 1942

My dear Phylabe—This is just the briefest of notes to say that your parcel arrived—long after all our hopes had faded away—last Tuesday, and I had the most glorious hour unpacking, tasting everything, deciding which bits I would send on to Mother and which bits I simply couldn't bear to part with. It was a most exciting and delighting parcel, and you were a perfect angel to think of sending it. Your two letters also were *much* appreciated and enjoyed, and a reply long enough to match has been brewing since the first one arrived, but my new job eats up my hours and my energy and I have fallen horribly behind with my letter writing. I will write more to you very soon, however, and this is to be regarded merely as an interim report on the arrival of two letters and one parcel safely! I will tell you what I am eating first—it is the delicious peach jam!! Scrumptious!

Till very soon—Lots of love
and many thank yous–Edith

✉ **4**
Central YWCA Club
Great Russell Street
London WC 1
13–2–42

My dear Phylabe

I have had such an exhilarating day that I feel I must write to you on the crest of the wave. Lately I've been working late o'nights and feeling so tired when I arrived home that letter writing was just a labour instead of a pleasure. So some of my friends have been getting very dull and even dismal epistles from Edith. But today, full of sunshine and clear frosty air, with my muscles well stretched from walking about, and with my mind cheered up by the tonic of a good and productive day's work, I ought to be in good trim! *Qui vivra verra!* [Time will show.]

Well, the first news is that the contents of that parcel from Greeley, Colorado, are just about consumed. All that remains, I fancy, is the buttons, and a share of the beans which Mother is saving until I go home at Easter. She has tried them out twice. First time, she says, she got them a bit too dry. Second time, perfect! The family approves whole-heartedly (if heart is the right section) of pinto beans as grown by Phylabe.

I don't remember whether I told you that the powdered lemon juice was spilt. Unfortunately quite a lot of it was wasted, but we salvaged enough to make some simply heavenly drinks. Most of us have not tasted real lemon flavour for a year or two, so you can imagine what a treat it was. I wonder why there has been no attempt to import powdered lemon (and presumably orange?) juice—it would take up so much less space in the ships, and would bring us the vitamins of which we are supposed to be going rather short. Perhaps they never thought of it (whoever "they" may be can take the blame!)—and now, I suppose, with the war spread so tragically much farther over the globe, we do not hope for any extension of imports at all, but are just thankful for what we have already got.

You asked what we thought about the lend-lease foods we have had from America. I have heard nothing but praise for them, and people seem to be buying them eagerly. They only came on to the market after I gave up housekeeping on my own, so I don't know an awful lot about them. But I have had spiced ham several times in restaurants, and it is excellent. I'm told the sausage meat is grand, being just about 100 per cent pork. Sausage here is limited to (I think) 45 per cent of meat, and what the rest is, I don't know. If I had a kitchen of my own, I should certainly try the American variety. The shop windows are full of Spam and Prem and various other brands of meat, but I regret to say I've not had a chance to taste 'em.

We still get lots of good things to eat. There is certainly a lot less "real" meat—beef and mutton—to be had. I never did eat much, so I don't miss it, but working men, who thought they couldn't keep up their strength unless they stoked it with beef, grumble about the shortage. I can't blame them for refusing to believe that a plate of lettuce and grated carrot provides them with just as much nourishment!

I don't want to write about the war. The news is so sad today, with Singapore almost lost.[3] But I do want to say how terribly sorry I am that America is involved in the war. We couldn't do without her, but all the same I felt that so long as America remained untouched, there was enough of the world left clean and sane to provide a good nucleus for a new world peace. The thought of Americans having to undergo rationing, blackout and defence-of-the-realm restrictions, to say nothing of the loss of their men-folk, and possibly the destruction of their cities, just makes me sick with anger. But I must change the subject.

Today I really feel I am going to like my new job. In the past month, I've not been feeling at all sure! There didn't seem to be a proper niche for me (even for my physical body! I've been slum-housed at a tiny table in a corner, in a draught and a bad light, with nowhere to stow my mounting pile of files, and no place to set my telephone without doing acrobatics to reach it). Three weeks ago I had a touch of food poisoning (or maybe it was a gastric chill—this winter's most fashionable complaint) one symptom of which is deep, deep gloom, and I lay in bed and laid plans for another change of occupation, probably into the Land Army at about thirty bob a week (if you know what that means!). But with convalescence I developed a better idea, which was to reorganise the Ministry on the staff of which I now occupy an insignificant position so that I *would* like it! So this week I've begun reorganising! How far I shall

---

3. Singapore had fallen to the Japanese by mid-February.

get before somebody says Hi! remains to be seen but for the time being I'm enjoying myself. [Four lines struck through]

On second thoughts, the Censor might not like that, so out it comes. I'm sorry about the mess, though.

Today my job took me way up the Thames—such a dear river! The sun poured down a golden daffodil light from dawn to dusk, and the birds and I thought the spring had come and burst into song together—the thrushes more melodiously than I. I went to two factories where girls are doing skilled engineering work—it was good to see how happily they were doing their unaccustomed war-time work, and with what pride of craftsmanship they took the silk-smooth bits of metal from their machines, running caressing fingers over them and exclaiming to each other "Look, isn't it beautiful!" The male manager of one of the factories told me he "gets more out of the girls" than out of the men who used to do the work, just because of the feminine pride in doing a neat and beautifully finished job. But they need a "personal touch" of individual attention—with praise attached—from the boss! Well, that's the sort of creatures we women are! I respond to a bit of praise from the boss myself.

One of my boy friends has just phoned to ask if he can come round and see me, so instead of continuing to write to you I shall have to clean up my day-dirty face and prink a bit. He's a corporal in the Royal Air Force, and stationed not far from here. He used to be on the rival paper in Newcastle 10 or 12 years ago; then I lost sight of him. He was on Mosley's Fascist paper, *Action,* editing it for a time;[4] but I don't think he found it a very congenial job. Then he started writing short, factual books for a popular series. Now, in the intervals of doing R.A.F. work, he is studying law in the hope of becoming a barrister after the war.

. . . (It is now a week since I typed the other side of the sheet). . . . Alas, my day of exhilaration, on which I began this letter, soon passed, and I have had a very hard and indeed dismal week. There is something not quite right about this job of mine—for one thing, there's an office feud going on, and poor innocent I seem . . . to be the cannon-fodder between the two sides. I don't think there's any personal animosity against me, but it's a curious—and

---

4. Harold Nicolson was the editor of Mosley's paper *Action.* It is not he who is intended here.

not altogether happy—position. Yesterday I even got to the point of telling my Senior I was going to resign. But she (who is always most kind and helpful) was quite distressed and said I must not think of it, so for the present I am still hanging on. But really, really—a girl has to take a stand somewhere! Don't you agree?

And there is our Bessie with a brand new job, too! I had such a nice long letter from her last week—full of news of blackouts, Christmas celebrations, . . . and other cheery topics. . . .

I'm terribly glad Bessie is still in Victoria, I must say. I'd heard . . . that she was due to arrive in Ottawa at any moment, and I was thinking with great disappointment, "Bother the girl. How can I go and visit her in Victoria, B.C. if she is going to live in Ottawa?" However, all is well. I am glad for her sake, too, for I can't think she would have been happy in Ottawa. Speaking from the abyss of dark personal experience I should say she'd have missed her home, her friends, her Club work, her old associations and all the fun of being a well known personage in her home town, and this on the top of all the difficulty and strain of taking up a new job. Often in the past have I preached to my young friends on the merit of being a rolling stone, garnering varied experiences to make a richly tapestried life (Ramsay Mac[D]onald could not have mixed his metaphors better!) and being enterprising, and cutting free from parental apron-strings, and so on, and so on; but now that I'm getting old and wise (?), I feel more like preaching the virtues of contentment and a quiet mind. . . .

March 4

Dear Phylabe, you put me to shame. Here I came back after a few days unexpected leave and found ANOTHER letter from you, before I have got any part of this one off to you. My head is bowed under coals and coals of fire. Please believe it is not lack of interest that stops me from writing—I just love writing to you and would enjoy a nice long evening with you. It really is just that I have extremely little time, and that time comes late in the day when I am tired, especially around the eyes, which are bothering me a bit just now. Also, I frequently need to bring work home with me, as I find it difficult to write articles in the office where the interruptions never cease. I've brought one home to do tonight, as a matter of fact (a leaflet to compose but I've decided to write to you first and then see how I feel!).

And after all that apology and explanation, seems to me I'd better get on with the letter! It may be a bit spasmodic, for I'm doing my weekly wash at the same time—leave things to steep while I write a few paragraphs, then rub, then write more, then rinse, then write again. Don't know whether my laundry system is ideal, but anyway, that's how I like to do it. Also, at this particular moment, I'm eating my supper too. I got home too late to have a meal in the cafeteria, which because of the war closes at the ridiculously early hour of 7.30 p.m., and as I often am too late for it, I keep a supply of biscuits, honey, margarine, and other such fill-gaps in my room. I also have my half-pint of milk—the ration has been four half-pints per week, though usually my dairyman has had enough to allow me a half-pint on five or six mornings a week. I used to use AT LEAST a pint of milk a day for drinking, apart from cooking, in the good old days, so the milk ration is one aspect of war I have NOT enjoyed. My main foods, in fact, were milk, eggs and fruit—just the things we can't get enough of now. I'd not SEEN an egg for three months till I went home on leave last week. I could have bought my ration of two a month or thereabouts, but have no means of cooking them, and fond though I be of eggs, I don't know that I like 'em raw! Fruit, of course, is hardly to be obtained. I had a pound of apples about six weeks ago, and now that rhubarb is coming into season again I am hoping some restaurant will some day produce a rhubarb pie. There seems to be a new supply of prunes in, and I have bought some, but I can only steep them and eat them uncooked, which I hope gives me the food value, though they are not so palatable as when gently stewed with sugar. There has also been a steady, though small, supply of sultanas.

The astonishing thing, Phylabe, is that we get so easily and quickly accustomed to shortages that we forget all about them. A year ago I should have said that I couldn't continue to live without eggs and milk—but I don't mind the shortage of them at all now! However, I must tell you that when I went home last week I said to Mother, "The thing I most want in the whole world is a fried egg." Her prompt reply was "You shall have a fried egg for breakfast every morning you are here." And I did, too. This was quite fair—I don't want you to think I gobbled up the whole family's egg ration for a month!—because when I gave up house[keeping] I bequeathed to Mother the pail of eggs I had put down in waterglass when eggs were unrationed and reasonably plentiful last spring.

Does this letter SOUND tired? Seems to me it is creaking badly, but maybe it is the distractions in the shape of honey, milk and soapy lather,—did you hear that our latest rationed commodity is soap? Somebody gave me a box of bath soap as a Christmas present, so I shall be able to keep very clean for a year at least. But I was caught napping with absolutely NO soap flakes or powder for laundry. And this is quite a problem, for the water in London is so hard that it simply eats up the soap flakes. The ration works out at 12 ounces per month of the soap flakes I use, which will be enough, but hardly too much. If I needed to buy toilet and household soaps as well, I think I should find the ration extremely meagre, and I am just waiting to see how the country's housewives are going to manage. There has already been a demand for extra soap for people like miners, who get very dirty at work, and for mothers with small babies who use a score of napkins (don't you call them diapers?) every day. But I must say that we in this country LIKE rationing, because it is so fair, and makes everybody alike and ensures everybody a share, even if not as much as they'd like. I am sure you will find it a good system too, in so far as you need to ration goods; but I imagine your food supplies will always be better than ours, as you are so much less dependent on shipping and have so much more agricultural land to use. Your sugar ration is twice as big as our $1/2$ lb. a week we get.

Oh—I am forgetting to tell you that I got my share of the beans. I told you Mother was saving some of them till I could go home, so of course they had to be cooked while I was there a few days ago. We had them on Sunday along with our dinner of roast mutton, baked potatoes, and sprouts, and I thought they were very good indeed. Of course they were cooked with a piece of bacon instead of with fat pork, and with golden syrup instead of with molasses, but I've no doubt the general result was much the same. We certainly liked them, and I must tell you that Father has taken a handful of the beans to plant in the garden so that we can (with luck) have a crop of our own. We enjoyed our dinner, there's no denying—and yet, your account of beans along with cornbread sticks, cabbage and apple salad and pie makes me think I would have enjoyed yours even more! That's just because it's so American—you've no idea what a passion this child nourishes for all things American. And that reminds me to tell you that I have this week seen two U.S.A. soldier boys in London—the first, surely to have taken their place here among the Canadians, New Zealanders, Australians, South Africans, Indians, Free French, Czechs, Dutch, Belgian and Norwegian soldiers, sailors and airmen who seem to make up quite half of our population these days of strange events and conditions. I wanted to rush up to your two compatriots and slap them on the back and say "Hail Columbia" in a very loud voice, but I maintained my English sangfroid habituel with an effort, though I hope the warmth of the welcome I sent them mentally may have just touched them a little bit.

It is most awfully kind of you to suggest sending more beans, and chili sauce and magazines and "anything else" that we'd like. You make me feel quite tearful with all your goodness and sympathy and generosity and I cannot thank you enough. It is lovely to receive things from you, partly for the gifts themselves, which are most acceptable, but far, far more for the friendship that sends them, and I only wish I could tell you what warmth of appreciation for American generosity flows around this country now, and how much our Base family joins in the general feeling as a result of the parcels and letters from Greeley, Colorado.

However, I do feel that the honest thing to say is that so far we are not in *need* of extra foods, acceptable though the delicious extras are—and to ask for luxuries like magazines (though my soul craves for them!) puts too heavy a burden on our consciences when we remember the sailor-boys who'd risk their lives to bring them for us. So thank you, very, very much, Phylabe dear, but we can manage fine, so do not you worry about us. When the war is over, I will send you an expensive cable and tell you all the things I want from America—magazines, and Ivory Flakes, and I. Miller shoes, and a Woodbury Facial Cocktail and a pumpkin, to mention just a few— and you can send me every one! But until then I will just do without.

There IS one thing I may write and ask you for soon, however, and that is a McCall dress pattern. I have always made my dresses, etc. from McCall patterns, which fit me perfectly; but now they are very hard to come by. I have some dress material waiting to be made up, and when I am ready to start dressmaking again, I will see the McCall catalogue at my pet store and send you the number of the chosen patterns. But at the moment I have all the clothes I need (in spite of rationing!). *McCalls* Magazine is one of my chief American weaknesses, and so far my newsagent continues to deliver it, with a few misses to which (like the eggs and apples shortage) I am becoming resigned. I should like some day to see a copy of the *Better Homes and Gardens* magazine you mention, and see how your homes differ from ours—but for that, too, I can wait till the war's won.

So you have been having a severe winter too. Ours has been "the worst since 1887" or some such year way back in the beyond. My poor Mother and Father have been feeling it rather badly, and Mother is a cripple with broken chilblains on her feet. She just cannot get her outdoor shoes on at all. It has hardly stopped freezing for nine weeks—a most unusual state of things for this sea-warmed little country. It was bitterly cold when I was home last week (I keep mentioning this holiday without explaining that our leave-year ended on Feb. 28 and I was suddenly handed four days' leave on a plate, to take at once before the year ended. It had never occurred to me that I should merit any leave after being there only 3 $1/2$ months)—but here in London it is beginning to be spring at last. The flower-sellers' barrows are ablaze with daffodils, and there are fat buds on some of the trees, even though the gulls and waterhens still *walk* over the surface of the ponds in the parks! The thaw has come, but the ice was too thick to melt quickly. Cold weather doesn't suit me—I just shrivel up. London's climate suits me a lot better than Newcastle's—for that bit of the North East Coast is the bleakest bit of all England; but I want something still warmer— Victoria, B.C., perhaps, or one of the Western States of America!

You say nice things about the British folk's courage, and ask if they are schooled from childhood to think of others. Don't know. I read somewhere recently an article on our Public School system (much criticized, and much defended, as perhaps you know). The writer gave it credit for turning out men who devote themselves to duty and public service and are "incredibly brave" but he pointed out that the same men were often rather stupid!! But it certainly is not only the Public School class who are brave, for this war has brought out the most astounding cases of bravery in all sections of the community. And apart from outstanding pieces of valour, the general courage and cheerfulness of people—housewives and old men and young boys, just everybody—is rather surprising. I'm sure they never *think* about being brave—they just ARE. I don't know that it's peculiar to the Anglo-Saxon—what about the Russians and the Chinese? Maybe it's heresy, but what about the Germans and the Japs? Courage, I suppose, is just one of the nobler attributes of mankind in general, and like all the other noble qualities, needs trial to prove its strength. I heard a story today that will help you to believe in the fundamental worth of man (I hope you are not in any doubt of it!). It's of a boy of 16 who went to sea on a merchant ship. The ship was torpedoed off the coast of Newfoundland in terrible weather and the boy spent I-don't-know how many days in an open boat, exposed to fearful cold. He suffered so severely from frostbite that both his legs had to be amputated.

Now the lad is back in England and has been fitted up with a couple of artificial legs. The Government, you know, has a scheme for rehabilitating disabled people, and this boy was one for whom the Government officers were trying to make a new life possible. They asked him what he would like to try to do. What do you think he said? He asked if he could be trained as a wireless operator and go to sea again!

And there is a girl up near my home town who lost both her hands in an air raid last year. She is now learning to write—and doing better writing with her artificial hand than she did before with her natural hand! She wants to be a telephone operator, so they are training her to do it.

That's the sort of spiritual courage that really does merit the description "incredibly brave," don't you think? It makes one think better of the whole human race to hear about it.

. . . It is long past my bedtime, Phylabe, and I shan't want to get up when the alarm clock goes off in the morning. So I must end this letter—temporarily. I will regard it as an installment and will continue with the next before long. . . .

Thank you, too, for the very interesting parcel of papers that arrived from you a few days ago. It's funny, but I hardly ever get a laugh out of the *New Yorker.* The jokes just seem to pass me by. Do you ever see our *Punch,* and does that make you laugh? I'd be interested to know, for it seems to me that Americans and English just don't have the same sort of fun-sense. But there was at any rate one of those drawings that tickled me to death—the lady with the very bare shoulders and top-of-bosom sitting at the far side of the dining table, and the other woman saying to her neighbour "Do look at Mrs. So-and-So when she stands up; she has the most beautiful gown on." Yes, that is a gorgeous one. . . .

By the way, you may get faint emanations from me through your papers. I often supply information about women in war work to American journalists here. It is part of my work which gives me a great thrill. But of course it is entirely anonymous.

MUST go to bed.

My very best wishes to you, and kindest greetings to your Mother and Dad.

Sincerely your
Edith

✉ **5**
Central YWCA
Great Russell St.
London WC 1
Easter Tuesday, 1942

My dear Phylabe

What a most lovely gift you have sent me! I've never seen such a beautiful scarf in all my life, and you have chosen just the colors I love—cream and green and crimson. I'm always happiest when there's a touch of red in my costume—red the colour for life and energy. It was such a loving and kind thought to send it—thank you so *very* much.

So you have "V for Victory" signs too! They have simply swept the country here—worked into costume decorations, used for advertising, scrawled on doors and painted on lorries. If only we could get past the slogan to the fact!

Is life much changed for you by the war? Looking back three years, I see that English life is *much* changed—denuded of so many graces and comforts and luxuries. Yet so much remains! Humanity soon adapts itself to new conditions. We have relatively little meat, so we eat more vegetables. Short of milk, we drink cocoa. Few cakes, so we take more bread. We had our first "national" loaf[5] yesterday, and I for one have no complaints to make! It is a sort of pale brown colour—not so dark or rough as the whole-meal bread we have previously spoken of as "brown." A very *very* great improvement on the "Standard" bread I faintly remember eating in the 1914–18 war. *That* was a dirty white in colour and pasty in consistency. But, wars apart, I have always been a brown-bread eater, so I am quite happy.

---

5. The national loaf was made from flour from which 85 percent of the wheat had been extracted.

This is being written on a train, Phylabe, so if you and Bessie have any more critical remarks to make about my handwriting, please make allowances this time! I have been spending a heavenly weekend in the Cotswold country, on the border of Oxfordshire and Gloucestershire, which I love above all other parts of England. It is such gracious, quiet country—golden-grey earth, golden-grey stone villages, the trees still, in this late spring, like sooty smudges against the gold. My Northumbrian eye—"From his castle walls a man may see the mountains far away"—loves an austere and wide-horizoned view; Southern England is often too bosky for me, too lush and green in summer. But this Cotswold country of gently sweeping hills and tranquil colors has just the perfect blend of simplicity and grace. Wish you could have been here this weekend! In Northumberland, the prevailing colour is blue—purply-blue moorland and hills and purply-black ploughed earth. Until you know it and love it, it is forbidding and fierce (though most beautiful). The Cotswold colour is yellow—the pale cream of new cut stone and the smoky yellow of lichen. *Such* a contrast. And I love them both, but Gloucestershire is where I would live.

Thirza West, my hostess, is a Hieland Scottish lassie, (usually to be seen in a tartan kilt!), but she is Cotswold-charmed too. Her cottage is 16th century, with a thatched roof *but* it has indoor sanitation and hot and cold water and a telephone and electric light! The village was there in times of Domesday Book making, and up the road is a Roman campsite. Around the hill is a Saxon burial ground, the skeletons laid all with feet to the setting sun. Now a charming little birch wood grows over it, and the Saxon warriors blossom this Eastertide in blue and white violets. Oh, I love this place! I lived here (it is rapidly sliding behind me as the train flies on) for two years once, on the staff of a magazine *The Countryman* which is produced from the Manor House of this tiny hamlet. I think it was the richest time of my life, (though there was much unhappiness in it too), and I made friends of the heart's best kind with several people as well as with the hills and woods. I never really want to live in towns— though I enjoy the concerts and meetings and plays and coming and going of a big city. But my sort of work seems to lead me always to cities. You are fortunate to be a farmer—you think so too? Tell me next time you write what sort of jobs you do. All I know so far is that you drive a tractor. Wish I was a farmer's girl! This morning Thirza and I were up at 4 a.m. by the sun (6 by our double summer time) and walked 3 $^1/_2$ miles to the station (no cars left running in the village! No petrol) while the moon grew paler and the thrushes tried their waking-up songs and finally, as we got to the railway, the sun flamed up behind the Tudor chimneys of the inn. I would have given worlds to stay! But in half an hour now I shall be back in the Great Wen—back in "Smoke," as Canadian Tommy calls the Centre of the World, back in my semi-basement, always artificially-lit room at the office. Oh dear, oh dear.

(But Thames is running past my left elbow all this time, and very lovely.)

I have been writing a long survey of the mobilisation of woman power in the war for Miss Frances Perkins' Department.[6] It will now be in Washington if the clipper did as was expected of her. It gave me a great thrill to stretch my pen across the ocean to your country. Wish I could have delivered the parcel by hand and come home via Greeley, Colorado! But here is a tidbit of news for you. A voice on the telephone the other day said, "This is Bill White of the New York *Herald-Tribune*"—and I am expecting to meet this New York Bill for luncheon any day, as he is a friend of a Newcastle friend of mine. Guess how I am looking forward to it!

Quite a number of American journalists (women) come into the office—Miss Harriman,[7] daughter of your Averell Harriman is one of them—and they are all so charming and all so extremely well-dressed, well-groomed and attractive! The more I see of Americans, the more I like them. Hope I see *many* more! There are American soldiers and airmen in London, though not many so far.

I think you would like *The Countryman* magazine which is all about country matters—crops and birds and folklore and tilling the soil, so I have asked Thirza to post it to you each quarter. Unfortunately it is only half the size of normal days, though there is still a lot of good reading matter. The "Northumbrian friend" mentioned in the Editor's reminiscences about Pace Eggs in the current number is me, and indeed all the information in that section (about Easter Egg

---

6. Frances Perkins was President Roosevelt's Secretary of Labor. She was the first woman in the presidential cabinet and served from 1933 to 1945.

7. Kathleen Harriman accompanied her father to London and got a job with the London bureau of the International News Service and later with *Newsweek*. She was in London from May 1941 to October 1943 when she left for Russia.

customs) came from my father and me. The Editor is a patriarchal old gentleman with a snow white beard, looking most benevolent and genial. He *is* a fine man, but he led his staff of girls an awful life when I was there! He was one of the only two people I have ever felt I hated! However, we are great friends now and all is forgiven and forgotten! (I started to put him in a book, but it would have landed me in gaol for libel, certainly.)

Talking about eggs, Thirza gave me an egg every day I was there—a great treat, as I never get eggs in London. (It's awful to think of the place food now has in British conversation!)

Coming into London now, so I must stop writing for the time being. Hope you can read my untidy writing (how I envy you yours!).

Thursday, April 9th

Time that all good girls were in bed (where I am, actually), but I must add a wee bitty more because your "interim letter" reached me this morning, along with the exciting programme for the opera festival. Did you go? It reminded me of the opera at Salzburg (we stood on the city walls and looked over the hills to Berchtesgarten) and all the music history hanging like magic about that lovely city's ancient stones. Mozart was born there—is not his story the saddest and most glorious of all men's histories? In Salzburg there are wonderful Baroque churches, and dreaming squares where the old men sit in the sunshine and the women wear (they did when we were there, before the *Anschluss*) their becoming national dress. But why am I telling you about Salzburg? Hitler rules there now, alackaday.

One point in your letter I must refer to—this broadcasting gallant who tells you we are reduced to eating sparrows and seagulls. What non-sense! I've certainly never heard of anybody eating such food, and there is *no need* to—we are not short of food (only short of *some varieties* of our former food). If any London shop had such birds on sale (both sparrows and seagulls are "varmints" which steal the sown corn from the fields and destroy the young shoots), it can only have been an impertinent experiment, and I feel like ringing up the BBC and protesting against any of their overseas broadcasters being permitted to say such things. Supposing Goebbels heard it—what propaganda material for him! And it's *untrue!* I feel quite angry about it!

I am sending you two letters I have just received from my young friend Marjorie Redfern, formerly on the Newcastle *Chronicle* staff, who has just joined the A.T.S. (women of the Army). . . . I'm so relieved to find she's enjoying the life, for she's the sensitive, fastidious sort and I was a bit worried. Don't send the letters back—but pass them on to Bessie if you like. She may be interested in reading them.

Went to the flicks last night and saw Gary Cooper (whom I protest I love) in *Ball of Fire*. Great fun! Also a Ministry of Information film called *Listen to Britain*—do go to see it if by chance it is shown your way. It brought a lump into my throat, just by bringing us pictures and sounds of Britain in wartime, with some lovely shots of Trafalgar Square (Nelson still on his column), and the Queen looking so sweet as she sat among ordinary war workers and such at a lunchtime concert in the National Gallery. It was she who made me want to cry. No more now except lots and lots of good wishes, and many, many more thanks for your lovely gift.

Edith

✉ **6**

THE BRITISH BROADCASTING CORPORATION
Broadcasting House, London, W. 1
23 April 1942

Miss E. Base
Central Y.W.C.A. Club
Great Russell Street
London, W.C. 1.

Dear Madam

I am writing in answer to your letter of the 12th April. We are grateful to you for bringing to our attention the regrettable inferences drawn from Mr. Robert St. John's broadcast to the U.S.A. in which he suggested that we are short of food in this country. Mr. St. John is acting as an American commentator from this country for the American network N.B.C. No censorship of such items is exercised on these commentators; they can claim complete freedom for comment on subjects which do not directly involve vital information, but we can draw their attention to the harm which any statement they have broadcast may have caused. Great care is, of course, taken in the BBC's own service broadcast to America that no such suggestions are made.

We should like to thank you for writing and can assure you that note will be taken of your comments in suitable quarters.

Yours faithfully,
R. M. Wellington
for Director Secretariat

This was the broadcast which told you we were eating seagulls and sparrows! I protested!

✉   **7**
London. July 13/42

Dear Phylabe

No time for a letter—but it struck me when reading my paper this morning that you might be interested to note the large proportion of space in our tiny wartime papers that is allotted to American interests. This day's issue is fairly typical. The latest fashion in everything here is American!—a new American restaurant in Leicester Square. "American coffee made here" on half the cafes, "Real American Hamburgers" at the eat-quick places, Fifth Avenue styles in the dress shops—an American soldier, if you can manage it, to give you his arm! How the girls love your boys! The nice British airman (a cousin of mine by marriage) whom I dined and danced with on Saturday said cynically "It's the money these chaps get—," but I don't believe our lassies are so mercenary—they are caught by the glamour of the "foreigner" (one never thinks of Americans as foreign) who speaks with their own tongue (though with fascinating differences); also by the smart uniforms, so much better than our lads' battle dress; also by the American boy's forthcoming methods?! It is interesting to see how an American boy out with a girl woos her boldly and unashamedly in public! The English lad always treats his girl with deference and discretion—such discretion sometimes that it almost looks like neglect!—in streets, cafes and public vehicles. No wonder the American way flatters our girls! I mustn't start another page! Mean to write very soon though.

Edith

✉   **8**
Central YWCA
Great Russell St.
London WC 1
August 1, 1942

My dear Phylabe

This is not a letter—just the briefest note to tell you your lovely parcel arrived, and ON MY BIRTHDAY, which was very delightful for me and extremely clever of you! . . . There was also an exciting surprise in the form of an airgraph letter from Bessie, so altogether it was a RED LETTER BIRTHDAY.

It was a delicious parcel—full of all sorts of unexpected pleasures. The red socks are something I was just needing and looking for—only if I'd bought them for myself they'd have cost me a precious COUPON out of my ration of 20; so think what you have saved me! I wore them today and felt VERY SMART. The lipsticks, too, are something to make eyes pop out of heads—rarer than foxes in the woods, are lipsticks! The colours are exactly right—oh, you are clever! Pectin I think is quite unprocurable here—so off it went to Mother to help with her summer preserves; she is in the thick of her jam and jelly making and will be delighted with the contribution. The beans and the apple and a share of the candies and gum also went home, and I expect you will hear about it. The lemon juice I am keeping to make up for all the fresh fruit I am NOT getting this year. (It is tragic not to be at home now, for they are having a record year with soft fruit crops—my mouth waters when I think about their strawberries and raspberries).

So you see you have given us an enormous amount of pleasure, and we do think you are the dearest girl to send us such lovely things and such kindly thoughts. I will write again soon, if my intentions and DESIRES make their due effect, but och, I am a busy woman these days, with a new job in the Press Office of the Ministry—a HECTIC job, but I like it—and a job on hand for the Business and Professional Women's federation as well. Not to mention fun and games of one sort and another.

A letter you must have quite soon, all the same.

Here are the promised photos of me. One from 1932, to show you what I was like, one from 1938 (coming by Cunard-White Star to America) and one of today—a "candid-camera" specimen, I'm

(*Left*) Edith Base, summer of 1932. (*Below*) Edith Base on deck of *Cunard-White Star*, crossing the Atlantic in May 1938.

Edith Base in Hyde Park, July
1942 (reference in letter 8).

afraid, and not much glamour about it. Still, I mustn't mislead you,
must I? . . .

On second thoughts, I'll send you a full set of the snaps taken of
me two or three weeks ago—in Hyde Park (note my Utility suit!).

My love to you
Edith

✉ **9**
29 Stanley Gardens
London W 11
24.11.42

My very dear neglected Phylabe
It is months and MONTHS and *MONTHS* since I wrote to you,
and I feel very badly about it. But 'tis not because I've not been
thinking about you! I think about you A LOT. But I seem to get

busier and busier, specially since I took to home-keeping again—don't overlook my new address. 29 Stanley Gardens is a large, imposing house on the curve of a quite imposing crescent in the very pleasant district of London known as Notting Hill Gate—part of the Royal Borough of Kensington. I have a minute small flat in this impressive residence, and simply adore it. Indeed, I've "flitted" twice within the past three months—and I hope that will serve as partial explanation of my long neglect, for it's made endless work, and I'm still not at the end of scouring and adapting, polishing and renovating, curtain-altering etc., etc., etc. In time I shall get so used to the *un*polished and *un*adapted misfits that I'll stop noticing them and they'll finish their days undone. But never mind.

I'm away from the house from 8:30 a.m. to 7:30 p.m. When I get home at night I cook a meal, eat it and clear away and by then it seems to be bedtime. Weekends are just hectic. Occasionally I wonder whether it was wise to take a flat again when I have so little time; but on the whole the benefits outweigh the disadvantages. It's heavenly to be able to stretch one's legs in front of one's own fire—just imagine, I went all through last winter *without* a fire to stretch my legs in front of! And it's worth a lot to be able to make a cup of tea whenever one's heart craves for a cup of tea. . . . But I fear me my social life will become even more tenuous and will probably perish altogether from attrition quite soon. Last week I was home in Newcastle (for my parents' Golden Wedding) and went to see a friend whose chief delight is to get her girl friends married off. "What!" she exclaimed, "you're in a block of WOMEN'S SERVICE CHAMBERS? ALL WOMEN? NO MEN!!!" She saw the calamity of the situation at once! But what can I do. There are MILLIONS of men in London Town. But they don't seem to have noticed me yet.

Incidentally, I've not made friends with any of your countrymen, though I see scores of them every day. Last night I was walking swiftly in the dark along Piccadilly on my way home. An American boy was walking at just the same pace about a yard ahead and slightly to the left of me, but my soles were rubber and silent, so he was unaware of me. Suddenly he turned right across my path and I had to halt on my heels to avoid knocking him over (or maybe it would have been me that was knocked over). "Excuse me, ma'am," he said with a soft slow voice that I took to be Southern and which charmed me because that sort of courtesy isn't often met with in English people. A short "Sorry" would have covered the situation for most of us. Being rather taken aback, I had nothing to say, but curse myself now for my slowness in not saying something pleasant. It was too dark for him to see by my face that I wasn't grumpy, but I hope he didn't think "Bah, these uncouth unfriendly English. . . ." I don't think your lads will have much chance to think that way on the whole, for they are most tremendously popular over here and most people go out of their way to be nice to "the Yanks." (Hope you don't mind being referred to thataway!)

Anglo-U.S. Combined HQ (Army) is in the same Square as my office, so there are always plenty of American officers about. Free French HQ is just down the street, too, so we hear a mixture of tongues. Your Officers have practically stolen away the cafe at the corner where I often used to lunch, too; unless one goes very early, there's never a place free. Occasionally I sit next to an American and chat slightly; but I'm a shy girl really! I had a nice American journalist in to see me today, to get more information about our women in their war work. He was Geoffrey Parsons of the *New York Herald-Tribune*—does his name mean anything to you?[8] Miss Harriman . . . gave me a bad half hour by requesting comparative figures of cost of living and wages, before the war and now. There was nobody in the Press Room when she came, as it happened, except me, so I had to "cope." But I simply hate questions to do with statistics! They terrify me, because figures mean nothing to me and I am always liable to add or subtract a nothing at the end of a figure. However, I delved bravely into old records for her, and HOPE she got her story across safely.

Last week, too, I met Professor Winifred Cullis, who is as English as I am (to all intents and purposes) but is in charge of the Women's Section of our Institute of Information in N.Y.[9] One of my jobs is to keep her New York office supplied with material about British women in the war effort, and it was quite thrilling to talk to Professor Cullis and feel that I do have quite a considerable link with

---

8. Geoffrey Parsons, Jr., was a war correspondent in London in 1941 and chief of the London Bureau 1943–1944. He became editor of the European edition of the *New York Herald Tribune* when it resumed publishing in December 1944.

9. Winifred Cullis was Professor Emeritus of Physiology of the University of London. She served as head of the Women's Section of the British Information Services in the United States, 1941–1943. She was the author of numerous books and scientific papers

America after all. Considering the stuff I have sent to Professor Cullis (through Ministry of Information channels) and the number of American journalists I have primed with information, I feel sure you must have read some of my sentences around sometime! They would be quite impersonal, however.

Well, Phylabe, dear, I had almost forgotten that this is really a Christmas letter, meant to bring you my cheeriest and best wishes for a bright, brisk and blessed Christmas time and the happiest New Year of all your life. It is hard to imagine Christmas here at the moment, as we are in the month of fogs and the blackout seems denser than ever, the shops all close at 4 p.m. and even when they're open there's hardly a sparkle from one of them, because we are all saving fuel (including light) so earnestly. We issued a Press Notice from the office yesterday that workers are to have two days holiday at Christmas or New Year—but are NOT EXPECTED TO TRAVEL. So I am not thinking of going home again this year. But who cares about a spoiled Christmas, or dark streets, or a shortage of Christmas presents or a milk ration of only two pints a week, now when the news every day is so marvelous! D'you know, Phylabe, you could FEEL the high spirits in the air that Sunday when your lads and ours were reported to have landed in North Africa [8 November 1942]. Fed-up-ness just vanished—if only I could tell you how everybody over here was just *aching* for the Allied Nations to ACT, to go in and WIN something for a change. They were getting more and more critical of the Government; even Mr. Churchill was being called hard names. "Second Front" was being chalked on pavements and walls all over the place, and we couldn't mention Russia and Stalingrad without feeling ashamed. But now everybody's got a new lease of enthusiasm, and production in the factories is going up sky high. Mother's got her flag all ready for Victory Day—won't there be some fun when it does come! I hope I'm in London that day—I want to see John Bull go wild with joy—if that's the way it's going to take him this time; he may just want to sink to his knees.

So this looks like being a happy Christmas, and I do hope that by the time this letter reaches you you will be plucking the turkey (or are you eating it tomorrow for Thanksgiving Day?) and looking in your stocking to see what Santa Claus has brought and generally be preparing for a really rollicking time. . . .

As a Christmas present I am sending you a book which I hope you will enjoy if you have any time at all for reading. Your last "interim" letter showed me a picture of a very, very hard-worked Phylabe with no time for lounging whatever; but I hope there is a little rest for farmers in the winter time. Have you had the sort of bumper harvest and crops that Britain has been having? It has been a wonderful year here. My Uncle Andrew in County Durham has the richest juiciest-looking stockyard he has ever had in his farming career, and everything he has planted has produced record results. Williamson will give you a picture of English farming life that you may find interesting to compare with your own. Of course he is also a prophet with a message, but it is more for his descriptions of the English scene that I send you his book.

Oh, this English scene! I am still wildly enthusiastic about London, which I am sure is the most typically English place of all, in spite of its cosmopolitan variety and size. I walk to work each day through the Royal parks—a crow-straight walk of three miles to the heart of London, Piccadilly, and in an English wood all the way! Isn't it wonderful? Never believe the people who tell you London is a place of cramped and crooked old streets, all smoke and grime and confusion. Tell them to take a walk from Piccadilly Circus to Notting Hill Gate by way of Hyde Park Corner, Rotten Row and the Round Pond—through Kensington Gardens where in this lovely autumn the elms have stood like dancers in black lace and gold spangles; or for a change to go by way of the Serpentine, and see the wild duck on the wing. Oh, it's beautiful, and captivating, and endlessly exciting. You must come—you MUST! . . .

Isn't this great news about our Bessie getting herself "tied up?" (That is her own phrase!) I was delighted to hear it, and am waiting for succeeding details most hungrily.

Now it's *the 25th*—I do hope it reaches you in time. I hoped to write pages and pages more tonight, but first I was late home, second I had to do a needy washing of smalls, third, my neighbour was talkative and I was too tired to resist, and fourth—it is now high time I was in my bed, so this is just a little paragraph to say Goodnight.

It's been a pleasant busy day. All days are busy since I moved out of Public Relations into Press Office. Reporters keep dropping in, the phones keep going—and each call usually means a lot of further telephoning and inquiring—and there's always a lot of reading to do, of newspapers, periodicals and Government Circulars. These Circulars are the chief pain in the neck—MILLIONS of them there seem to be, each one with a slight variation on some Regulation or another. My poor brain REELS. Today I also wrote a 1000-word article for a Turkish paper, planned a tour for a visiting American, and dictated large numbers of letters. By the way, I wonder whether you heard our Minister of Labour's speech last night?—he was to have broadcast it, but the atmospherics were wrong and the paper was read for him at the dinner in New York where he was to have been heard. Then did you hear a sort of Brains Trust broadcast last week in which my friend Mary Ferguson, a Fleet Street journalist, took part? There were two or three broadcasters on this side and a similar number on your side, the only American one I can remember being Eric Linklater.[10] Another transatlantic broadcaster I should like to think you had heard is Robertson Scott, editor of *The Country-man.* I believe he speaks to America quite frequently. At present I am minus a radio, so I miss an awful lot. They are hard to come by here nowadays, and even if there were lots, I have NO MONEY. But in the New Year, when I trust the financial crisis will have passed, I mean to get a set at the earliest possible moment. It's too awful an impoverishment to be without one.

I heard today from my *Countryman* friend Thirza that she is coming to spend Christmas with me here, so imagine me having a lovely time with a tall, near-redheaded Hieland Scottish lass in a tartan kilt. She is the Circulation Manager of *The Countryman,* and is awful keen on getting the circulation in America stepped up. Too bad that now the paper control limits the number of copies they can produce. By the way, would you like to continue to receive that magazine? I ordered it for a year, and think you will now have received the last copy, so if you enjoyed them tell me, and I'll repeat the order.

I hope your growing war restrictions are not . . . too irksome. It was awfully sad to read that you are only going to be allowed one cup of coffee a day—won't that be a severe deprivation to Americans? Our tea ration goes much further than that, and coffee is not rationed at all—but coffee is of course very much the secondary

---

10. Eric Linklater, author and university professor at Aberdeen, was assigned duty, under the director of public relations, in the War Office in 1941 and saw special service in Iceland and Italy. He later became rector of Aberdeen University. In fact, Edith may actually have been referring to the Canadian-born broadcaster Art Linkletter, who, in 1941, produced the "Cavalcade of America."

drink here. Our worst shortage is definitely milk. After that, as far as I am concerned, eggs and fruit. The meat ration of 1s. 1d. worth a week is ample for me—I usually take it in mutton chops and get three which, cooked in different ways, make me three good dinners. With Central London as my shopping ground, I've no difficulty in getting fish, liver, sausage and so forth, so please note that I am living like a lord! At the same time I'm losing weight, but that's just cussedness. At the Parent's Gold Wedding party we had 11 people to lunch and 17 to tea, and you should have seen the spread we managed! For lunch we had soup made of our own tomatoes, rabbit pie (rabbit not being on the ration) with lashings of home-grown vegetables, cheese and biscuits and coffee and apples (homegrown too). For tea we made large flat dishes of Swedish sandwiches with various non-rationed savoury and sweet spreads, home-baked scones with Mother's jams and jellies, and a REAL bride's cake made with the family's rations of eggs, butter and fruit. The mock almond icing was made with mashed potatoes or something odd like that, but it tasted marvelous. Milk would have been a difficulty, but mercifully our farmer guests from Uncle's farm brought their own. There was also a plentiful supply of Mother's famous apple cake, and various other bits and sorts of cake acquired from various sources. So you see it really WAS a party!

Well, here I really must stop, I'm afraid, or I'll never reach you by Christmas.

Have a LOVELY time, Phylabe dear, and may the Blessed Star shine on your path.

Lots of love and loving thoughts from
Yours ever
Edith

✉ **10**
Dec. 10, 1942
29 Stanley Gardens
London W 11

My dear Phylabe
What marvelous lucky packets you do send! Your last one (received Nov. 30) kept me from doing *any* work before

lunchtime—I just read and read and read, through letter (a *wonderful* letter), newspaper cuttings, Digest articles—the pictures were thrilling, too, especially the views of the Million Dollar Highway.[11] Have you driven along its entire length? Take me with you next time! Then we'll do the new Alaskan Highway (making Bessie the leader), and the Grand Trunk Road of India (did you read *Kim* when you were little?), and maybe finish up in England by following Watling Street from beginning to end, or the lovely Fosse Way (they were built by the Romans 1900 years ago) which is always scented with lilies-of-the-valley for me since I saw it first in spring when the wild lilies were abloom in the woods. But your packet—it too was an ecstatic experience, like the lilies along the Fosse Way, coming with surprise and delight. What a golden day you made that foggy November 30! I was three times my normal size all that day, being so enlarged with contentment and joy. . . .

I thought this was such a slack day in the office that I could start a letter to you, but since I wrote the top line a volcano has erupted . . . oh dear, tetchy people do make life difficult. Now all is peace again, (till the next spasm), and it's soon going to be tea time, so till then I hope we shall have no more interruptions.

I've just been doing a little bit of Christmas shop gazing. Can't say "shopping," 'cos I've not bought a thing. Our shops are gallant and gay and a little pathetic. The usual lovely Christmas luxury things are quite missing—instead there are bundles of *scraps* of old tweed, or artificial silk, or cotton, offered for sale along with patterns for making slippers, handbags, dolls and so on. I was looking for some bit of pink material to make a rag doll for a little friend, but found nothing. Last night I went through my wardrobe to see if there was an old garment I could cut up—but these days we wear our clothes till they're not even fit to make into rag dollies!—No— let's be honest! We're not really so badly off (though it's fashionable to pretend we are!). But it just happens that I've nothing suitable that could be cut up, so unless I spend two of my precious clothes coupons on half a yard of new material, it looks as if Mary would have to go without her doll. I had lovely schemes for *making* presents

---

11. U.S. Highway 550 between Ouray and Silverton, Colorado. The name probably comes from the exorbitant cost of paving this scenic road through the heart of the San Juan Mountains.

for everybody this year, but time is so sadly lacking. But to buy things to give is just impossible, for the most worthless little "fancy goods" are fantastically dear, and the good old stand-bys like handkerchiefs and stockings cost coupons, which few people can spare. Especially women, as furnishing fabrics and even such things as tea towels have to come out of our *clothes* ration!)

It's raining dismally today, but yesterday and for days before, the weather has been mild and gentle like—like—no, not like summer, but like the loveliest, softest December. Winter days have their own beauties—when I lived in the Cotswolds I learned to love November, with its hedgerows laced with mist-jewelled spider's webs, and February, flinging glittering gold hours out of azure skies and pearling the dykes with sudden hail. *Our* sort of hail! *Your* sort sounds too fierce by far. I remember once a hailstorm (thunderstorm hail) that killed some of our week-old chickens, but that was astounding— something to talk about still after 20 years like the snowstorm of 1884 (or when?) that my parents still talk of.

January 30, 1943

Oh Phylabe! What will you think of me? Two months today since your marvelous long letter (still being read and reread!) came, and still not acknowledged . . . over a week since your parcel—your lovely, exciting, delighting parcel! I owe you dozens and dozens and dozens of letters in return for all that—so here goes for a half-hour contribution, anyway, before I go to bed!

. . . I don't know where to start to tell you what pleasure you have given me, or what to say Thank You for first. So I'll say Thank you for Everything—and not least to Bessie for being so generous in sharing you with me! Supposing . . . I had never met Bessie, how much poorer I should be! And by degrees I get right back to a day some 15 years ago when with a very bad grace and fury in my heart I "did my duty" and went to the funeral of a man I had never seen.

The man was Bessie's grandfather, my mother's Uncle Joe. They lived in Leeds, and I happened to be on a visit to friends of mine in Leeds when Mother received news of Uncle Joe's death. Not able herself to go to the funeral[,] she sent word to me asking me to go, and I was very fed up I can tell, because not only did I scarcely know the Crowthers, but I had to miss a much-looked-forward-to picnic in order to go. But I went, unwilling and cross as I was. Well, the first part—going to the ceremony, standing in the graveyard, seeing the grief and tears, was depressing enough. But then Cousin Jim Crowther, whom I *had* met once or twice before, took charge of me, and was so kind and friendly that my black heart began to melt again. Then back at the house for tea *everybody* was so friendly and kind that I really began to feel very happy. Then Jim walked back to my friend's with me, and I thought it was a long time since I'd met anybody I like as much, and when he urged me to go and visit him and his family at Yeovil in Somerset, and meet his daughter Kay, I determined I would do so as soon as ever I could. But Yeovil was a long way from Newcastle, and it wasn't till I had left the North and was working on *The Countryman* in Oxfordshire that I was able to go to Yeovil and meet my charming cousin Kay. Incidentally, Kay, now married and the mother of two boys, is living at Gloucester and I hope to go and visit her there in three weeks' time when I have a couple of days leave falling due.

But if I had never met Kay, I should never have met Bessie, and if I'd never met Bessie—I shouldn't be sitting here in a brilliant red and orange Colorado pinny writing to Phylabe! All of which certainly points [up] the moral that one ought always to do one's duty even if it means forgoing a picnic; but this is a very long detour from saying Thank you for letters and parcel and friendship coming me-wards from Greeley, Colorado! But I am counting my blessings generally (and oh my goodness, I do have such lots).

I put on my bonny pinny (if you can understand Border English!) to show David, who came to tea, and kept it on while I baked an apple pie in the hope that Bill Gerringer[12] will be here tomorrow to help me eat it. Bill has twice been to London and twice failed to see me—the first time because he looked for me at the YWCA and I was no longer there (and the mutts didn't give him my address); the second time because I had warned him I would be much engaged that weekend (though if I'd known he was coming to town of *course* I'd have fitted him in somehow). But tomorrow I hope there are going to be *no* snags. I'm looking forward tremendously to meeting him and hearing news of Rose and you and feeling that you *are* real after all and not just a character I periodically read about in a charming book. Before this letter leaves me I may be able to tell you more.

---

12. Bill Gerringer was a college friend of Phylabe's.

I'd have liked David and Bill to meet. In your letter to [my sister] Chrissie . . . you said Bill was typically American and full of verve. Well, David is typical of a lot of things that I think are considered typically and exclusively English (though I must say I never met anybody but David that was so!)—and I think the contrast might have been rather piquant. David is tall, slender, dark, elegant and languid, and speaks with a really matchless English drawl. Today he wore pale fawn corduroy bags, a grey wool polo-necked sweater and grey tweed jacket and grey socks, and looked quite exquisite. He *looks* and *sounds* so tired and bored and lackadaisical—but what a deceiver! Did you ever read the Baroness Orzy's novels about the Scarlet Pimpernel? That's David to the live! He's not a lazy idle lounger, but an astute and intelligent advertising expert (was on *The Countryman,* and is now on *Punch*—or *was,* and *will be* again when the war's over); he's not a fop, but a London fireman and went through the blitzes of 1940–41 on duty, and saw the heart of London burn. He's also a devoted and quite selfless husband to my friend Joyce, who was also on *The Countryman,* and when Joyce suffered a mental breakdown after their baby was born, he cherished her with such patience and tenderness that I can hardly think of them now without a tear. Joyce and little Roger were evacuated to the country, and David only sees them for a weekend once in six weeks—but if Bill had met David today as I'd hoped, he'd have seen none of this in David's delicate, artistic form and amused, gentle smile, and I wouldn't mind betting a ha'penny he'd have thought the fellow was nuts. But maybe I'm wrong.

Anyway, David approved my pinny and I hope Bill approves my apple pie! He will also have a chance to eat a cookie made of four chocolate drops—what a fascinating idea, Phylabe! I could hardly wait to get the oven on and start mixing! I used up half of them last weekend and the rest today. I also made George Washington's Ma's gingerbread last weekend and ooh, was it good!!! I wish I had it left for Bill.

. . . There's no end of gale blowing round this house—and this afternoon we had a thunderstorm, of all queer things to happen in January. Heaven can show the Hun a thing or two when it comes to bangs! We've been hearing some of the Hunnish variety lately, too—an extremely noisy night a fortnight ago, my first notable London raid; then the next day [20 January] a daylight raid, in which a school was hit and nearly 50 little children killed. That shocked us all very much. I notice the tube stations (Underground) are full again at nights of timid people. A number have kept on sleeping in the Underground stations ever since 1940—mostly poor old things who, one suspects, are saving on house rent. They go down as soon as it gets dark, taking their bundles of blankets and all their possessions with them—it's pathetic but a little comic to see them fixing up old curtains round their bunks and making little private corners for themselves. But now one sees whole families in the tubes again. Probably they are people who've been bombed out once (or more) and don't intend to risk it again. But I hate to see children sleeping along the platforms crowded with people and noisy with trains and shouts. Curse Hitler and all his works.

Goodnight Phylabe. See you again tomorrow, I hope.

February 16, 1943 (just LOOK at the date!)

Two delightful things have happened today—first, a letter arrived from Phylabe (covering me with shame because this letter has never got off to you yet)—and I met (at last) Bill Geringer. . . .

First impressions of Bill were GOOD. We had about two hours together, and I am hoping to see more of him another time. He called for me at the office at 1 p.m. (I was taking a half day's leave) and we went to a well known brasserie on Piccadilly Circus for lunch. Considering that there's a war on, we had quite a good lunch—do you wonder what we ate? Tomato soup (large plates full), some excellent grilled sole (first I've seen in years) with creamed potato and anchovy sauce—no, not anchovy but shrimp— and a little blancmange-y sweet served with fruit syrup, and coffee. All right, eh? Then I took him on my favourite walk round my darling St. James's Park (where the crocuses are coming out and the ducks are getting gay), and I think his reactions were all right! I get so cross with people now if they *don't* react to dear, darling, beautiful, gracious London Town as warmly as I think they ought to! Dear London, how I do love her!

Imagine you getting out your maps and tracing my morning route (when I'm not too lie-abed and late) through the Parks. Now what Britisher would do that about Washington or New York? (They wouldn't have the maps, in the first place!) Ooh, Phylabe, you must come and SEE her. You can't IMAGINE how lovely and fascinating she is! . . .

No, I never met that Bill White. He rang me up one day and asked me if I'd meet him for lunch one day in the following week. I said Yes, he said he'd ring again to confirm the day—and I never heard another darned word from the fellow! Another *Herald-Tribune* man was in the office the other day and I asked for news of Bill White. It seems he is now in North Africa—but you are right in saying there are several Bill Whites in the Foreign Correspondents family. I had noticed reports from different places by "William White," so guessed there must be more than one. I wish I had met the one you knew.[13] A funny thing about the American reporters is that they always want FIGURES. HOW MANY women in the factories, HOW MUCH money are we spending, HOW MANY aeroplanes are we turning out—all the things we can't tell (and don't always know ourselves) on security grounds. This demand for figures is quite invariable on the part of your eager and practical-minded countrymen (and women)!

I've recently been reading William Shirer's fascinating and important *Berlin Diary*. What a picture! (My typing is so bad that I must admit I am terribly tired. The dearest of dear friends has been in Town for the past three days, and we have gone short of too much sleep. I promised myself an early-to-bed night tonight—but then your letter came!) But that *Berlin Diary* makes the life of a foreign correspondent sound so fantastically hectic that I wonder they don't all finish up in the madhouse! Flying about from capital to capital as I might go from Piccadilly to Leicester Square! I suppose man can condition himself to speed of that sort as he can to 400-miles an hour aeroplane travel. But what a life! Shirer's book was chiefly remarkable, though for its picture of the war through GERMAN eyes—and its view of the British pre-war goings-on, through the eyes of a neutral (even if a friendly one). I found it utterly enthralling.

---

13. The William White Phylabe knew was William Lindsay White, son of William Allen White, the editor of the *Emporia Gazette*. W. L. White, a correspondent representing the North American Newspaper Alliance and *Reader's Digest* in London, arrived in England during the winter of 1940–1941. He succeeded his father as editor of the Kansas newspaper and was the author of a dozen books, several written during the war years.

A William Chapman White was a foreign correspondent in Germany and Poland (1930–1931) and was with the Office of War Information in New York and London 1942–1945.

Next I read the charming book, *I too have lived in Arcadia,* by Mrs[.] Belloc Lowndes—the story of her own childhood and her parents' early married life in Paris during the Franco-Prussian war. Some of the descriptions might have been written today. Many of the stock French and British remarks—"the Germans are nothing but cruel, destructive brutes," "we must break up the German nation into small states again"—ARE being spoken and written today!

But Phylabe, how do you manage to do such a formidable war job as the one you have just taken on! Sixty hours a week! That is more than we like our women over here to work (though many of them do so)—and I am afraid you will find it leaves you with no time at all for many quite essential personal jobs. I find 52 hours quite enough, and I am not a farmer into the bargain! You sound so happy about it, though. I do think it is good of you to undertake this extra work when you have such heavy responsibilities on the farms. Now don't, for goodness' sake, go and make yourself ill!

Bill Gerringer tells me you are a mighty fine gal! Not that I needed to be told it—I knew it already from a thousand little bits of evidence in your letters. But it was nice to hear it in so many words from one who knows you. . . . I took great thought before going forth to meet Dr. Bill. Have you ever heard a woman say that she hasn't a rag to wear? That's my state at the present time—and it's a TRUE STATEMENT!!! So I looked at my red frock that had the moth in it and is full of darns and thought "Yes, it suits me, but if I wear it, I must wear my black hat and THAT makes me look middle-aged." So then I thought I had better wear my big brown felt hat, which is fairly becoming, but if I'd worn that I'd have had to put on my brown frock, which is dying of old age and is also full of darns, and my ancient llama-lamb coat (new to come to America in 1939 and worn steadily ever since), which really is *too* moulting and shabby. So the only choice left was my once-smart navy suit, bought in *1936* (believe it or not!) under my dowageresque musquash and a little navy felt of the same vintage as the suit. All this care and consideration, my dear Phylabe, was much less due to personal vanity than to anxiety for the honour of England! The nation had not to be let down *too* seriously. The plain fact is that I have had practically no new clothes (nothing "major", certainly—except a Utility suit which fits badly and was away at the cleaner's at the time) since before the war, and as most of my friends are in the same state, it doesn't really matter much on ordinary days. But

Meeting America is no ordinary occasion—and I am almost persuaded that I really MUST get myself some new rags before any more Red Letter Days loom upon the horizon. However, I've got loads of summer clothes, so I'll wait now till Autumn, then look for something really STUNNING.

Well, Phylabe, it's now February 24, and the state of my conscience just isn't fit to describe. It will serve me right if you cut me right out of your correspondence list—but please, *please*, Phylabe, don't do that! This poor letter is getting more and more dogs-eared as I carry it around. It has just been to Gloucester with me for the weekend, on a visit to Kay Crowther. I expected to write reams to you there—but a house that contains Kay to talk to, Jim to argue with and young Brian and Colin to listen to just is NOT the place to write letters in—and this time I decided to spare you the pains of reading a letter written on a rollicking wartime train.

When I got back there was a long lovely letter from Bessie . . . with news of the way she has been hobnobbing with a Ministry of Labour acquaintance of mine who was over there on a mission. I love the way she just phoned his hotel (having heard . . . that he knew me) and fixed up a dinner date! I just am tickled to death! Then it seems she took the whole British delegation on, inviting them to Charlie's and keeping them out of their beds till 1:30 a.m. Oooh, our Bessie is a rich one! And I'll bet those British Labour representatives wrote that evening up in their diaries with special-coloured ink! I enquired this morning and learned that the delegation has just arrived back—so I'm looking forward to . . . hearing what THEY think about it.

Spring is coming, Phylabe. I've just walked all the way home in daylight for the first time this year (blackbirds singing and lovers laughing all over the park!). Last summer was a joy—this one is going to be a thousand times better; first, because I live at this end of the parks now; second, because of all the new friends I've made. For one thing,—here is a piece of news for you—Thirza West is coming to live and work in London, because *The Countryman* has just been sold to *Punch* and will be produced in London in future instead of in the Cotswolds. She is to live with her married sister for a while, but we may decide to live together eventually. May not, though—for we're both rather independent people and like a fair measure of solitude into the bargain. But at any rate we shall live close enough to see a lot of each other—and a permanent heart's-

(*Left*) Phylabe Houston, c. 1938.
(*Below*) Bessie Crowther, on grounds
of Parliament Building in Victoria,
British Columbia, Summer 1941.

friend at hand's-reach is going to make a lot of difference to me.
Then in the past two or three months—since I had my own flat in
which to entertain them—I've found several other very pleasant
friendships consolidating themselves. . . . Thirza was here for Christmas and we had one whale of a mighty fine time, including a

party. . . . I DO wish you could have seen my flat in its Christmas decorations! Imagine my sitting room—ivory walls and fireplace, deep crimson carpet, covers and curtains in ivory linen covered with enormous bunches of crimson roses and green foliage, my nearly-all-green picture, a signed artist's proof of Ethelbert White's *The New Fence* over the fireplace, holly (thick with berries—I picked it myself in Epping Forest) along the picture rail, and a baby Christmas Tree in the corner. Two jars of winter jasmine as further trimming. Though I sez it wot shouldn't, it really did look gay and welcoming. We managed a mighty spread of food too, on and off the ration— sausage rolls, half a dozen kinds of savoury and sweet sandwiches, biscuits, several cakes, a trifle (without cream, of course!) and even a Christmas Cake with what LOOKED like almond icing (made of soya bean flour)—every bit home-made. Then practically every guest kindly brought a contribution, and the result was that we were giving food away and eating up the scraps for at least a week after the party!! Wouldn't old Hitler weep if he knew. After that, parties didn't frighten me any more, so whenever life is looking a shade grey round the edges now I throw a party and freshen it up again. Thirza came up again for ten days while she was taking a training course in preparation for reconstruction work in Europe (pre-Armistice!—But the *Countryman* changes may change her plans)— and over the weekend we threw one continuous party. Would you like to meet some of our guests? There's Jean Brown, petite and vivacious, with a delicious giggle and a taste in entirely frivolous hats. She's advertising manager for Maclean's Tooth Paste ("Did you Maclean your teeth today?"—know it?). Then there's Marjorie Hayward, tall and poised and elegant—formerly Publicity Officer for one of the biggest industrial combines in England, now an Officer in the Ministry of Labour, and a vice-president of the National Federation of B. & P.W. Clubs. Marianne, whom I used to push out in a pram at Whickham, works on Locust Research at the Natural History Museum; Frances, my charming and lovely little Syrian friend, designs shoes and a lot of other things and is an artist and an idealist in everything she ever says or does. Phyl is a Monitor at the B.B.C.—she is very tall, dark and quiet and rather shy. Cissie, who was Chrissie's friend rather than mine, but is mine too now, gave up her secretarial post at the outbreak of war in order to become a nurse. She has been at Middlesborough most of the time, and had a stern experience with almost nightly blitzes, but now she is in a

rather luxurious type of hospital near London nursing Service Officers. She's rather quiet, too, but she's a grand person. Marjorie Redfern, whose letters you have seen, has been a frequent guest, too, for
she has been at Windsor while in her Officer Cadets Training Unit—
she is now commissioned, a Second Subaltern, and the happiest
thing inside the Army or out of it! WHAT a difference joining up
made to that girl—both physically and spiritually. She has blos-
somed like a flower in the sun and it is a joy to see her revelling in
her full, busy Army life. If ever there was a good advertisement for
the A.T.S., she is it! Another friend I should introduce to you, as you
may very likely meet her again, is Margaret Mackendrick, a former
Countryman friend, now in the J. Walter Thompson Advertising
Agency in London. They are an American firm, and considered very
advanced and progressive here, and Margaret is one of their copy-
writers. She's a good sober, stolid Scot—I like Scots and half the girls
mentioned above are Scots! Maybe I am attracted to them because
I've lived so near the Border and known so many of them. . . .

I've been saving cuttings from papers and magazines for you
ever since I started this letter two and a half months ago, and now I
have such a pile that it would seriously embarrass our shipping! Also,
most of them are stale, so I must do some combing out. I will send
you, however, some views of Gloucester Cathedral, which I love
almost best of the cathedrals I know. It has something of
everything—a Saxon beginning, a wonderful Norman nave (though
if you want to see a Norman cathedral I must take you to Durham!),
some Early English, a lot of Decorated, and finally some additions in
the Perpendicular style which I love above all other Gothic architecture. How you would love the darling little churches of the Cotswold
country—nearly all of them in this lovely late Gothic style, the most
truly "English" (and I don't think Gothic took this turn in any other
country, so it really is an English style), and to me the most completely satisfying of all building. The Cotswold stone is of such a gracious, soft gold-grey colour, too, and the churches merge into their
village backgrounds as though they had grown there like the elms in
their churchyards. Lots of the Cotswold villages still stand as they
stood 300 years ago—virtually no change in them over all those
years. The war, sadly enough[,] is changing them a good deal—
soldiers and airmen and evacuated children and Army transports
and zooming aeroplanes and much, much ploughing-up of ancient
grazing ground. I wonder if England will ever be the same again,

and in many respects I must say I am a bitter opponent of change! I don't want Gloucester Cathedral changed one iota, for instance— and I hate with burning fury both the WEATHER and OLIVER CROMWELL, who both have much despoiled it! The empty niches mutely cry out against that earlier Dictator; the exterior carvings are worn almost level by wind and weather. That Cromwell, I think, destroyed more beauty in England than even the filthy Hitler-birds, and it doesn't matter to me one scrap that his motives were pure! Phylabe, there is one beauty you must not die without seeing—that is the loveliness, the inexpressible glory of the buildings that grew under the hands of the Gothic masons! I do not know of any art more moving. Music? It can uplift the emotions, excite them, shatter them. But architecture of this great kind, it brings you to your knees in holy awe, in ecstasy, in spiritual exhaltation. It makes me worship God and have faith in men—men who have praised God so sublimely with the work of their hands and through whom the sublimity of God's gifts to men has been made so nobly apparent. Well, Gloucester Cathedral had had much of its precious glass removed (to safety) and many of its monuments were buried in sandbags. But the spirit of God still dwelt within the walls—it is more potent than incense, and it endures longer than the stones and needs no roof to keep it in, and if you come with me one day to Lindisfarne (where first Christianity was landed in England) you will know the spirit is there though the arches raised so long ago stand now like rainbows against the open sky. . . .

That reminds me that you are now being food and clothes rationed too! Your list of points values was in our papers this week, and it doesn't look as if you'd be much better off than we are! Doesn't it make some of your people kinda mad to think they can't get canned fruit because it's coming to us? It would be very understandable if they did. Do tell them, though, if you come across them, that we've had *no* fruit until this month (and the apples we grew were all used up by Christmas). A month's points soon go— this month I expended my 20 points this wise—one medium size can of loganberries, 9; one packet shredded wheat, 3; one lb. sago, 4; one pound tapioca, 4. So for the rest of the month I can buy no more canned fruit, fish or meat, no cereals, no grains or pulses, no biscuits, no crispbread, no syrup, no dates or raisins or other dried fruit. But these are restrictions rather than lacks—there is always plenty to eat. If there are no tomatoes or lemons, there are carrots and cabbages galore; if there is little cake, there are potatoes! I must say I manage handsomely on my rations. I *should* like more milk, however, the winter ration for ordinary adults is 2 pints per *week*. (I used to drink at *least* a pint a day.) The dried milk is a great help, but hardly the same thing! Everybody would agree, too, about wishing the butter ration was a bit bigger. It is 2 ozs. a week—sometimes I have an orgy and demolish mine at a sitting, spreading it thick on bread or scones as a gesture to the horrid Hun! . . .

I'm glad my Christmas package reached you safely. We have been *extremely* well served by our sailor boys, don't you think? I don't know of *any* letters between us that have been lost.

Goodnight, goodnight

My love and very best wishes to you (A common wish to friends here is "Busy days and quiet nights to you!"—but though the busy days are no doubt a commonplace to you, it's good to know there's no special need to wish you quiet nights!)

Ever yours
Edith

1943
May 8, 1943–November 19, 1943

✉ **11**
29 Stanley Gardens
London W 11
5.8.43

How can Phylabe be? No news for *such* a long time! I'm feeling LONELY for the lack of an American greeting. Have some gone to the bottom of the sea?

Summer is being lovely here—hot and sunny, and sometimes (e.g. today) showery and cool. Roses everywhere, and now the gladioli and chrysanthemums beginning. Soon you will be able to come and see them for yourself, eh?

Hadn't thought of writing to you today, but the *News Chron[icle]* is so interesting and vital that I felt you *must* see it. So here is a wee note to tuck inside. No time to embark on NEWS—not that there *is* much. Life goes on tranquilly but so *monopolisingly*—no time for anything but work and Civil Defence, and a minimum of housewifery. Social life *quite* denuded. . . .

Did I ever tell you Marjorie Redfern was appointed to the A.T.S. Press Office in London? She is still here and we meet every few days. She . . . is at the age to enjoy the easy friendships of the Service and all the fun available to them in London. Makes me feel envious (some days) and pleasantly grandmotherly (on others).

Three new (*old* really) *McCalls* arrived yesterday, so I still garner a little American atmosphere here and there. Have also made an American WAAC friend—will send you a photograph of us together. She's a Personnel Officer, with a very interesting job, me thinks.

No more minutes, so nothing more except

Edith Base and an unidentified WAAC at a "do" at home of Caroline Hazlitt, President of Business and Professional Women's Federation (reference in letter 11).

Lots of love and good wishes
Edith

Mustn't write much more but must get my tired self to bed. I'm working a lot harder these days—enjoying it, and pleased to have some real responsibility at last, but I never seem to have time for relaxation or fun or even for sleeping! Awful state of affairs! Today, too, I've been called up to be a part-time Air Raid Warden. Not that I mind—I've done no voluntary war work since I left N/C [Newcastle], and feel anxious to do some; but oh dear, I shan't have time to sleep *at all* at this rate!! Never mind, I believe I'll be issued with a free pair of trousers, so that'll compensate me! . . .

Goodnight now, my dearie. I am wishing you all sorts of good experiences and gifts.

Love
Edith

I have been remiss and never told you how much I've enjoyed drinking *your* powdered lemon juice. It is *marvelously* good—and I am sure I owe something to it for the fact that I've not had a single cold this winter (touching wood hard!). Thank you so very much for it and for so much else.

✉ **12**
29 Stanley Gardens
London W 11
June 1st 1943

My dear Phylabe
    . . . I am going to start on a very-long-intended letter to you, though it's hard to say when it will get finished! It was so cheering just to see your handwriting, to be reminded that life is really wider than the small and ever-diminishing orbit of wartime days in a London office. Don't think we're downhearted—oh no! But life *is* a bit grim; it *is* restricted; more and more the cycle is just work-food-sleep-work. And one gets a bit astigmatic! So it's good to have a window opened on a wider world every now and again.
    It seems a long time since I heard from you. I know it's a long time since you heard from me, too! . . . My dear friend Thirza West . . . has just taken a flat in Stanley Gardens—we can wave to each other from our respective windows—so we shall be able to see much more of each other. She is such a dear—I wish you could know her. Her home is in the far north of Scotland and she speaks with a delicious Scottish lilt and rarely wears anything but a jacket and kilt. What is more important, she has all the "true and tender" qualities attributed to the folk from the North, ("oh dark and true and tender is the North"—was Tennyson ever one of your enthusiasms?) and I am always happy when I'm with her.
    . . . Thirza brought her sister and brother-in-law to look at her flat on Saturday and they came to tea with me. On the way home from work (finish 1 p.m. on most Saturdays) I met Marjorie of the A.T.S. for a picnic lunch in the Park, so she came to tea, too. It was a blazing summer day, we were all in summer frocks (even Marjorie, who was off duty for the day so got out of hot khaki), and we were all feeling merry and bright, *especially* as I had just had a bumper hour in the market and got *two* half pounds of tomatoes and a *pound*

of apples!!!!! You've no idea what that means to a fruit starved London girl! So we had a whopping big tea!

On Sunday I went to Southall for lunch, then Thirza and I went to Stoke Poges—heard of it? It's where Gray wrote his "Elegy Written in a Country Churchyard"—"The curfew tolls the knell of parting day" etc. We disapproved of Stoke Poges, however! Too tidy, too sophisticated, too many "keep off the grass" notices, too mercenary—they wanted 2s.—each for admission to a garden adjoining the churchyard. Still, it was lovely—tranquil and leafy, and smothered in roses and sunshine. So we registered a private protest against their shortcomings and betook ourselves to a silver and gold meadow where we sunbathed for the rest of the day. If you could only see England in her silver and gold dress—the late May or early June dress of cowparsley and may blossoms and buttercups! She never decks herself more ravishingly. The scents are so fresh and spicy then, and the birdsong so ecstatic and the whisper of breezes among the new leaves so comfortable and friendly. There's never been a spring and early summer like this one—everybody says so. No snow during the winter, no excessive cold and no bad weather, so everything green a month earlier than normally and now, on the first day of June, we are in full midsummer. The fruit trees have more blossom than had been seen in living memory. I was at home a fortnight ago and the apples and pears are so thick with tiny fruit that there is hardly room for the leaves. Given reasonably good summer and harvest weather, there will be record crops of everything. Even in the North the wheat fields were standing a foot high in mid-May, and the hay-making has already started. There are many people who say "God is on our side" and feel more confident still of victory because there have been the two best growing years together in history. The man-power shortage is the greatest problem—the bumper crops of fruit must be picked and packed, and the corn must be harvested but Britain's men and women are all in Forces and factories. But the housewives are being roped in for part time duties, the schoolchildren will be on the land in thousands, the factory and office workers are preparing to spend their holidays in the fields. It's all rather inspiring and exciting, the way the people pull together. If only the same spirit operates into the Peace, how easy the rebuilding of the world will be.

Pause there for tea. We had a birthday in the office today and the forfeit for having a birthday (oh! these penalties for growing old!) is to provide a cake for the tea club. So now I am full of sultana cake and tea. Cakes incidentally are one of our pains-in-the-neck. My colleague daily stands in queues to get a very ordinary and dull slab of cake for the office tea. Last week the last remaining frills— occasional chocolate coating, occasional mock cream filling (usually nasty) were docked by Ministry of Food regulation. Now there is nothing much but plain madeira or nearly-as-plain "fruit" cake to be bought. I manage to bake a cake most weeks—my fat ration *just* runs to it. I enjoy pottering in my kitchen, and find it the perfect relaxation after all-day desk work. Then I can invite my various "homeless" friends to come and eat the products. That's the chief joy of having my own wee house!

How goes the job, Phylabe dear? Are you still working so hard? It sounds important and worth-while, and I know you will get a lot of satisfaction from being at the heart of things. . . . Who does your work on the farm? I believe the labour shortage is acute with you, too, but I hope your farms are prospering. Is your Dad well, and able to continue his work without feeling over-harassed by the war difficulties? . . . Can you still run a car in your part of the world? Bessie sent on to me your enthusiastic letter about the visit of Margaret Bondfield,[14] which interested me so much because I have known her all my adult life. That is not to say she knows me! She was Member of Parliament for Wallsend-on-Tyne when I was a young reporter in Newcastle, and I used to see a lot of her as she addressed meetings and attended local functions. She was a notable personality, not only for being one of the earliest women M.P.'s but because she was the first (and so far only) woman Cabinet-Minister. It was regarded by most intelligent people as a tragedy when she lost her seat to the young and inexperienced Conservative candidate, Irene Ward. Certainly the country lost a highly responsible and progressive legislator; but it happens that Irene Ward (who is an old acquaintance of mine and whom I see often here, as she sits on Mr. Bevin's Women's Consultive Committee, the meetings of which I attend) has proved a good fighter, too, and not the mere Party-woman it was feared she would be. Irene fights for women as indefatigably as Miss Bondfield did, I imagine. Still, it is a pity we could not have had them both.

---

14. Margaret Bondfield, Minister of Labour in the Government of Ramsay MacDonald, appeared in Greeley, 16 February, 1943.

Irene, by the way, is shortly going to China on a lecture tour! She has seen a lot of the world since she became a Member of Parliament, all by going on Ministry of Information lecture tours. Wish *I* could see the world that way! But I fear I shall always have to be a tourist and pay my fares myself. (Even so, I hope to come and see you one of these days!)

. . . My American acquaintance does not expand at all, in spite of the *hordes* of your boys in London Town! Maybe you didn't know I am shy! I'm still rediscovering *old* friends, though, and very nice that is. Last week I met again Frances Rowe,[15] a vivacious and charming Cambridge graduate who joined the Repertory Company in Newcastle and used to come to my Claremont Terrace flat (long before you knew me). Since then she has played in various Rep. Companies in different towns, and now has just come to London in her first West End part—a part in the new play by J.B. Priestley and a great thrill for her, naturally. But poor Frances—she has had numerous introductions to film producers "but as soon as they see my face they turn me down!" She's what *I* call extremely pretty, intelligent and lively, but is not "photogenic." "But I've seen much worse faces on the films, and surely they need all types," I said to her. Apparently if you have a name first, your face doesn't matter much, but to break into films without *either* the name *or* the face is quite, quite impossible.

Another N/C friend, Gladys Boot, got her first professional stage part (at the age of nearly 50) in a West End success that has been running now for two years (*Quiet Weekend,* by another N/C acquaintance Esther McCracken),[16] and I hope these two will meet at my flat on Sunday, along with still another old friend, Veronica Nisbet, who is in Town for a short holiday and knew both these girls in N/C.

Now nearly time for me to go home. There have been many interruptions in the above, while I did necessary work. I'm "late man" tonight, but my three male colleagues have stayed late too,

---

15. Frances Rowe was to make her American debut on Broadway in Maurice Evans's revival of Shaw's *Man and Superman* (1947). She later made movies in Hollywood with Errol Flynn and Peter Finch.

16. *Quiet Weekend* had opened at Wyndham's in 1941. Gladys Boot was to appear in *The Cherry Orchard* and *The Cocktail Party.* She appeared in New York in 1949 and on television in 1952.

telling stories mostly (only mildly busy today). I'm going home to *try* to get some curtains hemmed. They've been waiting ever since I moved into the flat last October, but it's more than one evening's job, so I've shelved it and shelved it. Now that Veronica (who's an ex-interior decorator) is coming, I'm ashamed to let her see my bedroom hanging cupboard without its curtains! My meal is cooked and only wants warming up, so I should get a good start on the sewing.

6:30 p.m. now, so cheerio!

9 p.m. Have not done the curtains and must do some ironing instead! Also I intend going early to bed, to make up sleep lost last night when there was an Air Raid Warning (bombs dropped, but nowhere near here) and I had to go out on patrol. . . . (I do 20 hours a week, plus training and lectures, and quite enjoy the fun BUT don't like having to go out through the night!)

I have been reading (over my meal) John Gunther's *Inside Asia*—very illuminating to a Briton who normally knows little of the Far East. The BBC is just announcing that cherries are not to cost more than 1s. 8 ^{1}/2d. a pound Rhubarb was 11d. a lb., then 9d., then 5.—when it became 5d. there was none to be found anywhere! I have prowled and shadowed and stood in queues for rhubarb for weeks—shopping for scarcity goods is the very dickens, especially for one whose office hours overlap shop hours at both ends.

I am yawning and nodding—don't think I shall even do the ironing! I'll post this tomorrow, Phylabe, also *The Countryman,* and hope to continue shortly. I do hope there'll be news from you soon—you don't know how a letter from you lights up the week!

With constant loving thoughts and warm good wishes to you and yours always,

Edith

✉ **13**
19.11.43
29 Stanley Gardens
London W 11

My dear Phylabe

I'm making you a Christmas present but the chances are considerable that it won't be finished in time to reach you by Dec. 25, so this is just to ensure that at least a greeting does reach you by the right date.

Merry Christmas to you, Phylabe dear, and a New Year full of dreams realised and days enriched! I do wish I could hear from you! I'm sure you must have written to me. At any rate I don't *want* to think you've never written since the last letter I received in February! So we can only blame the Atlantic hazards. But I do feel starved of news of you and the feeling of friendship that had grown so strong and pleasurable between us.

How are you, dear? What job are you doing now? Have you spent the summer months on the ranch and do you now go back to your Air Force job? Do write to me. Tell me whether you ever finished your re-building plans or whether the war has stopped private building in your country as it has with us (from the very first week of war!).

Tell me about your countryside, and your weather, and how you plan your days, and whether you've time for any hobbies or reading or social life. I've been reading about Wyoming. It made me think of you—is there any real similarity? The novel *My Friend Flicka* about a Wyoming horse ranch is having a great vogue here, but I've not read that, only the sequel, *Thunderhead,* which has been running in *McCall's* (still thankfully received with only a few gaps). I thought it delightful (but it's true to say that I'd not have been nearly so interested in it if it hadn't constantly recalled you and made me picture you in some such setting and some such way of life). Last week I saw the film of *Flicka* but it was so poor (except for some tempting Technicolor views of ranges and valleys) that I'll say no more about it. I still read about the American scene and American life with deep interest and a sort of nostalgic longing. My one short visit can't be responsible for it all! America spells Romance, Castles in Spain, Fairyland for me. I must Come!!! It seems necessary to ride a horse, however, and I fear it is a little late in life for me to take to the horse! But perhaps there are other means of locomotion. How about "doing" the 48 states with me on bicycles?! I've just put in an application for consideration for Government posts in reconstruction overseas, but alackaday, America seems about the *least* likely place I'd arrive at! However, I may be able to get to wherever it is *via* Colorado. Visiting a sick friend last night, I found another friend there who volunteered to "tell our fortunes" with cards. The very first thing she told me was that I was going on a journey overseas almost at once. Later on she discovered a "dark elderly man" was going on the same journey. It appeared that the end of *his* journey was "money" and the end of mine was "heart's content." But of course there's no guarantee that this will all work out according to plan!

Life is awfully quiet for me these days—seems to be bounded by office (where I'm often bored because I haven't enough work to keep me on my toes) and home (where the chores never quite get cleared because time's too short). I've not opened a book for a fortnight (though I had started, during a period of sick leave, the enthralling Russian novel *The Don Flows Home to the Sea.* Can't recall author's name). One's clothes and household possessions are all on their last legs and always require mending. Visiting my sick friend last night, I took a torn sheet with me and "turned" it there, sitting on the floor with her sewing machine on a stool. I never go anywhere without my darning bag, and oh! the heartbreak when a darned and better-darned pair of stockings has at last to be recognised as no-more-darnable! *Everybody* wears stockings with darned knees, and runs sewn up—you just have to, or go stockingless and its too cold to do that now. Have I sung this song to you before? I probably have, for it's a dominant theme! What a nation of "make do and mend-ers" we have become. Chrissie writes that she's making a new dress out of a Japanese kimono she made for a fancy dress party about 19 years ago! I'm joining the good bits of two nighties together to make a new petticoat slip, and my friend Nancie is making a shirt blouse out of the tail of an old shirt of her husband's. It's all very commendable, but it does take *time,* and among all our rationing and doing without these days, the greatest shortage of all (especially for women) is TIME.

November 24

Such a lovely day it is today! Cool and clear and sunny and sparkling—not quite frosty but a lovely bite in the air! Four days ago we were obliterated by fog and the next day we had pouring rain, so our climate doesn't lack variety! A friend of mine was commiserating with a Canadian soldier from the far west on coming to a climate like ours, but can you guess what his response was? "The only people who complain about the English climate are the English! We think it's grand." Anyway, today is grand from all points of view—if you've got a warm enough coat on. I went into St. James's Park for my lunch-time walk. It was so lovely—the trees mostly bare now, and beautiful against the gentle blue of the sky, and the sun low enough, even at noon, to throw a gleaming golden ladder across the pond. The air was full of the sound of seagulls, scrambling after the food people constantly throw for them to catch on the wing, and the smell of woodsmoke from the little piles of burning twigs and leaves. I wish you'd been there, to stand on the bridge with me and look down at the ducks, and turn both ways to see those two delightful views over the pond, one towards Buckingham Palace, where the Royal Standard was flapping the news that the King was up for the day (he was opening Parliament this morning—and the traditional search of the vaults for a Guy Fawkes bomb was carried out most *un*traditionally by Home Guards!—) and the other way across the water and thickets to the gracious buildings of Whitehall. I'm still in love with London—have you gathered as much? Tired and sober and in Utility dress as she is, poor darling! Here and there you see a newly painted house (paint can be obtained only if essential to prevent property going to ruin) and realise how unkempt and dingy the rest of the place now is. Here and there (but even rarer than the paint-fresh houses) you see a glamour-dressed woman—but when you turn to look at her you don't think how plain and unattractive everybody else is but how unseemly *she* is! Simple wartime dress seems appropriate to our mood these days—it's very odd that except for nostalgic moments one doesn't *want* to dress up! I don't mean to imply women are *badly* dressed—in the main they're not, though their clothes may be old (as all mine!!). The general standard is remarkably good—but always simple and quiet and *practical*.

I've been indulging in a new coat—*really* needed, as my last new one was pre-war. It's a Shetland homespun as soft as swansdown (surely), in a wide herringbone of dark red and black. It's a home-made one—I didn't make it myself, though I meant to; a friend who is much cleverer at dressmaking (this was really tailoring) than I happened to be free of a job at the time, and did it for me. It's terribly nice! I'm wearing it today as I'm going shortly (when I leave the office, where this is mostly being written in spare moments) to help Thirza celebrate her birthday. Cecil, a *Newcastle Journal* colleague recently come to Reuters in London, is coming with us, but it was all very hurriedly arranged an hour or two ago as Thirza is just out today after a dose of flu. The programme will be a quick meal and perhaps a flick if there's time, but I have to go on ARP duty at 10 o'clock. I'm hoping horribly there won't be a raid—we've been bombing Berlin this week, and they nearly always retaliate, and, willing though I am

Cecil Bacon in his office (reference to Cecil in London in letter 13).

to take my share, I can't deny I simply hate getting up at dead o'night and going out on patrol with perhaps gunfire going on all around. We've had a lot of raids recently, and the Underground stations are full of shelterers again. It's amazing to see them—as soon as it's dark (about 5:30 p.m. now) they begin to go down, with their bundles and the babies and their picnic baskets. How they can stand it I don't know—heat, draughts, crowds, noise, discomfort! But they tuck themselves in on the wire bunks—hang curtains all round sometimes and make tiny little chambers of privacy for themselves in the turmoil. At one station I go to there are more shelterers than bunks, so the odd-men-out spread newspapers and blankets on the concrete platforms, and lie there, with the feet of train passengers all round them. One of my colleagues was just telling me of an elderly married couple who have nearly split their partnership on a shelter problem—Madame goes down-under every night because she has made friends with a group who play bridge every night, but Monsieur wants to stay at home. And this has been going on since the Blitz of 1940! But I don't think they're typical! Time to go now!

 Goodnight until tomorrow!

25.11.43

It's an even more exhilarating day today—crisp and clear and shining bright. I walked across Green Park to the Soroptimist Club luncheon and wanted to jump. *Did* do a little hop-skip in fact when nobody was looking.

A soroptimist from Houston, Texas, was at the meeting—tall, elegant and beautifully dressed. One might have said "American" at first sight of her. I'd have loved to talk to her but there was no opportunity. The luncheons are always a bit of a rush and today I wanted to chat to an old Newcastle Club member who is now head mistress of a London high school and came along as a guest. One of the nice things about Soroptimism is that it enables paths to cross again! We had an interesting meeting—after a luncheon of lentil soup, grilled fish and apple trifle and coffee, we had a debate on problems of postwar education. The two chief developments demanded were nursery schools for the 3–5's and young people's colleges for part time continued education of young people who leave school at 14 or 15 and go straight into employment. I love the meetings—they're always invigorating; and I love the members, each and all! I was looking for the Denver Club in "The American Soroptimist" this morning. They meet at noon on Wednesdays in the Denver Dry Goods Tea Room, and the Chairman (or President) and secretary are Miss Marion Smith, Chamber of Commerce, and Miss Lois Phillips, State Capitol Bldg. Is it too far away for you to join?—Greeley apparently has no Club. Do you know either of those ladies?

The birthday party was a great success last night. It was Thanksgiving Day—a new festival for us since the American Army came to town—so what do you think we had? Pumpkin pie! Very good, too. Served with a flop of what passes these days for whipped cream. We *didn't* have turkey. Probably all the available birds were being consumed in American messes. We like our turkey best on Christmas Day—but they're *fearfully* expensive now!

Tonight's excitement is choir meeting. I've not told you, have I, that Thirza and I joined the Morley College Choir and are having the time of our lives singing with it. Michael Tippett, a notable young composer, is our conductor, full of dash and enthusiasm, and full of fun, too.[17] We sing his own wildly experimental part songs, Elizabethan madrigals, chorales by old Bach—such an exciting variety of classical and modern. Some of the loveliest things we've sung so far have been madrigals by Monteverdi, so lovely and so little known are his works. At the moment we're learning carols for a Christmas Concert—modern carols, modern arrangements of old ones, and traditional carols sung as they were written three or four or 9!! centuries ago. We give concerts in mighty places—the National Gallery, the Wigmore Hall and such—and get appraising write-ups in *The Times* and other august publications. But it's glorious, glorious fun. We're to broadcast, but to South America and Central Europe, not on home lines so far as I know.

I shan't be going home for Christmas. Travelling is unpatriotic, and the holiday is too short. Thirza and I shall probably combine forces, for culinary and entertainment purposes, and I'm hoping to throw a party, probably on the Sunday. Or, if we have holiday on the Monday, have the party on Monday and on Sunday go to hear *The Messiah* sung at the Albert Hall. In any case it will be quiet and mostly stay-at-home. Wish you could pop over! I shall think of you, anyway.

Now I'll end this letter and get it into the post, so that with luck you will receive it by Christmas. *Do* write to me! I look every day for an American letter and a Canadian one, but they never come.

Many, many loving thoughts, Phylabe, and best and cheeriest Christmas greetings.

Yours ever
Edith

---

17. Michael Tippett, composer of symphonies, operas and oratorios, was in charge of musical organization at Morley College (a working class institution in South London) from 1940–52. He was knighted in 1966.

1944
January 26, 1944–December 28, 1944

✉ **14**

29 Stanley Gardens
London W 11
26.1.44

Phylabe my dear

I was *so* relieved to see your writing on an envelope at last! You can't think how sad I'd been at never hearing from you.

But, my dear, I'm dreadfully sorry to know the reasons why you've not been able to write.[18] Please accept all my sympathy and loving thoughts. You have had such a sad year, and I'm so sorry. I hope your Dad is feeling better now—though I know that one doesn't get over such a loss at all; but I hope the relief from anxiety will help his health. I am wishing very much for you that this year will be a happier one, and that your own personal load may be lightened, dearest Phylabe.

Your letter reached me before Christmas, and I should have sent you an acknowledgement straight away. I kept on hoping, though, for time to write a real letter, but there never *is* time, so I will just write in snippets and send you what I can in a few days. This is my lunch hour, but it is pouring rain, and as I have my best coat and hat on (I'll tell you why in a minute) and no umbrella, I'm reluctant to go out (though my lungs and muscles scream for fresh air and exercise!). But *chiefly*, I have a really nice pair of silk stockings on, and if I go out I know I'll splash them up to the knees! I would groan at

18. Phylabe's stepmother died of cancer in 1943, after a long illness.

this state of affairs if it didn't offer me a chance to start a letter to you—but here goes!

I'm going out tonight—supper and flick—with Marjorie and a boy friend. Feel I am being greatly honoured to be let in on a nice party *a deux,* so must do my part and go looking as little like somebody's Aunt Matilda as possible! Marjorie has quite a circle of boy friends, but this one seems to be looming large on M's horizon at present, and I'm not sure whether it's the boy or Aunt Matilda who's being produced for inspection tonight! Anyway, in case it's me, I mustn't have splashed stockings, must I? Marjorie is still posted in Surrey, and likes to come to Town for her days off. She usually arrives at 7 one evening and stays till 9 next evening, giving her two evenings and one really good day in Town. It's too bad it's raining like this for her today—there'll be nothing to do with the boy friend except more and more flicks. She's still the dearest of young things—doing well at her job and expecting another promotion (third pip) at any moment.

Thirza has been in the hospital for the past three weeks, so I've been kinda lonely. I'm a lonely soul by choice and don't soon tire of my own company, but I'd got so used to having Thirza about the place that there really is a gap when she's not here. This week she's left the hospital and gone to her sister's in Middlesex to convalesce. She's got a trying complaint which is apparently going to mean constant dieting and care, which is very distressing, especially for a girl so proud of health as my lively Thirza. But we hope that with care for a year or two she *will* recover eventually.

We had such a happy Christmas. It will be a long time past before you read about it, but still, I'll tell you. On Christmas Eve we were very domestic—made mince pies, hung up the holly and decked the Tree—with Cecil . . . to lend a manly hand with hammer and nails and a long reach where necessary. On Christmas morning we cooked a lovely Christmas Dinner—roast chicken, with sausages, sage and onion stuffing, baked onions, potatoes, carrots and swede, and brussels sprouts. Then plum pudding and mince pie, and coffee. Also, although we're both next door to teetotal, we had a bottle of Algerian wine which Santa Claus had brought me, so it really was a festive occasion. Picture us in Thirza's big bright sitting room in front of a blazing log fire—off-white walls, a polished mahogany table with gay flowered pottery plates, "cottage" brown pottery serving dishes, gleaming silver (Thirza loves silver and has been collecting pieces for years), lots of holly and Christmas cards, silver and gold witch balls reflecting the fire flames and all the colour and warmth of the scene caught and held and multiplied tenfold in Thirza's lovely red and cream and green and blue Persian rugs. She has such impeccable taste, and all the "bits" in her flat are beautiful things, and mostly rather unusual and exciting things, though they all fit into the "Thirza" background. Her own colouring is fresh white and red and gold, so it is right for her to have a background of light and brightness and warmth. Her flat always makes me feel that mine is a fearful hotch-potch—though I'm fond of mine too! However, whenever I have guests I want to impress, Thirza lends me her table silver! Mine is more or less all Woolworth's.

Well, replete with Christmas delicacies, as they say in the novelettes, we sat in front of the fire and listened to the King speaking and all the round-the-world Christmas broadcast. Then, as it was five, we went walking in the Park. Then Cecil (who's "alone in London" and in very dull digs) came to tea—and I wish you'd seen our display of cakes, tarts and cookies! We even had a real Christmas Cake with icing on the top! After that, we went to a dance-party at the YWCA and had a merry time. Next day I had a party—in my flat this time. Nine of us, all girls, playing party games, talking, eating, talking, eating. I love giving parties; love contriving nice food out of the Spartan wartime ingredients. Thirza helped, of course. We started at 4 p.m. with tea, and had supper at 8, and Thirza and I finished off with tea again somewhere about 11. One of my guests was a girl, Frances Rowe, whom I met first in N/C when she was playing at the Repertory Theatre there. Now she's in a West End part—or at least has just come to the end of one and in the interval is in a film of the play (J.B. Priestley's *They Came to a City*) being made at Ealing. She kept us all laughing over her account of the trials of film actors—how they mercilessly shave off your eyebrows and pull out your hair, build your face up with putty and file off your teeth. She made it sound funny, but we all decided we wouldn't be film stars after all!! All the same, Frances looked blooming on the treatment. The third day of the holiday I was again the cook—roast pork and stuffing, and plum pudding this time—again with Cecil as guest, and after a brisk afternoon walk, we went to see a popular musical comedy (but found it very boring and decided we were now too old to get lost in such fantastically unreal romances!)—so you see it was a Merry Christmas indeed. Santa Claus was very kind to me—I had a number of books (which I never have time to read), a silver spoon, a beautiful hand-crocheted red macrame handbag from Chris, a patent gas lighter (*much* appreciated, as matches are so scarce) from Marjorie, the promise of a pair of sheets from Mother (also very scarce and precious things), a Christmas Cake from Mother, and a lot of other nice things which at the moment I can't remember. Most of the gifts I *gave* were in promise-form! I'm still knitting the Fair Isle gloves to match Thirza's kilt and the wash leather gloves for Cecil aren't begun! Yours, too, is still just a promise! But they *will* all get finished!!!

I should think you've heard enough about Christmas now to assure you that we're not suffering from any particular depression in London just now! Everybody's full of beans, indeed. Theatres are booming—seats have to be booked weeks and months ahead. The play of the season is *There Shall Be No Night,* with Alfred Lunt and Lynne Fontanne, from New York.[19] Haven't seen it yet and probably shan't, as I don't feel I can afford West End theatre prices except on special occasions. The tax on entertainments is heavy, and a reasonably good seat costs 10s or 12s. The ballet is cheaper, and I would go often and often, but getting seats is almost impossible unless one has hours to spare for queuing. So I go to the flicks in my suburb and get all the fun I need! *Prefer* flicks to stage plays, in fact. The illusion is always so much stronger—and the standard of production and acting generally higher. Needless to say, I choose my films very carefully and don't enjoy *bad* films. But there are plenty of good ones. Tonight it is an old Bette Davis one we are going to see— *The Little Foxes*. We all missed it when it was new, and I never miss Bette Davis films if I can help it because they're uniformly good and she's not merely a good-looker but an actress. Also, as I'm still regularly told I resemble her, I like to imagine it's *me* looking so elegant and romantic! Gives her films a sort of importance personal to me!

I was telling you about London. It *is* getting brighter. Here and there a house newly painted, here and there shops and blitzed restaurants reopening. That's not to say the place is [not] still *fearfully*

---

19. The Robert Sherwood play, *There Shall Be No Night,* had opened on Broadway in 1942 and run two and a half years. The original plot involved Russia's invasion of Finland, but was changed for the English opening in 1943 to the Italian invasion of Greece because Russia was now an ally. The play closed because of the V–1's.

shabby. Poor old London Town. Soldiers were filling in trenches in the Park the other day. Does that mean the war is going to end? On the other hand, we had a nasty night last Friday—two very noisy raids, from 9–10 p.m. and from 5–6 a.m. "Like the good old days" said our neighbours as we sat on the stairs two floors down (I'm just under the roof, and there was so much flak flying around that I didn't feel safe. 'Twould be such a waste to be killed by a bit of our own shrapnel). Our barrage is something to write about these days, Phylabe—shells going up like machine gun bullets. I'm sorry for the Germans up above. The noise is terrific. But more, *much* more sickening is the noise of our bombers going out, which they do most nights. For an hour or two hours on end, without a pause, the roar of them goes on. It's horrifying. We know it's got to be done and that we didn't start it, but we hate it. I don't know anybody among my acquaintances who likes hearing that Berlin's been bombed again—though people did write "Bomb Rome now" on the walls a few months ago. Everybody does feel the European war is getting toward its end now, though all the same we're polishing up our Air Raid Precautions and mending our gas masks in expectation of some bad spots first. I think what we're most looking forward to is a cessation of the blackout. It is *so* trying. I notice that when Americans come over here they seem to be astounded by the blackout. More important longings of course, for most people, are to get their families together again, to get back home—but I'm only talking about the little things. My own chief longings are for more milk (2 pints a week only gives you enough for tea, really), more eggs (hardly ever see one), more marmalade (orange), and nicer cakes. Not that I couldn't do without them indefinitely! Then I want (so does everybody!) shorter working hours and more leisure. We're all more or less tired, I think.

I must stop very soon now and do some work, but I'm glad it rained!

I've seen no more of Captain Gerringer, but I'd a nice note from him a few days ago. I'm not sure where he is, but apparently he comes very seldom to London. . . .

Bless me, I've forgotten to mention our Bessie! What do you think of her?! I'd a lovely long letter from her last week, telling me all about her wedding and her home and her husband (who sounds a LAMB and really nice enough even for our Bessie) and her wedding presents, and sending me snippets from her wedding costume and coat. I'm delighted to know she's so happy, and as I've told her, it made me feel GREEN as GRASS with envy! Has she described the view from her window? Imagine having a BAY and a MOUNTAIN outside your sitting room windows! I would give a lot for the sight of SEA this minute. Wouldn't you? Let's both go and call on Mr. and Mrs. C. L. Smith, the minute the war's over. Shall we, Phylabe?

Are you fully occupied on your farm again, Phylabe? I picture you always in a setting with wide horizons and clear air, and can't feel it right or happy for you to be shut up within four walls, pounding a typewriter. If it's necessary in the war, all right, but farming sounds such a wider, richer life. I know nothing of its tedium or drudgery, and maybe I'm all wrong, but I felt happy for you when you told me you were going to work on your ranch again. It's very important war work—ask any Briton, who knows he couldn't have survived without the food you sent him! Dear Phylabe, we *are* so grateful—even though "Spam" is a national joke and dried eggs are the very divvil to mix smoothly! But the chief thing is for you to be happy and fulfilled, and that is what I am hoping for you with all my heart.

I'm also hoping that in the process you'll have a *little* more leisure and will write to me! For I do so love your letters. And now I *must* stop—my "in-tray" is piling up and I must get it levelled down again forthwith.

With warmest love and wishes for a marvelous year for you,

Ever yours
Edith

✉   **15**
29 Stanley Gardens
London W 11
23.2.44

My dear Phylabe

The packet of magazines arrived yesterday—so joyful to see your writing on the envelope! Thank you so much. I've already devoured the clippings and am looking forward to enjoying the *Digests* at leisure over the next fortnight or so.

Incidentally, I met at Thirza's one evening recently a delightful girl who is assistant to the *Reader's Digest* director in Europe. She told us amazing facts and figures about the *Digest*—can't remember 'em but they all seemed to run in millions!—and I remember I envied her her job! But the English edition is a lot smaller than yours these days, owing to paper control. Miss Greene was full of excitement because they'd just successfully launched their newest baby (if you'll pardon the mixed metaphors!)—a Cairo edition. As you probably know (though I didn't till I met Miss Greene), the magazine is now produced in nearly every country and nearly every language in the civilised world.

Now, Phylabe, I must tell you that . . . there has been no sign of the Christmas parcel you mentioned as being "on the way" in your note inside the Christmas card. Making all possible allowances for a slower parcel post, I'm afraid it looks now as if the parcel has been lost or maybe stolen and I can't tell you how terribly disappointed I am. Not only for the nice and exciting things it contained, . . . but because you too will be so disappointed. . . .

February 28

We're having lively times here just now. . . . We've had a succession of raids, . . . some of them rather serious. Two nights my flat was ringed round with fires. Thirza counted eight from her bedroom windows. I have no view from mine but it was as light as day in the glare. It's all very horrible, Phylabe, and very alarming, too! The din is terrific—chiefly from our guns, of course, and we don't mind that; but the sound of bombs falling is just *sickening.* Our street fortunately is untouched (except for showers of shrapnel, but it hasn't done much harm). But two of my friends a few streets away had an incendiary in their flat. "What on earth did you do?" I asked them— they were both at a B & P Women's Club-meeting the next evening, looking very spruce and cheery. "We got a stirrup pump and put it out," they told me. But not before their sitting room had been pretty well ruined with fire and water. Then they went out and helped to put out fires in three other houses. I should add that they are two little elderly bodies of about 60! And that they were completely bombed out in 1941 and had only just got a new home together about five months ago!

On Thursday morning I arrived at the office to find part of it had disappeared![20] My room only lost one pane from the window,

---

20. This letter was severely censored. The ministry office was in St. James Square and St. James's Palace was also damaged in a February raid.

and the odd thing was that we had put a bottle of milk out on the window sill overnight to keep cool and it was immediately outside the blasted pane. But the bottle was quite whole! Presumably the blast slid round the bottle, but the window, because it offered resistance, was broken.

It was a bad do, though. . . . bombs were dropped. . . . Our H.Q. building (in which I work) is modern steel and brick and concrete, and all we suffered was broken windows—(there was glass everywhere!). But we had recently taken over two of the fine old town mansions in . . . and outhoused some of our expanded staff in them. These two are completely gutted. . . . I'd like to tell you of one very historic and picturesque building that's much damaged, though not beyond repair, but the Censor might object so I'll mention no names. But I wept . . . it—partly with misery at the destruction of so much . . . with anger. Ever since I've been in a state of seething anger about the whole beastly, senseless, savage business—and I don't care whether it's London, Augsburg, Rome or Helsinki that's being destroyed. . . . Don't you too, and mustn't all reasonable and normal people feel the same? To see . . . but modern buildings are . . . in looking at them . . . or . . . only five hundred years old perhaps, . . . old buildings can be, done down over-night by some dastardly stab-in-the-back night raid. It's murder, isn't it. As much so as if flesh and blood were involved. Perhaps more. There's enduring life, enduring spirit, in the great works of man's hand and their destruction impoverishes us all. I felt as if I'd lost my husband, child and wife when I came on this one building the other day, suddenly and unprepared for it, as I didn't know it had been hit. However, they'll patch it up quite well, I should think, and by the time you come to London there'll be little to notice. If they ever get the Abbey or St. Paul's, though, life will hardly seem worth living. So much will one's personal life be robbed—as by the death of a dear friend.

Poor London! She gets shabbier and shabbier. Dirty and down at heel and dishevelled. I often see parties of American soldiers being conducted round, especially around the Westminster and St. James's areas where there's lots of historic interest and a fair bit of war damage. What can their impressions be? "Is *this* the capital of the world—this neglected, untidy place of boarded up shops, rusty water tanks, unpainted woodwork, crumbling stone, waste sites?!!!" Each spring it looks worse. Each spring the Royal Parks drop one stage back into the wilderness. Each spring there's less grass on the

Squares—Leicester Square, that was a green oasis in West End cinema-land, now a weed-patch; Berkeley Square, where "the nightingale sang," now trampled down hard and grey and barren. Yes, the Mother of Cities has lost her teeth and her waistline and her hair and most of her charm, and your soldierboys must think she's a disappointing dame indeed. BUT,—she will recover! and *how* I'm looking forward to that time! *How* I hope I'm lucky enough to be in London for, say, five years after the war ends, to see her colour coming back and her lamp lighting up and her flowers all abloom again. What a time it will be. Heaven send it soon!

Chris was coming to spend Eastertide with me, but in view of the raids we think it better to make other plans. I should be worried stiff if she was here in a bad raid, and so would Mother, but it's very disappointing. But by April the Second Front may at long last be in operation and civilian traffic would be undesirable on the railways anyway. Don't know when I'll get home for a visit. I'd like to see Mother. All being well I shall hope to go home in the early summer. I may spend some of my holiday time too at Bangor, in North Wales. My friends Aura and Claude, who were evacuated there with Claude's school from Liverpool at the beginning of the war, have just bought a Preparatory School with 24 boarders. They'll therefore have 24 spare beds out of term time, and I'm cordially invited to keep one aired whenever I like. May Phillips, my Cotswold friend, is Aura's sister and we three were an inseparable trio in my *Countryman* days. If May can be at Bangor at the same time as I, we'll have a lovely time. I spent many happy days, during an in-the-main very *un*happy period in North Wales, visiting Bangor and crossing over the Menai Bridge to the Isle of Anglesey. I can still recall the scent of thyme and the feel of spring turf underfoot as one walked round the shores of the island—a lovely place. Halfway across Anglesey is the place with the longest name in Britain. Can't remember it all but it begins Llanfairpwllgwyngll . . . and ends ogogogoch. Isn't it marvelous? Known generally as Llanfair P. G., for a mercy.

The women of the businesses and professions have been celebrating international night—quite brightly, in spite of raids though hardly with peacetime *éclat*. To begin with, it was a tea time gathering instead of a suppertime one, for nobody likes to be away from home when bombing time draws near. About 400 of us gathered in the ballroom of Grosvenor House, one of the monster Parklane hotels, and we had for speakers, Miss Irene Ward, M. P., just returned from a tour of China; Helen Kirkpatrick, your (*Chicago Times* -or *Sun?*) war correspondent, who has had thrilling adventures in N. Africa, Sicily and Corsica;[21] and Dr. Lena Madesin Phillip of New York, International President of B. P. Women's Clubs.[22] I must say that except for Miss Kirkpatrick's the talks were very poor, especially Irene Ward's, which was deadly dull. Perhaps we were all affected by the putrid tea this luxury hotel served us!—miserable fish-paste sandwiches and "cake" (in name only) that quite definitely was not fit to eat! I hope Dr. Madesin Phillip took due note, for the following reason. I lunched before the meeting with Nancy Anderson, national organiser of BPW clubs in Britain, at a rather expensive and fashionable St. James's Street restaurant, Pruniers. Nancy told me that our Elizabeth Hawes, international liaison officer for Soroptimists, gave a small dinner party there for Dr. Phillip and the fare included oysters, lobster, very good wines and other luxury foods (which *can* be obtained at a few restaurants and hotels but *only* at considerable cost) and that Dr. Phillip had remarked that lend-lease hardly seemed necessary. This worried us considerably, because only a very small proportion of our people can possibly afford such meals. These luxury foods are extremely scarce, and the Government has made regulations which very much restrict the restaurants in supplying them. In ordinary reasonable-price restaurants the food is really *not* very good. Very little variety, mostly made-up dishes, very short in meat, fish and other basic foods. If Dr. Phillip wanted to see how the English feed, she shouldn't have gone to a banquet at Pruniers! So if you hear anybody saying "I hear the English feast on oysters and roast turkey so why should we go short to send them food?" do please say that you have been assured by an absolutely honest Englishwoman that food *is* short (although we're not by any means starving) and that without your tinned meats,

---

21. Helen Kirkpatrick was the first woman foreign correspondent for the *Chicago Daily News.* She was in Prague when Hitler invaded the Sudetenland, covered the Balkans, Italy, Poland, and France, and was one of the press planners for the Normandy invasion. She was awarded the French Medal of the Resistance and the U.S. Medal of Freedom, and was later to hold executive positions in the State Department.
22. Lena Madesin Phillip, an attorney and, after 1935, editor of the *Pictorial Review,* was founder and president of the international federation of Business and Professional Women (1930).

dried milk and dried eggs, to mention only three foods, we should have been in very sorry straits indeed!

My own B & P Club, the Regency, planned an International Night celebration of its own for next Monday, but is moving it to the following Saturday afternoon in view of the renewal of raids. I'll enclose the original notice for you to see—it was going to be quite an event. The change of date means I can't go, as every Saturday afternoon (and every Thursday evening) till March 19 I'm rehearsing, with the choir I'm a member of, for a performance of an oratorio, a new and topical work by our conductor, Michael Tippett.[23] It's to be given on the 19th in the Royal Adelphi Theatre. Really it's an impassioned protest against the persecution of Jews in Nazi Europe and against the conditions that make persecution possible. The musical idiom is strange and difficult to sing, but we're beginning to feel, now that we know it better, that it's tremendously powerful and beautiful. It's punctuated by Negro spirituals as Bach's oratorios are punctuated by chorales, and the whole thing is impressive and moving. I wish you could come and hear it! A week ago we gave a very different sort of concert—anthems and choruses by Purcell. Do you know the music of that early English composer? Very lovely it is, and balm to the spirit in these restless days. This choir is a great joy to Thirza and me.

I'm having too many interruptions now to be able to continue this letter satisfactorily, so I think I'll end it here and hope to start another one quite soon.

Every good wish to you, Phylabe my dear. I hope to hear from you soon. I hope the "long letter" you said you were writing was not in the parcel and is not lost. It would be *too* disappointing.

My love to you, and kindest greetings to your Dad.

Yours aye
Edith

---

23. Michael Tippett's oratorio *A Child of Our Time* tells the story of a young Polish Jew who killed a Nazi in Paris.

✉ **16**
March 14/44
29 Stanley Gardens
London W 11

Oh Phylabe, Phylabe, Phylabe,

The parcel has come!!! Isn't it marvelous? Four months to a day
since the Greeley postmark, but here it was when I came home
tonight—all intact, all so lovely, all so *EXCITING*. . . . Phylabe, I just
can't tell you how much joy you bring me and how I bless the
chance that brought me Bessie and then you and now all my feeling
of identity with you and Colorado and America and indeed the
whole world! What a unifier one letter from you to me turns out to
be! I love you as YOU and my own very dear friend but you are also
a symbol—hope you don't object!—and having found *you* in my
heart I find all America is there, too, and having learned to love
America I know there is room for France and China and Italy and
Russia and Germany too. Not that I'm forgiving the enemies of
mankind. I hate 'em and wish 'em ill in whichever nation they
belong! Only I find it more and more difficult to divide mankind
into British, German, American and Japanese and easier by far to
think of them in groups as spiritually enlightened or living in outer
darkness. Some of the latter category (the anti-Semites, the anti-
French, the anti-Yanks) live in London and no doubt many of the
other group failed to escape from Berlin—nationality has little to
do with it, though I condemn the kind of aggression that came out
of Germany with my whole breath and feel absolutely certain that
we are fighting unavoidably, necessarily and for the right. All the
same, and while realising the military necessity, the bombing of Berlin fills me with horror because we are all alike, as John Donne
declared, "involved in mankind," and in destroying Berlin, Rome,
Tokyo we destroy a part of ourselves. "Send not to learn (ask?) for
whom the bell tolls"—we all know part of the quotation now!—"it
tolleth for thyself. Every man's death impoverishes me, for I am
involved in mankind." Which is why each day's news of the slaughter
of Germans on the Russian front, and the hell's din of guns and
probably bombs that's going on above at this moment (for there's a
nasty raid in progress and I'm writing this in the air raid shelter in
the cellar) fills me with fresh sadness, and new horror and pity for
poor mankind that has got itself into such a mess.

I've got a long way from your Christmas parcel, but it was a logi-cal excursion for you are all the above misery in blessed reverse. You are all the glory of mankind united and friendly and free, and your token-of-love parcel lights a candle in this world of naughty deeds. Oh Phylabe, personal friendships sometimes seem the one stable and reliable and healthy thing left unassailable in this tottering, wretched world—the one assurance that the good things, the holy, pure and right things *are* the strong things that will endure. Maybe midnight in a cellar under an air raid isn't the best time to be writ-ing a letter to a Friend in America, but I'd like you to know that one woman in such circumstances felt the hand of her American friend reaching her with almost physical comfort and upholding, and was freed of many unhappy thoughts in consequence.

Phylabe dear, I have another letter partly written to you upstairs (on real note paper!—please forgive this office scrap-pad, which fortunately happened to be in my bag, or I shouldn't have been able to write to you now).[24] It goes haltingly because I never dare spare time from the clamouring jobs of cleaning and mending and mak-ing. But in small stages it will one day be completed and will come to you with news of 1944 London and Edith's Lighter Moments. There's also a new *Countryman* ready to set out for you. You have been doing me proud lately!—three separate packages from you in the last two or three weeks! Not counting the parcel. I've said thank you for them in the other letter so will only say so again quite briefly now. It was lovely to have them, and do please thank Virginia very warmly indeed for her letter. I want Thirza (and she wants) to write to Virginia, because I mustn't be selfish and keep all of you to myself and because I'm sure you'd both like Thirza an awful lot and I'd like you to.[25]

Now I must *hurry* to bed. The raid is over, we're still intact, and I'm beginning to feel angry because I've been done out of the long night's sleep I'd promised myself tonight and because I've not enough milk to make the cup of tea for which I'm panting and a cup of water seems poor consolation! (I'd better get to bed before I start throwing things about!)

---

24. This letter is written on twelve small sheets of a scratch pad made from cut-up 1936 government forms.
25. Virginia Fowlkes, a friend of Phylabe's, was a school teacher, who served for a time in the Waves.

Goodnight, Phylabe dear, and thank you a million, million times for your wonderful parcel and all your other tangible and intangible gifts.

Ever yours
Edith

✉   **17**
29 Stanley Gardens
London W 11
March 8, 1944

Dearest Phylabe
. . . How lovely to find a note in your own blessed hand tucked inside the *Digest*—but oh dear, my poor Phylabe, I do hope you're better! Flu is such a *beast*. I do hope it didn't last *too* long (but what a time to choose to have it—Christmas and New Year!!) and that now it's quite removed itself and left no unpleasant evidences behind.

Was yours a brand of the same epidemic that we had, or do you have a brand of your own? Ours (mercifully I escaped) seemed to wear itself out in 4 or 5 days and wasn't on the whole very serious. Yours sounds a lot worse. But it's poor fun anyway having flu, and I'm full of sympathy for you. . . .

This can only be the *start* of a letter, but start it I just had to tonight while my delight at receipt of yours was at its height. I'm eating my supper while I write (can you smell my lease-lend egg omelette?!) and am going on air raid duty at 10 so must hustle round now and wash up the dishes *etc etc*. We've had one or two more raids since I wrote you a week ago, but the last few nights have had peace, due, they say, to the dear old moon. By next week the moon will be rising late again and no doubt the enemy will take due advantage of the fact.

10:30 p.m. Believe it or not, the sirens went just there! All over now, though (no excitement; no planes got through tonight) so I've come home, and am going to bed in faith that they won't come back. Am on duty till 7 a.m. but as I live just opposite the Post I'm allowed (so far) to spend the time at home unless there's an Alert. Very convenient!

But no more letter tonight! What a pity. I must remember to tell you about the Queen. Goodnight, Phylabe.

March 24

A lot of mornings have dawned since I wrote that Goodnight! In between, your lovely Christmas parcel arrived and I wrote to tell you so, and I hope that has reached you. I've been enjoying your gifts so much! Especially the scarf. Curious women on buses speak to me about it, and wherever I go, eyes follow me! This is all entirely true—don't think I'm exaggerating! I've never worn anything that attracted so much admiration. . . .

Summer suddenly came yesterday and caught us all napping. I went rambling with a party of girls in Surrey, all of us wearing sweaters and scarves and winter coats. Then the temperature shot up to nearly 90° in the sun—and as we were on the downs in full sunlight (not a shred of cloud anywhere on that exquisite blue sky) from mid-morning till sundown, you can imagine the strip-tease acts that kept taking place! Oh, it was heaven. The blackthorn (which, in case you don't grow it in Colorado, sprouts lovely little white flowers thickly all over its black stems before any leaves show) was coming out in the hedgerows, and in the cottage gardens the almond trees (bright pink) were in blossom and the daffodils a-blowing. What a breath-taker spring is! I could jump off housetops and take to the air. The land is frightfully dry, however. We've had no snow and hardly any rain, and although we were on uncultivated down-land all day yesterday our shoes were smothered in *dust* with no *mud* at all. I read in the paper that in many villages the water supply has dried up, which is very serious at this time of the year. The town reservoirs are lower than they should be, too, so we are all urged to limit our baths to 5 inches of water!—but that is mostly to save the fuel involved in pumping and heating.

I reminded myself at the beginning of this letter to tell you about going to see the Queen. We (Ministry) were running an exhibition at the Royal Academy of severely disabled men back at work (we have a scheme of rehabilitation and training of people who lose limbs, sight, etc., which is having remarkable results) and the Queen visited it one day. The Press Office went over more or less *en masse* to see her—and she was *lovely!* She really is the prettiest and sweetest woman—no photograph that ever I've seen does her anything like justice. She stopped to talk to every single man and woman working in the exhibition, with such *interest* in her face and her voice. Everybody was enchanted. Incidentally, it was much commented on that two DARNS were evident in the Royal hose—so now you really know how hard up we are for stockings!

We've had a succession of air raids since I last wrote—very disturbing ones. The amount of damage done has been small on the whole, but nasty in the districts concerned. All of us now are careful to get up and dress instantly when the sirens go—nobody wants to be caught out in a flimsy nightdress and bedroom slippers! As a matter of fact, when bombs were dropped near the office a few weeks ago, a woman came into the office fireguard room in great distress in nothing but a thin dressing gown. She'd been taking a bath when the bombs fell! But all these broken nights, and the fact that one delays going to bed as long as possible in case there's an early raid, leads to an awful tiredness. By the end of the week—till Sunday gives one a chance to make up some of the lost sleep— everybody is yawning! I feel it worst in my eyelids, which develop a continuous twitching that nearly drives me crazy. A small affliction compared with what many people are suffering, but annoying all the same. *Three* of my friends have had incendiaries in their flats, poor things, but they're amazingly philosophic about it. Did I ever tell you about Nancie, my friend since childhood and mother of one of my goddaughters?—they live at Sunderland, County Durham, which has been bombed and better-bombed for years. One night a bomb fell near Nancie's home, blew all the windows in (the flying glass cut her curtains and carpet to ribbons, buried itself in the furniture, slashed the walls, brought the ceilings down, shook all the soot out of the chimneys and left them little but the walls of their house. Nancie and the children were safe in the shelter. When I cried out with horror and sympathy at sight of it she said "none of this *matters*—we're all unhurt!" and quite plainly, the loss and the mess and the discomfort were blotted out for her in thankfulness that the major calamity had been spared them. Don't know whether I'd be so angelic! I hate the thought of losing all my precious bits and pieces, my comfortable bed and my bonny red carpet and my beloved books! Still it wouldn't really matter.

I can't remember, by the way, whether I was able to add to my last letter, one I wrote during an air raid, that during that raid our beautiful parish church was burnt out. Fortunately its particularly lovely tall steeple is undamaged and as the outer walls are standing no doubt it can be restored after the war. But for the present it's just a shell. A Roman Catholic church in the same road was hit again after being almost entirely destroyed the previous week. In two or three places on my way to the office next morning the road was pitted and splashed all over with the white ash of scores of incendiaries. At one point I had to make a detour around an unexploded H.E. (high explosive bomb). Marvelous days we live in! Two or three nights ago another of our historic old city churches went up in smoke. May God forgive us all.

Do I sound a bit miserable tonight? I'm feeling sad, and a bit scared. Don't like the way the world's going. Just had an argument with my boss that frightened me—because he talked like a Nazi, and I feel more and more people do, without in the least knowing it. Some shipyard apprentices are threatening to strike unless the Minister of Labour will promise them something or other. "I would put a dozen of them up against a wall and shoot them" said my boss—said it with hatred and fury. And when I protested, added "A little more Totalitarianism would do some people in this country a lot of good." He spoke in patriotism, because the apprentices may hold up the war effort. But oh, it frightens me when people forget what we're fighting for and begin to copy unconsciously in their thoughts the ugliest and most sinister ideas of the enemy. I'm alarmed, too, because apparently they're going to remove Mr. Eden from the Foreign Office, and one suspects it's because he's too good an internationalist and too honestly a pro-Russian. The Second Front seems as far off as ever—Mr. Churchill in his broadcast speech last night seemed to push it back *months* again. We can't understand it—is your country, too, wondering? The end of the war seems a long way off yet, and each month that it continues increases the danger—to persons, property and—ideals. It's the last I get most worried about.

But I mustn't make you think my morale is wearing low. As a matter of fact, it's not. If anything, it's a lot stronger than ever it was, because in the past five years I've had time to get my ideas sorted out and clarified until now, as never before, *I'm quite* certain what *I'm* fighting for and what I'll have to continue to fight for so long as I live, on the small battlefield of daily life and personal contacts. It's such an obvious thing—one shouldn't have to fight for anything so patently right at all; just the equality of all men in their right to life and liberty, and the thing that Edith Cavell[26] had in her mind when she said "Patriotism is not enough; I must have no hatred or bitterness in any heart." It's the fear of hatred and bitterness, of dark destructive forces a thousand million times more horrible than air raids, that saddens one. They could—no matter who wins the war—blot out the beauty and light of life for centuries to come. I have faith that mankind, in the long—the *very* long—run, ascends, but one lives for such a very short span of that long run, and I (for one) don't want to die while the world is on a downward stretch. One could die contentedly if it was plainly moving towards its goal.

Don't think me a horridly belligerent kind of creature! I don't really want to have to fight for anything at all; *hate* fighting. Just want to live in the sun and have nice friends and listen to music and in general "cultivate my garden." *Wouldn't* it be nice to live like that!!

March 28

Lunchtime, and have just been for a turn round the Park with Thirza. She's staying with her sister out of London just now, waiting for a reluctant new baby to make his entry into the world, so I'd not seen her for some days. The Park and the Mall and Trafalgar Square were crowded—it's Salute the Soldier Week, a week of campaigning for National Savings, and there are parades of all sorts going on about the place. The weather is still miraculously lovely and it's brought the people out in thousands. Yesterday there was a march past the Palace, with the King and Queen and the Princesses taking the salute, but not knowing anything about it in advance (on security grounds it was kept dark, in case Hitler came and bombed it) I missed all but the verge of the crowd as it all ended. Don't like martial displays, anyway—except Highland pipe bands!

All this long while and I've never mentioned your Christmas present! It is rapidly nearing completion!! Yes, really!!! A few more air raids and it certainly will be finished! I'm awfully grieved that it's been so very long in coming. I began making you a present in November, and would have got that off to you sometime before Christmas, but when I got it finished it seemed to me rather small for you, so I decided to start afresh, and gave the small one to

---

26. Edith Cavell was an English nurse who helped more than 250 prisoners escape from Belgium to Holland and other Allied territories during the First World War. Though not herself involved in espionage, she was executed as a spy under international law because those she helped may well have carried valuable information. Her story was made into a movie in 1939.

another friend who is very small. By that time my schedule was well and truly out of gear and I had to start frantically making presents for the family and other friends over here. *Most* of them, I'm afraid, got promissory notes on December 25 and the actual gifts a *long* time afterwards. I've been steadily making Christmas presents ever since, and still have a pair of gloves to make for my favourite boy friend after I finish the present I'm making for you! I know the whole thing is deplorable, but it's no good feeling too bitterly ashamed of myself, because I really haven't *wasted* any time—it's Hitler's fault, for making us have to work such long hours and spend so much time mending and cooking (instead of just calling at the shop for a new pair of stockings or a cake or a cooked dish). But I do hope you will forgive me, all the same. It really will be coming along soon—in about a fortnight, I should think.

We had a great day last Sunday week, when we sang in the first performance of Michael Tippett's new Oratorio. . . . He's becoming known as a leading contemporary composer, and this new work had a marvelous reception. There was a crowded theatre for this first performance, and the critics have devoted unusual space to it and written of it with enormous respect. I wish I could send you a programme, but I could only get hold of one, which I want to keep. It's difficult to form an opinion on the work myself, as we only heard it from behind, so to speak, and indeed we only heard it *whole*, with orchestra and soloists, on the day of the performance, and the choir part is a bit disjointed without them, as you can imagine. Besides, I have to admit I don't understand the technique behind modern music well enough to appreciate it, and I only *feel* I don't much like it because it lacks beauty and grace. But that's because I'm old fashioned! (What's perplexing is that our Michael is steeped in Purcell and Bach and worships at their feet and *yet* writes his own queer stuff!)

Anyway, we had an enthralling day. It was exciting to sing with the London Philharmonic Orchestra and be rehearsed with them by dynamic Walter Goehr—thrilling to realise what a master he was and that he was working *through us* to give a creation life. Interesting, too, to see the aristocratic members of the Philharmonic being drilled and occasionally told off! We had a gruelling morning. (So had poor Walter! Trying to make us mutts sing like angels!!) Then ate our packed lunch in the stalls while the orchestra rehearsed a

Mozart Symphony; then a quick walk on the Embankment in the sunshine and back for the Great Performance! It really was a thrill.

Now we've started work on two sets of Elizabethan madrigals, for a College concert next month, and I must say they're a rest cure after Michael's dissonances and syncopations.

I'd another letter from Bessie this morning—full of anger at a Wages Control Bill she felt to be unjust, and of indignation at one or two other things, but so blessedly full of beans that even just reading it I felt I'd had a tonic. Isn't it grand to know she's so happy and eager about things? I'm so happy for her. Mr. Ratcliffe, in this office, who met Bessie when he was over in Victoria with a trade delegation a year or more ago, came into the Press Office this morning and I showed him Bessie's wedding snaps. He said of Charlie "Such a *shy* boy," and of Bessie, with a gleam in his naughty old eye "That's her—ah, I remember" and left me to imagine *what* he remembered! But I gathered he was impressed.

I wonder what you're doing with yourself these days, Phylabe my dear? I've heard so little of *you* for so long, though so many packages have come from you. They don't tell me enough about you. . . .

I'm sorry to say I must now start to do some work—not that I've anything worth doing today really! Things are very quiet this week, with the result that I'm bored. I just can't bear sitting here and *making* little useless jobs to fill in the time—but I mustn't get onto that theme!!! We're just having a birthday tea at the moment—one of my colleagues is celebrating. . . . This time it's a *real* cake—a home-made fruit cake with real orange peel in it! Ooo-er! Did I tell you we'd had two allocations of oranges? I got one pound the first time and two pounds the next, and made marmalade, which is delicious. This week I'm living luxuriously—felt lonely on Sunday evening, with Thirza away, and Marjorie and Cecil both away in Newcastle, so I looked in my store cupboard and found one remaining treasured pre-war tin of Aylmer's peaches! Talk about rapture! Only it seemed a pity to have them when there was nobody to share them with. I tried to persuade Thirza to dash home with me tonight for a meal before going out to her sister's, but she thought the baby might just decide to arrive tonight, and not even peaches could deflect her.

Now I must stop, Cheerio, Phylabe dear, and lots and lots of good wishes to you. Please give my greetings to your Dad.

With such and so much love to you
Edith

✉ **18**
29 Stanley Gardens
London W 11
18.5.44

Dearest Phylabe
    You shall have a Christmas Parcel even if it *is* May when I dispatch it and July (probably) when you receive it! Dear Phylabe, I am a *villain* to have kept you waiting so long. Please be indulgent and forgive me this time! Though I can't promise it will never happen again!
    I do hope the collar and cuffs will fit *something* of yours. Do you remember I told you the original collar I made for you turned out too small?—*This* one is really too *big!* I started it one night in the air-raid shelter when I hadn't the book of words with me and rather than pull out what I'd done I just continued on the large scale. So the final result is a yoke rather than a collar, but it is not overwhelming on *me* so I hope it won't be on you. The Mince Pie card has been waiting to come to you since December, but the Tree book I just discovered on the stall yesterday. Do you have horse chestnuts and beech trees in Colorado? It is rather important that you *should* have, if I am to come and see you, for those are trees I just can't spare from my landscapes! Especially in the month of maying. The chestnuts are heavenly in England just now. And all the May trees are out—oh, so exciting and ravishing everything is just now. The bluebells are just passing. Phylabe—you should have seen them! When bluebells are out in the woods you just can't see where the flowers stop and the air starts. They blow their blueness up in a magical haze and the air floats down and mingles shimmeringly with the flowers, "annihilating all that's made to a *blue* thought in a *blue* shade" (to misquote Marvell) and turning you drunk with delight. I long to see *your* wonders and joys but can't forbear my own! Wouldn't ever want to give up an English spring—not for anything! They're so few and far between, and get more terrifyingly precious each year as they fly past. Do you ever get into a panic because of the things you are missing? I am in one now because for three weeks I've not been able to go into the country and what I have missed is too terrible to think about. No cherry blossom, no apple blossom, no voice of cuckoo—o-o-o-oh!
    The little book on European architecture is a recent find, too. These Pelican and Penguin and Puffin books are easily the best

book things obtainable in England at the present time (when paper shortage limits quantity and quality of publications most sadly). They cost no more than ninepence (as against 8s. 6d. at least for a new novel) and the contents are always (nearly always) beyond all value in money. I wonder if this one will thrill you as much as it does me? I am wondering what your feelings about Gothic architecture can be. Something akin to mine about the antiquities of Peru? I don't know. I only know I long to show you some of ours— especially our lovely beloved serene old village churches; but also you must someday, before you have to give account to St. Peter at the Gate for all life's chances you've failed to grasp (do you know the story of the dream that chased Baden-Powell off to Japan?[27])[,] stand in an Early English cathedral and let its soaring arches draw your eyes and your spirit up to Heaven.

Now I have got so far and haven't yet said Thank You dear Phy- labe for all the *Digests* that keep coming so quickly that I can't keep up with them and that I enjoy so much. Thank you indeed!

But your long promised letter still lingers—you treat me nearly as badly as I treat you!! I don't know how you are or what you are doing—please, please tell me soon!

Such and so much love—and many merry Christmases to you!

Aye
Edith

✉ **19**
Office—4 p.m. Sat May 20/44

On duty this afternoon and v. busy! But have just put the kettle on and am taking 5 minutes holiday till it boils. Here are some snip- pets to tell you how the world wags hereabout. . . .

Tomorrow I am going picnicking with four of your countrymen! (And three of my countrywomen). Am looking forward to it so much, but the weather is dingy. We plan to go to Windsor, see the

---

27. Lord Baden-Powell, founder of the Boy Scouts, dreamed he met St. Peter at the Gate of Heaven and in a conversation was asked how he had liked Japan. He told St. Peter he had never been there and was chastised for having failed to take advantage of his opportunities. The warning to do so before it was too late did not fall on deaf ears, and the already middle-aged man immediately embarked on an extended lecture tour of the United States and the Far East.

Castle and walk in the Great Park. *How* I hope it's a fine day!! Will tell you about it later. Two of the officers are from Seattle, so maybe they have walked on the same pavements as our Bessie.

Must return to my work now!

Lots of love to you, aye,
Edith

✉ **20**
29 Stanley Gardens
London W 11
Aug. 1st, 1944

Phylabe dear—

Just found a nice little book of pictures for you so will scribble a wee sma' note to tuck inside it—but this isn't the letter I mean to write you one of these fine days! Life gets more and more tied up—this time it is doodlebombs,[28] which I really think are a good enough excuse to offer for almost all sins of omission! There may be a time soon when I can tell you more about these abominations, but in the meantime I'm sure the Censor won't mind if I tell you they are a blankety blank blank nuisance and one can't get anything done for them. My evenings now consist of making my meal, eating it and clearing it away, all quite likely to an accompaniment of sirens and buzz bombs and bonks, then listening to the 9 p.m. news on the wireless, then carrying rugs and pillow down to the basement and making up my shelter bed and getting myself ready to dash to it when the moment comes. Three nights a week I am an Air Raid Warden from 10 p.m. to 7 a.m. and recently this has meant very broken nights (there is a siren sounding now—just after lunch) with a total of perhaps 3 or 4 hours sleep, so that most of my so-called waking hours are really spent in a state of semi-sleep. ("Danger imminent" signal

---

28. The first V–1s, jet-propelled flying bombs called "doodlebombs" among other things, began to fall over southeastern England on 13 June. Before the attacks ended in March 1945, property damage and civilian casualties had been extensive. The first flying bomb was launched on 13 June and in the first fortnight 2,572 Londoners were killed and 400,000 houses destroyed. In all, more than nine thousand were launched against England and just under half were destroyed by interceptor planes, anti-aircraft fire, or balloon barrages. The last was launched on 29 March 1945.

just gone, so I have hied me down to the office shelter. These fiend-bombs pounce on you so suddenly sometimes, the engines having cut out perhaps some miles away, that I believe in taking shelter when the D. I. goes. However, I must tell you that the majority of the staff doesn't bother—and it *is* a bother when it happens several times a day!) Sleepiness and shelter-itis—the aches one develops from sleeping on hard bunks and shelter beds—are chief topics for jokes these days. I wish you could come spend a buzz-bomby day here in London—I think it would interest you profoundly and amuse you quite a lot. It is so comic to see normal life and emergency life running along together quite comfortably. Everybody takes precautions—but not if it interferes with other plans! Everybody tells awful stories of terrible experiences—and laughs at them. Everybody says this is damnable and diabolic and the Government ought to do something about it—but firmly believes that the Hun is whacked and can do no more than bruise our heels. But all the time poor old London is getting more and more battered and dishevelled, and there are casualties and sad destruction. One of my close friends has lost her home and all her possessions—she and her husband and children were dug unharmed out of the steel shelter on which their house collapsed in rubble. I had a letter from her yesterday from Whickham (we were childhood friends together and she has gone back there to relatives) saying "I went to church to give thanks for our life." A large number of friends have lost windows and doors and suffered damage to furniture, two others were in a hotel that received a direct hit but miraculously escaped without a scratch; and three American officer friends who were staying in the same hotel were back on duty the next day, though one was so full of flying fragments of glass that it took the First Aid people two hours to pick it all out!

Still, we are anything but down-hearted and, as I said just now, I wish you could spend a day or two here, for I'm sure it would do your heart good!

(By the way, I came back to my desk about the middle of the last page!—Raid over.)

Phylabe, Phylabe, Phylabe—when am I to have news from you?! An airgraph from Bessie this morning expresses anxiety about you—she is waiting anxiously for a letter too! What is the matter, dear Phylabe? Is this bad old world too ignoble for you!—or are you over-busy?—or are you not well? I do so long to hear. I know I am a miserable correspondent myself and pots ought never to call kettles black—but even though I don't deserve a letter, please, please send me one. There's a dear!

Mustn't embark on any more news this time or I shall not get letter posted today. This is just an interim note to let you know I'm still thinking of you. . . .

Do take care of yourself, my dear Phylabe, and don't work too hard or worry too much! I am thinking a lot about you, with love and gratitude for your friendship.

Ever yours
Edith

✉ **21**
29 Stanley Gardens
London W 11
Sept. 3, 1944

My dear Phylabe

I'm on a train, so feel like writing a letter. The writing will be abominable—I hope you don't mind too much.

I'm on my way back to London after a week at home. It has been a lovely week—beautiful brilliant, clear late-summer north-country weather, with a high wind to blow the clouds about and make dramatic purple-blue shadows on the green-gold-azure picture of land and sky. Whickham, you know, stands high, and there is always a wind there. I love it, and used always to love to get higher still on to the fells and feel the wind and my muscles battling against each other to hold my body straight. Also from the fell top you can look both ways over the world and see the Cheviots (hills) holding their wall against Scotland to the North, and to the South a wonderful patchwork of fields and moors stretching across Durham County and reaching into Yorkshire. This is the month when views are most brilliantly clear and colourful, and I wish you could have been with me to see the English high-summer scene and feel the kind, stimulating North of England wind streaming off from your figure. My abominable new pen has run out on me. I lost my precious Onoto pen, gift of my dear old editor some 20 years ago. I used my handbag as a pillow while I sun-baked in the Park one day and my pen must have fallen out. Fountain pens are difficult to get these days, but I was lucky (I thought) in getting a second-hand one. But it isn't very good and it is always running dry. It seems a pity to stop writing when I've just begun, so I'll continue in pencil, though it's not very satisfactory.

It's been a lazy holiday, because I was in need of a rest after 10 weeks of flying-bombs. It was marvelous to go to bed and know nothing would disturb you till morning! Previously I'd slept only twice in my bed in 10 weeks, and most of my nights had been short and much broken. It's surprising how accustomed one gets to sleeping only in snatches. I suppose mothers of babies do it! But I *was* tired when I came North, and to be quite honest I'm *still* tired and don't feel at *all* ready to go back to hard-and-fast hours and work. Whickham is full of evacuees from London—mothers and children mostly. My own friend Hilda and her two children, who were bombed out of London and lost their home and everything, are billeted with a neighbour. Mother and I had a day at the coast on Tuesday and as we waited for a train in Tynemouth Station at night a train load of evacuees arrived there—mothers and children again; all very excited and not a bit cast down! Wardens and First Aid workers and Boy Scouts were dashing about, full of excitement too as they welcomed the visitors, and the ever-present Women's Voluntary Service was there with a tea-wagon—no English scene is ever complete without a teapot, you know! If you wonder what has upheld the Briton's morale, I can tell you—TEA! Nothing like it! The noise of bombs is ever drowned in the rattle of teacups, and the true English expression of sympathy—everything said and everything understood—is "There, dear, drink this nice cup of tea!" What wouldn't I give for some this very minute! Halfway down England, on a train crowded to the limit, hot and sticky and panting and no prospect of anything to drink—having emptied my luncheon-flask of coffee—til I get home some four hours hence! I drink some 10 cups of the stuff daily myself—3 with breakfast; 2 for elevenses; 2 for afternoon tea, and 2 or 3 in the evening. I drink it very weak, without sugar, so it won't do me much harm!

It is exciting to journey down England just now and see the corn. The fields stand so thick with it "that they do laugh and sing." England used to be a *green* country—most of our fields were meadows for grazing or hay; but now it's a yellow one, for all possible land is growing corn. I've never seen so much wheat! Last weekend when I went North it was mostly standing, now it is cut and stacked—beautiful to see in either state. There seem to be stupendous crops again—though the farmers are having trouble getting it let, for there has been rain every day (between the fine spots) to keep it constantly wet. My farmer auntie came to see us on Thursday (Mother's birthday) and said they were beginning to be anxious about their oats, which had been cut 10 days. Yesterday and the previous night it rained without ceasing, so it will still be un-led. It must be maddening to be a farmer! How do you keep your patience, you farm folks?

Now we've got to Peterborough, last stop before King's Cross (London)—about a 2-hour run. I gave my seat for a while to a man who'd stood all the way from Newcastle—like a lot of other people. Travel is *misery* these days. There's another man who looks as if he would like a seat and I think he must have mine shortly. Also it's raining again—oh this *silly* weather!

Phylabe, will you do something for me please? I am *most particularly* anxious to know if there is published in America any notable magazine for adolescents (15–19 years or thereabouts), with cultural interests. If there is, I'd be most awfully grateful if you'd send me a copy. I'll tell you more about my reasons later!

Oh dear—horrid overcast sky now. I hope this doesn't mean a lot of flying bombs tonight.

I may have changed my job before this reaches you! I've been fed up with my present one for a long time, as I've probably told you. I haven't nearly enough to do and it just isn't a useful job any more. I'm as rusty as can be when it comes to writing, and I've never been so bored in my life. So—with due regard for wartime regulations of employment—I'm looking for a new job and may possibly have got one. I expect a letter to be waiting for me when I get back. If I *do* get it, it is general reporting for a newspaper combine with a chain of papers all over the country, and I shall be dashing about with a notebook again. How I shall love it! I can't tell you how it has irked me to sit still for three years! I began to feel like a bedridden patient who fears she'll never walk again!

We're all looking forward to victory soon. Won't it be heaven to be at peace again? Our men have done wonders—yours and ours. And our spirits are rising daily—hourly! I was looking through various packages of books, etc[.] that I'd left stored at Whickham, and came on a long, soft parcel I didn't recognise. "What's this?" I asked Mother. "Oh, that's the flag for Victory. Leave it out!" said Mother. She's all set to have it hoisted before Christmas, and she's coming to London to celebrate. *How* we'll celebrate!!

You may receive an anxious request from a friend of mine shortly, and I hope you won't be too much bothered to help them, Phylabe dear. Do you remember I told you that my friends Geoffrey and Jean Edwards gave me an introduction to the American correspondent Bill White whom you know? They have lost touch with him and are anxious to get a letter to him and—I hope I did right—I gave them your address and suggested they should send a letter to you and ask you to forward it. Their only child, a daughter of 12 was laid up with a T. B. hipbone two years ago (she is now able to get about on crutches) and Bill was awfully good to her and before he left Britain sent her a huge box of puzzles and games for which they've not been able to thank him. So if you *can* help I know they will be most grateful.

Do you ever get English films around your way? If so, do look out for two—*The Canterbury Tale,* which will give you some lovely glimpses of Kentish scenery; and *The Tawny Pipit,* which was made partly at Fifield, a village I lived in while on *The Countryman,* which will give you some idea of the Cotswold country. Goodness knows whether they will get an American showing though! It appears that film monopolies prevent the showing of more than a very few British films in the U.S.A., these are two inexpensive and unassuming productions. But they are full of charm and naturalness, and have something typically English about them, and I'd like to think you could have sight of them. What you are much more likely to see, I fear, is Noel Coward's film *This Happy Breed.* It makes us look such a dingy and *un*happy breed! It got my dander up, I can tell you. I assure you that English family life is a *much* more cheerful affair! Noel Coward is clever but the general tone of his thought is dingy. I am *not* one of his admirers!

I seem to have got to the end of my news—life has been dull lately. Or maybe it is just Edith who's dull—so I will end my letter and let the little man have my seat. Cheerio, Phylabe dear. *Write to me soon!!!*

Lots and lots of love to you
Ever Edith

✉ **22**
Wednesday November 15

Here I am again! Snivelling this time, for I believe I'm starting a cold. I used to love the Winter, and I do if I can be out of doors when the sun shines and by a nice fire when it doesn't, but to have to spend my days sitting at a desk in a room which is draughty whatever we do, doesn't seem to me the most sensible way of putting in the three coldest months of the year! However, they will soon pass.

I've just packed up a little book, which has some rather nice pictures in it, to take the place of a Christmas card. THE COUNTRYMAN (Winter issue) won't be out till about Dec 10 and will not reach you till the New Year. Now that the news of V2 has been allowed to come out, I can say something about them.[29] It is a long time since strange, unexplained explosions began to happen. We were told they were gas mains and at first it seemed possible that one or two gas mains were faulty after the various periods of strain put on them but later this began to be a joke and we used to speak of 'flying gas mains.' The bangs were obviously coming from V2 which had begun to arrive but the news wasn't let out, not even in any of our home papers, so we all joked about flying gas mains. These things come so fast and from such a height that no warning is possible. They travel faster than sound and though they do much more concentrated damage where they fall it isn't so wide-spread as the doodlebug devastation. Not many get here. Goodness knows if they explode up in the stratosphere or where or if not many are sent. Last night wasn't so good for we had more doodlebugs. I think probably it was a reprisal night for the sinking of the *Tirpitz*.[30] That was a good job well done, wasn't it?

---

29. This letter was not finished, but was included in a later letter. The V–2, another of Hitler's "vengeance weapons," was a liquid-fueled rocket that traveled at supersonic speeds. Because it could not be detected in flight, only the explosion of its one-ton warhead gave notice of its arrival.
30. The *Tirpitz*, a 42,000-ton German battleship, long a threat to northern shipping routes, was finally sunk on November 12 near Tromsö, Norway, with the loss of a thousand lives.

✉ **23**
29 Stanley Gardens
London W 11
Dec. 28, 1944

My darling Phylabe—

At last, at last you have come back to me! I thought I was utterly abandoned—unloved, forgotten and cast out! And now comes a SPATE of darling letters, dating back to March 19*43*, incontrovertible proof that you *have* given me a thought from time to time and do really want your English Edith to keep a place in your heart. O rapture! You know, it's no good denying I've been horribly disappointed never to hear from you all these long months. You have first to understand what an enrichment it was, three, four, five years ago, to have your friendship, your long intimate letters, the light of your new-world mind on my cribbed insular one, the sense of romance and adventure in having a hearts-friend overseas and a lively link with that astounding and exciting country I had just had a tantalising glimpse of on one brief visit. If you first understand all that, then you will have a glimmering of what the impoverishment was when you went away. Then, when I learned that Bessie also was hearing no news from you, I began to worry about you frightfully. The war *hasn't* done you down, dear, has it? Oh, *don't* let it. I'm so relieved by your precious letters, which are just as natural and youish as ever—even though you do get angry with your B. P.-ers—but that's a sign of abundant health and vigour, mental if not necessarily physical. I am sad about your tiredness, and about your poor eyes, I can truly sympathize about both troubles, having known personally their utter misery. I do hope the operation and the new glasses have ended your eye trouble, and I am hoping the conditions which make you so tired will soon be altered. But the end of the war seems to recede daily farther into the distance, doesn't it? However, my dear Phylabe, . . . I am much less pained on account of your real troubles than I had begun to be over the ones I imagined! I was afraid you had sunk into such a state of melancholy or despair that friends and even life itself had no more meaning for you. I have a friend, too sensitive and loving, who tried to take all the cares of the world on to her shoulders, and now lives in a pitiful shadowland where none of us can reach her anymore. The first sign of what was happening was that she ceased to answer my letters, and could not be cajoled, bullied or won into writing. So you

see how my fears about *you* began to take form! Oh, blessings on
your dear head for being just a too-busy woman! I'll always accept
that excuse for silences quite happily, darling. But *do* keep well and
try not to over-work!!!

Phylabe, I shall be SACKED, THROWN OUT, GIVEN THE
ORDER OF THE BOOT if I go on writing to you any longer. I began
writing when I began my breakfast, with a slice of toast and marmalade in one hand and my pen in the other, my pad on my lap and
crumbs everywhere. Breakfast is long eaten and it is much, much
more than time that I was on my way to my office. But I *had* to *begin*
a letter. It won't get finished for ages, for I am just at the beginning
of my busy fortnight, so perhaps I had better adopt your installment
plan and send you a letter page by page. I have such heaps to tell
you. But here endeth Chapter I.

Much and such love to you
Edith

December 28

Same day but cauliflower-cheese supper now instead of breakfast
crumbs. . . .

You would have laughed if you'd been here last night. Your new
letter to me was full of vexation about the Deweyites, and Virginia's
to Thirza equally furious about you Rooseveltians. I began to hold
forth on your side but Thirza broke in, "I must defend my Virginia
. . ." So she did, most eloquently, for a few minutes, till my dander
was good and roused. "But my Phylabe says . . ." "Yes, I know; but my
Virginia says . . ." till in sober truth we nearly fell to tearing each
other's hair. You girls must really get your political differences settled or you'll be having me and my pal at daggers drawn!

Thirza and I, like 99.99% of other Britishers, are ardent admirers of Mr. Roosevelt. We think he is one of the Great Men of all ages,
and that his work for justice and the good of all men will take a
large place in history. Because of his personality, AND because he
and his party have been so generous in their support of us British,
we (all Britain) were *desperately* anxious he should be reelected.
BUT—we know next to nothing of American domestic politics and
quite honestly are not competent to judge the merits of the respective Parties. No doubt Republicans have some merits!—just as no

doubt our Conservatives have, though on the whole I think they're a menace to the whole future of civilisation. (But for years I was a firm Tory and viewed all Socialists with horror!) These days I'm a Liberal, but that Middle Party has little power and few Personalities (the notable exception is Sir William Beveridge, whose Social Insurance scheme gives them a marvelous plank for their platform). There has not been a General Election in this country for 10 years, and up till then I had never exercised my right to vote because I never could decide which side I was on. Next time I shall almost certainly vote "agin the government"—*c'est-à-dire*, against the Tories; but I must confess I'm not terribly enamoured of our Labour people (except my Mr. Bevin, whom I admire and trust, even if he *can't* talk King's English!). I would always rather vote for personalities than parties, but of course that may add one's mite of weight on *quite* the wrong side of policy! I don't really like party politics at all—especially when there are more than two, and here our progressives are split into three, or four (Liberal, Labour, Communist and Commonwealth), which is fantastically silly and will inevitably put the villain Tories in. I hate politics, lock, stock, and barrel; but unfortunately for me I recognise their importance and my responsibilities! I don't know how America feels now about Mr. Churchill, or how your feeling has been affected by this tragic Greek trouble.[31] His stock (not as a War Minister but as prospective Prime Minister for peacetime) has been declining rapidly here for some time, and Greece has nearly done for him. Few people withhold their tribute to him for the way he has led the country through the war. Everybody also concedes his personal honesty. But his views are those of a capitalist and royalist and general old reactionary, and there is great apprehension among forward looking people that his personal popularity will put him back into power, with his Conservative Party, for the postwar period on which everything depends. If we *must* have a Tory Government, we'd rather have Eden at its head for, although

---

31. In December 1944, the British intervened militarily in Greece to prevent a takeover by the communist-led National Liberation Front (EAM). Although this policy was unpopular in Britain and the United States, it was ultimately successful—the insurrection was defeated in six weeks. However, the atrocities committed by the communists on the civilian population would long be remembered. The communists renewed their insurrection in 1946, after the restoration of King George II by plebiscite, and were not finally defeated until 1949.

he is a traditionalist in many ways, he is progressive too, and, above all, he is an internationalist of rare sincerity. But enough of politics—I really hate the subject, though I think one *has* to be interested because so much hangs on it. Don't worry about getting all het up about your reactionary BPW friends in your letters to me. We have 'em too! My goodness, the smugness and fatheadedness and selfishness and general imbecility of some folks! The small-mindedness and ignorance and blindness of them! It's enough to make one crazy and despairing and defeatist and wretched! But "God does not yet despair of man" and why should *we!* Men (generic term!) are such pets individually. My own belief is that to date, on balance (in spite of these devilish things that still go bump in the night), we've progressed, and, even if sometimes in the dark watches of the night, I think our hold on sanity (as a race) is fantastically precarious, in normal moments I'm full of faith in the future. Now I am *definitely* going to change the subject.

The cauliflower gave place to mince pies and the mince pies to coffee, and the carpet is literally besprinkled with all three because my eye was not on the ball, so to speak. Living alone is shocking bad for the manners and I never eat (alone) but off a tray at the side of my armchair. Even that today is complicated by the awful freezing cold which leads me to sit practically *in* the fire and so be still less well placed for tidy eating. Phylabe, I want to go on writing to you for ever and ever, but I have so many jobs on my conscience. The ironing is urgent, and if my finger nails don't get attention I'll have to pretend I'm wounded and wear 'em bandaged; also I'm in the middle of a frock (making it, I mean), and I NEED it, so MUST get on with it. And the mending—oh, *mending!!* If ever I'm made a belted earl and take unto myself a family crest, the centre piece will be a large darn RAMPANT, surrounded by thousands of holes couchant. Holes and the necessity of filling them in just dominate one's life these days. You ask—*so kindly*, Phylabe!—about our shortages. Honestly, in the way of food we need *nothing*. Our dietary is dull, but there's plenty of it, and though we complain (but naturally!), we really don't go short of essentials. Really, the provision of food to this people during the war has been a *miracle*—it certainly seems beyond just brilliant and imaginative organisation. The one Government Dept. against which *no* hard words are flung is the Ministry of Food. *Everybody* admits the rationing system, which ensures every single person a sufficient minimum of essentials and ruthlessly cuts out luxuries in favour of good plain necessities, has been a masterpiece of good management. Of course I'd like to have lots more! Who wouldn't?! But we manage fine. I wonder what you know about our rations? We get (each person) per week—8 ozs. fat (2 oz. butter, 4 oz. margarine and 2 oz. lard), 4 oz. bacon, 3 to 4 oz. cheese, 8 oz. sugar, 2 oz. tea, 4 oz. preserves, meat to the value of 1s. 2d. (my ration runs to about two pork chops or three mutton chops or an equivalent piece of stewing beef, with "offal"—liver, kidney, heart, tongue etc., extra *when you can get them*, which isn't often). Also 2 pints of milk in winter and 3 $^1/_2$ pints in summer, and eggs according to supply—perhaps 12 or 20 in a year!!—*BUT* we have a generous supply of dried eggs from your country (I *hate* mixing 'em, but we all bless heaven for sending them), also a good deal (but never enough) of dried milk. Milk is the only shortage that really bothers me. It is *awful* to have only half a pint of milk on Sunday, Monday, Wednesday and Friday, and none at all on Tuesday, Thursday and Saturday. I used to drink *quarts* of milk. Now one *never* drinks milk! (I should tell you, though, that children and nursing mothers get an adequate ration, and get it free if they can't afford to pay; and I daresay we husky middle-agers can get along without it all right.) Then we have 24 "points" a month to spend on foods such as tinned meats, tinned fish, tinned fruit (but there never is any—now *there* is a *great* miss!), dried fruit, biscuits, cereals, treacle, marmalade, rice, lentils etc., and various other things that I can't recall. You can imagine that 24 points don't go very far round all that lot! For instance, last month my 24 went like this—2 lb. tin of treacle, 16; 4 oz. sultanas, 3; 4 oz. biscuits, 2; packet of Shredded Wheat, 3. Total, 24 in no time! But the tin of treacle will last for weeks, and next month I may indulge in a tin of salmon or Spam (bless its heart) and a pound of rice and some prunes. Shopping is *such fun* (she spat the words between her teeth). However, grim as it all sounds, we manage extremely well. (Oh, I must mention one horrific lack—nice cakes. Your soldier boys over here must think we don't know how to make 'em, but the truth is that we aren't *allowed* to make 'em for sale in shops or cafes, and our personal rations don't leave a margin big enough to allow us to home-bake more than a very occasional cake. Those that *are* on sale are in the main *quite distasteful*. I *mean* it. And of course they cannot be iced or decorated at all. But I had a miraculous Christmas Cake from Mother— iced with a concoction of soya flour and trimmed with silver cachou and angelica that must have come out of the Ark.)

So you see, dear Phylabe, there is *no* need for you to send us food, though I can't tell you how enormously we appreciate your loving thought. Coffee and cocoa, I forgot to say, are not rationed; nor is bread; nor are vegetables; which are plentiful but devilish dear (except potatoes, carrots and turnips, which are cheap enough). Fruit is very hard to come by, though I have not been short of apples for months now, and I bottle like mad whenever I do come upon any fruit (only *that* is expensive, too! The Govt. does not encourage us to eat fruit, which if imported is poor value for shipping space, so the price is allowed to rise—though controlled. Carrots and potatoes, which we can grow plentifully here, are made cheap enough to encourage us to eat lots of 'em. Oh it is all very wisely done!).

The clothes shortage *is* serious, however. Our stocks have shrunk to almost nothing after 5 $^1/_2$ years of war, and the ration is painfully small. The Utility scheme is a sound one and has done wonders in maintaining an *equal* supply to all people whether rich or poor; but the quality of the Utility goods is far below that of even such a moderately well dressed person as myself. The non-Utility clothes (only a small percentage of the total manufacture) are heavily taxed (100% in most? (many) cases) and far too expensive for people of my income level (because our incomes are taxed too, at 50% mostly, so that our spending power is terribly restricted). I am driven to make my own clothes in order to get good quality at reasonable cost, and fortunately I'm a good dressmaker and love doing it. But home dressmaking doesn't save coupons, because you spend as many on materials as on finished garments (in fact more sometimes, if you want a lining, or a fuller skirt than austerity regulations permit in made-up garments), and as we are all vain peacocks, we spend our meagre supply of coupons on *top* clothes and most of us go ragged underneath! Shocking but alas, too true! I wear vests that would make you cry aloud in horror. They're not ragged, because I mend and mend and mend. But they are literally a patch work of bits from one garment joined up with bits from another to make one reasonable whole. I'm certainly not exceptional in this. We are all alike. At hen parties when the girls bring their mending the most amazing garments come on view. Before the war, one would have been ashamed, but now, needs must! Things like handkerchiefs, scarves and gloves come out of the precious clothes ration, too. Phylabe, I even darn and patch my handkerchiefs!!! (But four separate Santa Clauses among them sent me

SEVEN hankies this Christmas, so I wear a smile as big as a dinner plate just now.) Much to women's fury, household towels of all sorts also have to come out of the clothes ration. And, of course, stockings! I don't suppose there's a girl in Britain who wouldn't tell you her greatest clothes problem today was stockings.

Phylabe, it is BEDTIME, and I have not done the ironing; have not put a stitch in my dress; have not even washed the supper dishes. I am *astounded* at the time, and I must fly. *MUST* do the ironing. Goodnight, my sweet. Shan't see you tomorrow because they are broadcasting Shakespeare's *King John* tomorrow night—a rare performance indeed—and I want to listen and sew at the same time. And Saturday I shan't have much time as in the morning (don't work on Saturdays now!) I do the shopping, in the afternoon am going to the opera (*Così fan tutte*) and in the evening do a duty at the ARP Post—but perhaps may write you from there. Anyway, by-bye for now. Does this letter sound grumblesome? I do hope not—don't mean it so. We are all really very content and cheery.

A Happy New Year to you! Shall post this and promise you more in a day or two, so that you too shall have a SPATE and see how nice it is!!

Ever and aye
Thy
Edith

1945
January 27, 1945–December 14, 1945

29 Stanley Gardens,
London, W 11
27.1.45

My dearest, kindest Phylabe—

Your marvelous parcel arrived three weeks ago, and I cannot tell you how it enraptured us—me and the folks at home, and Thirza, and a whole flat-full of girls at a tea party just after it arrived. If I'd had sense I'd have sent you a scrap of a note straight away . . . but I wanted to write such reams that I waited till I had more time ahead—and now three weeks have passed and nothing's been said and I still haven't any time ahead at all. But this morning I'm at the hairdresser's and for half an hour at least I shall be under this drier with nobody to bother me. So here goes!

Hinney (which is Tyneside's own special term of endearment), you are *marvelous!* What imagination, thought and care you put into that magical box of presents! . . . By good fortune my friend Cecil was with me when it came so I did have somebody to share the fun with. He enjoyed it as much as I did, and you should have heard our exclamations of surprise, joy, wonder and amusement as we delved deeper and deeper into the Aladdin's Cave. Cecil had been invited in to supper, but supper was delayed by at least an hour! But our appetites were doubly whetted by excitement, so you did us *two* good turns! Then we wrapped everything up again as nearly like your way as possible, so that the Whickhamites could have fun too. That process had to be repeated several times, because every fresh visitor to the flat had to be shown Phylabe's wonder-box; but eventually it went off to Whickham, and I think they got all the thrills too. I sent the whole box with instructions that they were to keep everything they wanted, but I did put in a special plea for the pyjams because they were a perfect fit for me and because my summer nighties all mended their little lives into a sleep at the end of last summer and left a sad gap in the wardrobe. So back came the pyjams, now laid away in state till the warm weather comes, and back came the biggest half by far of all the other things, so, although I feel a little greedy, I also feel extremely lucky! Mother is wearing the orange fascinator to keep her warm these icy days; Father is to plant the seeds in the garden, Chrissie fell in love with the little red lamb on the plastic brooch and is keeping him, but I think I am the fortunate one to have everything else, even the gloves, because they were my size but too small for the others. I *adore* the little finger ring and wear it every day. I had been longing for a ring for my little finger, and here is just exactly the one I'd have chosen! . . . By the way, the gift of this ring was foretold me 3 1/2 years ago!! In 3 years time I was to receive "across the water" a silver ring handmade by dark-skinned people in a sunny land. I thought *I* was to be across the water, and it's disappointing that I'm not, but maybe that will come true later.

    —Later, 8 p.m. Now I'm at the post, with two hours' duty ahead and nothing much to do—unless!! It hasn't happened yet in our Sector, and I devoutly hope it never does. The beastly things keep going off all around. One at teatime made me jump, but it must have been a long way away. Oh, Phylabe, will it *never* end! Each bang means perhaps dozens of homeless families, and many dozens more who though not homeless, have their homes so blasted that living in them in this bitter weather must be killing. Each bang also means *some* deaths and injuries, even if not many. The father of an acquaintance of mine just disappeared the other day—they identified a glove, but otherwise there was no trace. But they knew his movements and knew he would have been waiting at the bus stop for his bus home just at the moment when the bomb dropped.

    It has taken me 1 1/4 hours to write the last paragraph. Too many callers at the Post tonight! Now we've been notified of a fire down the street and my colleague has gone down to investigate, so for the moment I'm alone. I hope nothing happens!! But in any case it isn't going to be much of a letter I get written to you tonight! I've been BUSY today (though I'm *always* busy!). I've made MARMALADE.

Edith Base c. 1945, about the time of her appointment as editor of *The Corsetry and Underwear Journal.*

There have been two allocations of sweet oranges, 1 pound per head, this month, but the distribution isn't very good and I never saw any at all. But I *did* manage to get 2 lbs. of Seville oranges, and it has made 8 lbs. of marmalade. The trouble was that I hadn't enough sugar, and couldn't borrow any because all my friends were wanting their sugar for the same purpose; so my marmalade wouldn't "jell!" I had to boil it and boil it—down to about half its original volume. Heartbreaking to see it disappearing! But the remaining 8 lbs. are lovely! At the same time I was trying to finish the black dress I'm making, as I want to wear it to go out to lunch tomorrow! Then my neighbour came in to ask my help with a shirt she is making, so the work party degenerated into a gossip. 'Fraid I shan't get the frock done in time, which is a pity as my only other frock is away being cleaned.

I've not told you anything about my new job, have I? . . . I'm now editor of *The Corsetry and Underwear Journal*!! Does that make you smile? It makes *me* smile—with happiness! I simply love it, and all my frustrations, inhibitions, repressions and furies of the past three years have just vanished into thin air. It seems a little comic that anybody's reason for living should be to edit a corsetry journal but here you are! Everything feels right and worth doing and runs smoothly in the groove now, as it did NOT when I was in a Government office doing "work of national importance!" Inscrutable are the purposes of providence! It's not *easy* work. There's a tremendous lot to do and only me to do it (with a part-time secretary) so that my time is well filled; and in addition there are quite considerable problems of industry and trade to grapple with. It's all a new world to me—though my Ministry of Labour experience helps enormously (and indeed that miserable period is now explained and justified; without it I should have been ill equipped for editing such a periodical as mine! My Philosophy of universal life is incomplete and unsure as yet, but there has certainly been a force controlling my movements from the very start and bringing me by logical steps to just this point. When I've wilfully strayed from the path, unexpected things—a man's sudden death in one instance—have happened to yank me back. It's startling, and fascinating, and sustaining. Do *you* feel yourself moving according to a pre-determined pattern? I most certainly do—though again I must say the provision of a corsetry editor seems an odd thing for the life force to bother itself about).

I'm sending you a copy of my January issue, in which my appointment is announced, though in fact this is the *second* number I have produced. (It's a monthly). I think you'll agree that it's a handsome publication—and please bear in mind our stringent wartime restrictions. People who know the British press very well tell me that our magazine is far and away ahead of all other trade publications. Forgive the bragging! I'm like a hen with a new chicken. *Every*body says the photograph doesn't do me justice!!

February 2nd

. . . I am getting on very slowly with this letter, Phylabe dear. Now it is midnight and I've just written these few lines while I sat down to drink a cup of tea after a very busy evening. First I had a visitor for an hour, then I cooked supper, then did the week's washing, then started some soup for tomorrow, made pastry and baked an apple pie and a jam tart, and stewed some apples for breakfast. Doesn't sound so much, but it has kept me busy till now. Saturdays I don't work now, so glory be, I can sleep in tomorrow morning. I've a date for 10:30 to go shopping with Thirza, who wants to buy a new dress; and a date with Cecil for 2:30 to listen to a concert; and in the evening there are three competitors for my company and I've got to work out the solution amicably if possible! Also I've brought work home to do, as Mr. Smedley (my magazine owner) has been working in my room this week (normally he's at Leicester) and I've not been able to get on with my own jobs for sharing in his. He's a lamb, incidentally—or perhaps a better description would be a shaggy sheepdog—lots of intelligence and hard sense, a good hearty Midland manner and accent (Londoners would say "no polish"), but a great sensitiveness and real artistic talent under his blunt, bluff exterior. We get on well, for I'm enough of a Northerner myself to share some of his characteristics. I'd better go to bed—I keep writing down the wrong words. My brain is more than half asleep!

February 15 now—oh dear!

But this is going off in the post tomorrow as ever is. I'm ready for bed, and sipping a cup of tea and sampling the biscuits I've just been making. (By "biscuit" I mean a wafer-thin crisp, sweet thing; I believe you mean something quite different.) I'm giving a party (hen) on Sunday, and this is Part I of the preparations. I've had a busy evening (as usual), baking a cake (which is smelling handsomely at this moment but which I can't bring myself to take out of the oven. Do *you* know when a cake is done? I never do; go through agonies trying to decide. This one *looks* done, and the hat pin comes out clean, but all the same I suspect it still has a heart of dough!)— also making curranty biscuits as aforementioned, also mixing large quantities of pastry ready to be made up into pies on Sunday. In the middle of it all Thirza and Alix came over to see about tickets for a concert by "our" choir on the 28th—I'll enclose a bill. Thirza is singing at it, also by an odd chance, my advertisement manager, Doris Pickering, who is in the Leicester choir. We have taken a block of 15 seats for our friends, and we hope they'll all come home with us afterwards for coffee.

Sniff, sniff—my cake! Yes, I've certainly left it in too long. Bother. However, it's not actually *burnt!* I don't make 'em often enough to develop good judgement—can't; rations don't run to it.

Oh Phylabe, these cursed rockets still keep falling. Yesterday two fell near enough to me to turn my knees to water. Every time one goes off, one thinks of the terror of the people caught under it. And the crashing masonry and flying glass, and the black clouds of debris and dust that rise high up into the sky. You cannot imagine how *horrible*. And I am sure you can scarcely imagine either the shabby, battered mess that London is in. Although Victory seems so near now and our hearts are tranquil, I don't think many of us are *joyful*. There is too much to be sad for. But don't think London is gloomy! Far from it!! Even *I* am full of beans (largely due to Bill Gerringer's vitamin tablets, I am sure!). Last night I was at a Press Club party, tomorrow going to see the new Bridie play[32] with Marjorie and another, Saturday going to the Greater London Soroptimist Club's 21st birthday party (we are the oldest club in Europe), and Sunday giving a party myself. Who couldn't say we aren't gay? Also I'm just the teeniest bit—lightly and delightfully—in love with a certain red-bearded Scot, so you SEE . . .

The love of my life is Corsets and Underwear! Today and tomorrow I'm pasting up—a lovely sticky game which I adore. Monday I start all over again, like the Queen of Spain, on the April number. I always think I'll never find anything interesting to put in—but it comes! Lovely, lovely game!

Not by miles and miles have I caught up on all your Christmas letters, but this is meant to be only an installment. More will follow fairly soon, I hope. Keep well, my very dear, and please don't get overtired if you can help it. Are the eyes relieved now by the new glasses? Please do take care of yourself. It is very important!
With much and such love to you,

Ever
Edith

✉ **25**
29 Stanley Gardens
London W 11
March 18/45

Dear beloved—I hope you'll not dislike this photo too much. Nobody here likes it and my best friend has disdained to accept

---

32. James Bridie's *It Depends What You Mean* opened at the Westminster Theater 12 October 1944. It contained a devastating parody of the *Brains Trust* type of celebrity panel. (See note to Letter 27).

one. But the camera never lies. No resemblance to Bette [Davis] whatever, is there? Nevertheless in Manchester last Wednesday an advertising agent I went to see said, in the first 2 minutes of our meeting, "Forgive this very personal remark, but how like—" Two things from you last week, angel girl—your letter and the packet of papers. Is the sinus trouble mended, my poor dear Phylabe? I do hope so. Has the spring come to Colorado? It's being very tardy in Lunnon Town. I hope all the lambs and piggies were safely born. A siren has just unpleasantly punctuated my breakfast, but the bang was a long way off. A near rocket yesterday morning interfered with our Sunday dinner preparations—hit the water main and temporarily stopped supply. Soon mended however. Monday morning— and I love 'em now!!

Best wishes ever and aye
Edith

✉ **26**
29 Stanley Gardens
London W. 11
26.3.45

Dearest Lass

Two letters from you in one weekend have demoralised me! This Monday morning I ought to be getting right down to work on my April number, but look-see! Here I am writing to you. Just one page—because I just can't resist it. Then WORK. This is the time of the month I don't like one little bit—starting to think out features and stories for a new number. I always feel franticly panicky that I CAN'T DO IT. Can't THINK of anything. Will NEVER do it this time. Next week, of course, I'll be feeling fine, but *this* week is AWFUL.

Which is one reason why I'm writing to you—'cos I'm a lazy idle girl and don't want to start putting pressure on my poor old addle-pate. I wish I had nothing else to do but write to you! How I should enjoy it! Isn't it wonderful to get letters from you within three weeks? As a matter of fact, it embarrasses me—it used to be convenient to let the blame for delay lie on the Post Office or the Fleet or the Hun—now I shall be shown up in my true colours as a wretched procrastinator and putter-offer and general ingrate. . . .

Spring has come to London—though we are told it is only a temporary call. It has been the silliest winter—record cold, record frosts, then record warmth. We freeze and frizzle alternately—go without stockings today and get back into all our winter woollies (if we have any) tomorrow. Fortunately weather never affects me very much and I like it all as it comes. But burst water pipes ARE a little trying. Today, however, it is spring. The crocuses (or are you one who says croci?) are putting up their little flames in the Park and the unaesthetic sparrows are eating them as fast as they know how, drat 'em. At 12 noon I'm meeting my Scottish Rufus—all among the crocuses and the sparrows and the garrulous St. James's Park ducks—with a double nosebag—so OF COURSE it is spring— Whooopeeee!

Life is going off like a one-o'clock gun all the time. It is intoxicating and enthralling and fulfilling—and all due to corsets! I can't believe it. Still, *you* must remember what a semi-morte I was even just six months ago as a Civil Servant! I hardly knew *myself,* and all my friends think I've gone off my head. So I have—and it's glorious! Oh dear, do forgive me! There'll be an awful slump shortly, I'm sure but in the meantime I *do like* being slightly mad!

And there are hardly any bombs these days. Oh, touch wood for me—HARD. They do still come over and always there are some people killed and many made homeless. My friend Hilda brought her children to tea with me yesterday. She was bombed out—I probably told you at the time—last summer, and has just now been allotted a new flat and a sum of money to buy furniture. But there isn't much furniture to buy and she's having an awful job finding such things as kitchen utensils and crockery and cutlery—there just isn't any. Then [there's] my friend Mary Jones, who was in a hotel that was bombed (when our American officer friends were there also). She wasn't injured at all—but she is now suffering horribly from neuritis and insomnia, and her memory plays extraordinary tricks on her—all due to the shock, of course, but she is not listed among the casualties, and there must be many thousands like her. But of course even people who've never been right in the track of a bomb are finding themselves with all sorts of nervous troubles; or maybe just grey hair like poor me; or with a feeling that they're a thousand million years old and youth is something vanished and irrecoverable. However, we're getting better every day and one of these days there'll be NO bombs and NO terrors and NO heart-numbing separations and NO more tears.

This letter must be like all the others I've ever written to you— all about bombs and trouble. I'm a poor liaison officer, am I not? My propaganda is all wrong. I should be telling you how calm and cheery we all are. So we are, of course. You'd be surprised. A bomb goes bang in the next street and you don't even pause in your conversation. A second later and you've forgotten it fell. Now stop it, Edith. NO MORE BOMBS. But I don't want one to hit me now— not when life's so ecstatic and satisfying. Now STOP it!

My (part-time) secretary has arrived and put the kettle on . . . and it looks to me as if I'd get very little work done before I go out to commune with the croci! So runs the world away. I've not even said how delighted I am by the snaps you've sent me—I love them; especially the ones of you and of your home. Oh, I want to come and see you! . . . Did you hear yesterday—9 hours from London to New York in your new fliers. . . . We SHALL meet, Phylabe hinney-love. SOON.

Aye
Edith

✉ **27**
29 Stanley Gardens
London, W 11
April 25, 1945

Dear my love—

Nearly every day something occurs to make me think "I must start that letter to Phylabe." This morning there was your Easter card with the note written inside it; last week there was the lovely book about Colorado which I have so far only skimmed through but which will be most thoroughly and rapturously devoured whenever there is a day when I can really sit down to read a book instead of just picking at one over meals; then there was President Roosevelt's death, which came as a terrible shock and filled us with gloom, for we looked on him as the hope of the world; and last night there was a phrase on the wireless which delighted me so much that I decided then and there a letter *must* be written to you before I forgot everything that had been happening.

We have a delectable 45 minutes every Tuesday evening listening to the *Brains Trust*—a panel of various erudite people who give impromptu answers to listener's questions.[33] I expect this type of programme originated in your country, so I needn't describe how it works. Last night somebody asked a question as to the desirability of setting up an English Academy like the French one, with the object of keeping our language pure, and it looked a lively discussion on a subject which has always enthralled me—our wonderful language and where it is going. Of course somebody referred to the "debasing" effects of American—meaning the current slang, which is silly and sometimes crude but which will pass like current British slang; unfortunately it is all that most English people know of the American brand of English. Then one of the erudite leaped to your defense, my Phylabe, and talked about the "Elizabethan richness" of your tongue. How I loved him for that phrase, which expresses all I feel about written American (very distinct from film-spoken American!). When people exclaim against the Americanisms creeping into spoken English I always try to persuade them to read some of your modern writers. I get almost the same tingle of excitement and pleasure from their daring, imaginative and novel use of words as I do from rehearing a Shakespeare play and opening my nervous system full out to the delicious enrapturing shocks of *his* language. I don't know any pleasure more intoxicating! Bless all you Americans for giving our wonderful lingo a new lease on life with your vigorous word—dynamite! Mind you, I curse too sometimes, when you monkey about with spelling that loses its roots and its meaning when you "simplify" it. What sense in making words easier to spell if by so doing you obscure their history and meaning? I'd even like to retrogress a bit on some of our spelling. "Daisy" is a falling off from Chaucer's "days-eye" for the little miniature sun with its gleaming petal-rays; but if the simplified-spelling people try spelling it "dazie" because it sounds that way, then they ought all to be sentenced to talk sign language for the rest of their days! Don't you agree? The correct treatment with foreigners who object to learning our language because it is difficult to spell is not to simplify (mutilate) the

---

33. A BBC production of Howard Thomas, *Brains Trust* derived its name from the term used by President Roosevelt to describe his advisers. The panel (originally Dr. Julian Huxley, Professor Cyril Joad, and Commander A. B. Campbell (R.N. retired), and later Dr. Malcolm Sargent, the famous orchestra conductor, Sir William Beveridge, and Col. Walter Eliot) fielded questions put to them by Donald McCullough. The program attracted some four million listeners.

spelling but to teach them Latin, Greek, Anglo-Saxon, Norman-French, Danish and Dutch as well, so that they can recognise the origin of the English words and glory in its richness. Let's start a Movement! (There's an article in my paper today by a German who has fought with the British Army since 1939 and was writing a little nostalgically about the circle of culture in Berlin in which he grew up. He tells of the grammar school where he learned Latin—"and did not dream how useful it was going to be to him when he came to English spelling." So, you see—)

I don't really know an awful lot about your contemporary writers—I'd like to read lots more but there's no TIME. Even up to Sinclair Lewis they're not really different from English writers—it's the writers who are young now who are putting the new wim and wigour into the language. Dorothy Canfield and William Faulkner are two who write richly; Saroyan and Damon Runyon are too individualist, probably, to be good indicators. Lots of your journalists and better-grade magazine writers have that knock-you-in-the-eye vividness of expression, too. All very exhilarating! . . .

By the way, has your BPW club heard from Miss Carruthers, the International Secretary of mine (Regency, London) yet? I took two of your letters along—or rather, as I could not go to the International Night meeting for more than an hour because of ARP duty, I gave them to Miss C., who read extracts to the Club. It was then decided that Miss C. should write to you from the Club, and I hope she has done so.

By the way again, could you do anything for my small goddaughter Helen Chapman, I wonder? She horrified me by telling me in a letter recently that they didn't learn geography any more at her school because they couldn't get a teacher (there's an awful shortage of teachers in this land of ours at present)—so I tried to help by sending her some of your cuttings, photos, cards etc. Result—she is thrilled to bits and would adore to have an American pen-friend too. Have you any young friend who would like to correspond with her? She is a dear wee thing, age now 14, but not a very advanced 14—like a 12-year-old, perhaps. I enclose a letter from her to me which will tell you something of her. She is, in type, gentle, sweet, good, a little shy, a most conscientious worker at school and a dear dependable little helper at home. Her mother, my schoolgirl friend Nancie, has a problem in not putting too much of a burden on Helen because she is so willing whereas her two sisters are less so and try to evade their share of duties.

April 30

I am writing this at the ARP Post, and be it recorded that we have
just received an order to "stand down" from midnight. Isn't it marvelous! No more duty, no more sleeping at the Post, no more
bombs! It's rather fun being on duty this last night of civil defense
service. The District Warden has just been round—shook my hand
and patted my shoulder and said "Thank you for all you've done."
I've not done anything except "stand by," but we all felt a little senti-
mental. Now the Post Warden (who incidentally is a delightful and
most handsome actor—most of the voluntary wardens at this Post
belong to one or other of the Arts, as the area is one in which literary and artistic people live) has just said "Wouldn't you like to go
home?"—; but I said "No, not on this last night!"—and didn't tell
him that it's no good going home as I've lent my bed to Mother!!
She and Aunt Annie are spending a holiday with me—at long
last!—and my spare bed is a tight fit for two; so as I was due to sleep
at the Post tonight I moved Mother into mine for the night. Tomorrow my goddaughter Dorothy wants me to put her up, too; she is
coming up from Leeds for an interview at Bedford College. I had
planned to come again and sleep at the Post and give Dorothy my
bed at home, and now the war has come to an end too fast! So I
shall have to sleep on the floor, I expect. But nothing matters so
long as the war *does* get to an end. As I write—it will all be over by
the time you read this—as I write it seems that tomorrow, or the
next day, we shall hear that Germany's defeated quite and we can
count the European war over. There is going to be a hullaballoo—
everybody intends, it seems, to abandon work and take a holiday for
a couple of days! It will be chaos—but it will be glorious!!! Oh
dear—feelings are very mixed. Are we too tired to feel elated? I
don't feel elated at all—just glad to be able to relax, though at the
same time horribly out of the habit of relaxing, from anxiety and a
sort of numbing sub-conscious fear—not fear so much as apprehension. My chief feeling of thankfulness is that now Westminster
Abbey and St. Paul's Cathedral are presumably safe. Both have had
bombs and some damage, but nothing irreparable. We were down
at St. Paul's today (I took a half day's leave to take my folks around).
A bomb came right through the roof (in 1941 or 1940) and fell
right through the floor and into the crypt—but didn't explode! A
gallant group of Bomb Disposal men removed the fuse (it was a

delayed action bomb) and saved the Cathedral at risk of their lives. We sent out a silent "Thank You" to them today.

May 14

And a week since *Victory!!* Oh Phylabe, isn't it marvelous! Did you weep, or shout, or laugh, or pray? I did all four—with due British reserve, of course, but every bit from the profoundest depths of my heart. It is difficult to know just *how* one feels different. Life goes on its day by day round *exactly* as before—but there are subtle changes which mean a lot. The bombers still fly over, but now they are carrying repatriated prisoners, not bombs. I have moved my bed back to its proper place under the window now that the danger of flying glass and explosions is over. I leave my curtains open with the lights full on at night. The sandbags and the blast walls are gradually (but slowly, because there is no labour to spare to do the work) disappearing from the fronts of buildings. I came home the other night to find the black paint had been cleaned off my kitchen skylight and all the windows on the stairs. Slowly the busses and trains are getting their windows cleaned of the beastly anti-splinter net which stopped one's view. The bunks are disappearing from the Tube stations. But these are all little things, and in essentials life is still hidebound by wartime restrictions. However, it is perhaps just as well that the relaxation is gradual. To jump right back into 1939 luxury and laxity would have been too much for us all at once.

I am *furious* because Thirza wrote to her Virginia hot after the celebrations and her letter will reach Gin before mine reaches you. It is TOO BAD, and I have told her I practically HATE her. As a matter of fact, Victory couldn't have chosen a worse two days to fall on in my view! My closing date for the June number of the magazine was May 10, and I had *oceans* of work which *had* to be done on May 8 and 9. I curse it, but there was no dodging it. So work spoiled my pleasure, and I'm rather afraid that pleasure spoiled my work! But it was beyond me to abjure all pleasure at such a time. Besides, I couldn't leave Thirza to go celebrating all on her own, could I?! We had a marvelous time—it was simply wonderful in London. I wouldn't have been anywhere else for worlds. In fact, I was in Leicester on Monday, May 7, and would normally have stayed overnight, but I was determined to be back in London "in case," and I cut a meeting that at any other time I'd have considered important, and got back to London just after 8 p.m. No announcement had been made so, being tired and grimy, I bathed and got into my (your!) pyjamas, and was just starting on my supper when the 9 o'clock news started and—it happened! Thirza came flying over—"Come on, Hebe, we *must* go out and see the fun—" so, feeling my years and wishing I could just go to bed, I climbed into my clothes again, and out we went. Golly, was it thrilling!!!!! I wasn't old or tired any more—just ageless and excited and happy as a pancake. We took a bus "to Trafalgar Square"—but the buses weren't going within miles, because the crowds wouldn't let 'em. So we footed it into Piccadilly Circus, and laughed at the girls waving flags and the boys climbing lamp posts and the fireworks going up and the planes dropping flares. Everybody was cheering everything, so we cheered everything too—and it was glorious to be silly and know everybody else was silly at the same time. We ploughed steadily across the Circus—it took us half an hour; and flowed with the crowd along to Leicester Square. One of the cinemas had ALL ITS LIGHTS ON. It just went to our heads—everybody's heads. You have to have lived through five years of black-out to realise what THAT meant! Some gay young things started dancing, some formed into a crocodile, with a tail that grew longer the farther it went. Another plane dropped flares and we all cheered again. Whoopee, wasn't it glorious! We flowed some more and landed in Trafalgar Square. On the other side the lamps were lit under Admiralty Arch, and behind the excitement we began to feel the deep *beauty* of London. We hadn't seen trees with lights among them for *years,* and the loveliness of London's limes and plane trees in May sunshine is surpassed by their loveliness under the lights in a summer twilight. It was enchanting to see them that way again. We set off along the Mall, along the avenue of trees that leads to the Palace, but suddenly we were stopped short by a stupendous sight—Big Ben with his faces all lit up like monster moons! It was more than a girl could resist! So we forsook the mall and dashed down Whitehall to see old Ben at closer range. He *is* a lamb! He looked so benign and kind and comfortable standing there in the starlight with his beaming bright face—very closely akin he seemed to the two very typical London policemen standing at the end of Downing Street—kind and good humoured and utterly, utterly immovable, even by the crowd that wanted to go and serenade Mr. Churchill at No 10. I would have kissed old Ben on the top of his nose if I could have reached it, and

I'd happily have kissed both policemen, only of course one wouldn't ever *dream* of doing such a thing, even on Victory night. But we beamed at the bobbies (Bobby being short for Robert, which is short for Robert Peel, who established police force—all of which I expect you know as well as I do)—and we walked round Big Ben and admired him from every angle, then, before we popped down under for the last train home (London's last trains are still 11:45—last buses, about 10 in summer) we walked on to Westminster Bridge to look up and down the river. "Earth has not anything to show more fair"—if Wordsworth could have seen it then, he'd have written an even greater sonnet. But he'd have kept the line—"a sight so touching in its majesty." That was one of the moments when my tears were very near. There were no hilarious crowds on the bridge—only the light of bonfires and the first of the floodlit buildings reflected through the trees in the quiet water, and the stream flowing so tranquilly and eternally; at one end of the bridge, the shell of St. Thomas's Hospital, bombed and burnt in ever one of the blitzes—and at the other end the statue of Boadicea, who centuries ago fought the aggressor with her people behind her for this same London town, and is still a symbol of resistance and courage.

Oh dear, it is long past bed time, and I've not got up to VE Day at all yet! In a way, it was anticlimax—our deepest emotions had been stirred on that first night. VE Day was in comparison only a holiday—but what a holiday! The weather was royal, the crowds were stupendous—one paper had a headline—"Trafalgar Square—not room for a pigeon." It was literally true. The poor old pigeons had to fly up beside Nelson on the top of his column before they could find room for their little pink feet. They must have wondered whatever had gone wrong with the world! The fireworks and rockets (the kind that go *up*, not the sort that come down!!) sent them wheeling out over the Square, and the searchlights picked them out as they flew. The floodlighting was *magical* on VE night! You can't *guess* how it stirred us. I can only explain it by the five years of blackness—the light intoxicates us now. We still have only the *dimmest* of street lighting, I must explain, and even on VE night it was turned off at 11 p.m. for economy's sake. So floodlighting is fairyland for us still.

Most of V day, I worked hard, but at 7 o'clock I went to Thirza's for a celebration supper, not only in honour of Victory but to celebrate the engagement of Alix, who lives with Thirza, to a nice

Canadian Major. Jim produced a bottle of champagne (he was home on leave from Holland), so we had the right drink for the occasion! After supper we joined the throng in front of the Palace. How many hundreds of thousands of people there were there I shouldn't like to guess! Once again, no room even for a sparrow. Yet when the King's voice began to speak through the loud speakers, the silence was absolute. Oddly enough, the only sound came from the sparrows. Their chirping seemed terrific against the utter stillness of the people. When the speech was over, we yelled like everbody else "We want the King," and when he came—with the Queen and the princesses—on to the balcony, we cheered our heads off. I've been to a news theatre tonight with Marjorie and seen the film of the celebration. It gives a clearer impression of the crowd and the fervour than we got from our tightly crowded little corner, and we certainly didn't see so much of the Royal Family as the film shows.

After the King, we walked for hours—along the Mall, lined with tired people too limp after a day of trafficking to do anything but sit and watch; across Trafalgar Square and down on to the Embankment, where all was peace. Up again into Fleet Street, where a dozen bonfires of ticker-tape from the newspaper office windows were burning; and up Ludgate Hill to St. Paul's, the most magnificently beautiful sight of all. ATS girls with mobile searchlights were floodlighting it. The last time St. Paul's was lit to the top of the gold cross over the dome, it was the fire blitz of 1941 that illuminated it.

But I must go to bed. Shall I post this, or keep it till I've told you some more of the things I've been saving?

I meant to tell you of the day Dorothy Thompson came and spoke at our Women's Press Club,[34] but it seems a long time ago now (the day before President Roosevelt died—and I haven't told you how we grieve over that. So *much* is involved. Has your new President got any strength?—enough to hold your Big Business men in check? We fear not—Truemann to us is a nonentity—I can't even

---

34. Dorothy Thompson was bureau chief in Berlin in 1925 for the *Philadelphia Public Ledger* and the *New York Evening Post*. After an early interview with Hitler, she dismissed him as insignificant, but soon changed her mind. She was expelled from Germany in 1934 and wrote a column in 1936 against Hitler for the *Herald Tribune*. In 1941 she moved to the *Post* but was dropped in 1947 because of her opposition to Israel.

Posed picture of a winter lunch time group at the Women's Press Club;
Edith Base and Cecil Bacon left of center.

remember how hc spells his name—but maybe he will grow to the
size of his responsibilities. Oh, why did Roosevelt have to die! He
was the *only* one I would have trusted—of the Big Three, I mean.
Over here they talk of the Big Two and a Half now—in dismay
rather than disdain. How I hope we are *needlessly* afraid!

Tonight your latest *Independent Woman*[35] arrived. Thank you, my
kind Phylabe. I don't deserve all your trouble and devotion—I'm a
wretched correspondent these days. I'm truly busy—my job takes too
much of me, really. Sometimes I want to run away. For the next fortnight, my secretary is on holiday, so I am staffless. Worse, my Director and his wife who keeps the accounts—have come from Leicester
to work in the London Office, and I have to run around after them

---

35. *Independent Woman* was a monthly publication of the National Federation of
Business and Professional Women's Clubs, Inc.; the subscription was $1.50 a
year. In the autumn of 1956 the publication changed its name to *National
Business Women*.

as well. It is next door to impossible to get any writing done in the office, so I have to bring it home to do. I don't at all *mind*, but sometimes I just feel too tired to care whether I do the work or not.

And that reminds me that I *must* go to bed now!

Goodnight, my Phylabe. I hope you are happy, and well, and that your labours may shortly be lightened by the return of some labour to the land, and that I will go on hearing from you even when I don't deserve it, and that our meeting is going to be SOON. . . .

Much love, dear lass, What are you doing at Whitsuntide? I am going cycling—with Thirza and two others—in the *Countryman* country, staying with another ex-*Countryman* colleague who won the Newdigate Prize for poetry when she was at Oxford University.

Goodnight—Edith

✉ **28**
29 Stanley Gardens
London W 11
July 12, 1945

My dearest Phylabe

I am longing to have a chat with you and have so much I want to tell you, but it is late—11 p.m. and time I was going to bed. Thirza and I have just walked home through the Parks—a wonderful way of finishing a wonderful evening. British Double Summer Time means that at 10 by the clock it is still only 8 by the sun, so to be in the Parks from 8 to 11 as we have been on this lovely summer evening means we had all the gentle lengthening sunbeams and the flowing sunset and the exquisite twilight and now the first soft amethyst shades of night. The limes are intoxicating in this warm air, and the blackbirds are singing their heads off,—and life has a kindness and restfulness about it because the fear of sudden death no longer weighs on us and destruction is stayed a little. My heart is very full tonight—of a good old mixture of emotions, I must say, because such a lot of different things have been happening to me lately and after having been all stirred up I'm now gradually quietening into the pleasantest and nicest state of serenity for a very long time.

I will tell you the end of the story first—the part about tonight. Have I ever mentioned my friend Lyla Grainger, who has worked among lepers in Nigeria for 25 years? She is beautiful and noble and kind, but also delightful and gay, and I think she is simply wonderful. Tonight she invited Thirza and me to dine with her at the Overseas Club, and she brought to meet us another most wonderful woman, Dr. Ruba Lengar, head of another leper colony in Nigeria, who arrived here on furlough only a few days ago. She too was beautiful, elegant, full of spiritual grace, and gay. Gay in spite of her story. Her family moved in Court circles in old Imperial Russia and were driven out after great suffering during the Revolution. They settled in Belgium and the young girl Ruba was helped by friends to take a medical course. I don't know what made her interested in lepers, but for the past 10 years she has been medical director of a colony of 3000 lepers. Don't you think it's wonderful that the dear old Colonial office (British) allows a woman to hold such a post? And with an all-woman staff? (Although the patients are preponderantly male.) I was staggered, because our very conservative Civil Service isn't usually so enlightened about women. But in this case, hats off! But during the war, and the German occupation of Belgium, Dr. Lengar has had no news of her family till now. Her father is dead, her sister was killed, her two brothers were taken away to Poland and have not been heard of since; only her mother is left. Can you imagine the pain and anxiety? She is going over to Belgium on Tuesday, but it must be a terribly unhappy homecoming for her.

However, I told you these women were *gay* and I meant it. Their spirit and gallantry and above all a sort of deep and utterly unassailable serenity they possess, make me want to shed tears of—of I don't quite know what: worship, thankfulness, humility and a lot of other deep emotions.

What makes the evening specially significant for me is that it is contrasted with a very different sort of evening yesterday. But really I must go back another day to Tuesday in order to build up this story (Indeed, I ought to have begun about 3 months ago) in order to convey the particular stew-pot state of my emotions. For some reason, or none, most probably in reaction to the tense control that had to be maintained by everybody during the war and the raids, I've been running somewhat amok—mentally and emotionally only! Have been wildly unhappy, darkly despondent, wickedly irritable, and generally a pain in the neck to my friends and myself.

Something *had* to happen to get me out of that! Even Corsets failed me, and the situation there was only saved by the sudden and unexpected entry of Thirza into the Corsetry and Underwear world. She's now my Assistant Editor!! Isn't it wonderful!

(This is the news I hinted at in my last far-distant letter—after I'd posted that I thought: "Oh my goodness, Phylabe will think I've got myself engaged to that red beard I indiscreetly talked about!" I hope you will not feel too much let down! The red beard was nice while it lasted, but quite evanescent, and can now be forgotten. Thirza is a much more permanent treasure and blessing.) Where were we? Oh yes. If it hadn't been for Thirza, I'd have thrown myself out of the nicest job I'm ever likely to find, and possibly into the Park lake into the bargain! (Not really, of course, but I *was* in a bad way.) But that's all over.

"Came" last Tuesday. I was going to a party thrown by Emily Yooll, my predecessor as Editor of the C. & U. J. and president of our BPW Club. I knew I was going to enjoy that and wouldn't want to leave early, so I was a wee bit disgruntled when Doris Pickering, my advertisement manager, arrived from Leicester, couldn't find a bed, and asked if I could put her up for the night. However, she volunteered to go to the flicks while I was at the party, so that was all right. Then the phone rang—who do you think? An old Newcastle journalist colleague of about 15 years ago, who went out to Nigeria and disappeared out of my ken. He's home on furlough and, for no reason at all that I can think of, troubled to dig me out one Sunday recently and with a friend take me on a day's whirl of pleasure which ended as suddenly as it had begun. Living in London one gets used to such happenings, for everybody comes to London some time or another and, feeling perhaps a little bored or lonesome, says to him/herself "Don't I know *any*body in this darned town? I wonder where that girl . . . What was her name? Edith Something— I wonder if *she's* around anywhere."

Well, that was weeks ago, then the phone rang on Tuesday, and it was K . . . again, wanting to meet me that night. Why *do* things always happen in a heap? Then one goes for months and *nothing* happens! Well, all I could suggest to him was that he come for a late sausage-and-mash with Doris and me after I'd been to Emily's. Then I went berserk and decided to throw a party, and collected an assortment of others, and inspired Doris to dash home and bake some tarts (marmalade—nothing else to put in them these days), and we had fun.

Next night (last night) K . . . besieged the office again. I thought London *must* be empty of girls this week, but I put on my most glamourous shade of lipstick (a Phylabe one) and sallied forth for an evening's fun of the kind K . . . apparently thinks good. So *many* people do, and I simply get *no* kick out of it at all. A drink, and another drink, and another and another to fill in the time from 6 to 8:30 (though nothing on earth will make me drink more than two cocktails. And *those* bore me stiff). Then a long tedious dinner with more drink, and a little unanimated dancing between bites, and the dim lights and inane music softening one's resistance to that mood of wholly false sentiment that tends to work up on such occasions. While all the time the sun was shining outside, and the Park there to walk in, and all the unread books in my bookcases waiting to be read! What a waste of time!

I'm an ungrateful puss, am I not? There was K . . . doing all the "right" things to give me a pukka evening, telling me I looked younger than I did 16 years ago and he'd always thought I was wonderful (both plain fibs), and buying me melon at fabulous black-market price (hadn't tasted any for literally years), and everything. And all I could say when Thirza asked me this morning if I'd had a nice time was, "Thirza, I'm grieved, and I'm *terrified,* because people live so profligately, and aimlessly, and take their pleasure on such a low level."

Then I went to the Soroptimist Club luncheon and there were some lovely women there, and a grand woman spoke on post war education with wisdom and gentleness and love. And walking back across the Park I counted my blessings, with Education (or at least literateness, which opens the thousand windows of books to the spirit's eye) at the head of them. And when Thirza asked "How was the lunch?" I told her "I feel clean again."

And after the man from Nigeria last night, there were the two women from Nigeria tonight. *What* a difference! What a *healing!* I can't *tell* you how much more I enjoyed the simple meal, and the walk in the Park, and the laughter over Dr. Lengar's merry tales of native patients, and the quiet talk about Colonial problems, than I enjoyed the glamourous pleasures of the May Fair Hotel the night before. Thirza said "I've enjoyed tonight more than—more than I enjoyed my Christmas Party!" So now you know something more about both Thirza and me!

Heavens, girl, I must go to bed! I could write to you for ever, but when my alarm clock says buzz at 7 a.m. tomorrow (today—for it's already tomorrow!) I'll be one whale of a sleepy baby.

So good-night, my dear, and thank you for your friendly ear this night! I'm a shocking correspondent, am I not? And I will be a worse one for the next 3 months, for I've an awful lot of work on hand producing an enlarged *Journal* and an *Export Annual.* Yet when I do write it is all about ME and not about anything vital or important or interesting. I am sorry. But your *Countryman* is waiting to be posted and this will travel with it, inadequate though it be. Forgive me, and keep on loving me, and write to me sometimes, because your letters are a great joy.

Love, aye,
Edith

✉ **29**
29 Stanley Gardens
London W 11
Sept. 19th 1945

Dearest Phylabe

Today is Reste after Toyle, Porte after Stormie Sea. Yesterday I finished off a most hectic fortnight's work on getting the October number of the *Journal* "away"—hectic because a month's work was compressed into 2 weeks after I'd taken a holiday, and because, Thirza being away, I was without help. Yesterday I just about decided to resign (again! I have been doing it regularly for the past 3–4 months, since the Proprietor of the paper came to work in my office, monopolised my secretary and too much of my time, and generally got on my nerves!). Today I have done no work at all (feeling that was due to me!) and today I decided (again!) *not* to resign because I'm much too fond of my *C & U Journal* to bear to part from it! So all is Peace again. This morning I let off steam about all my troubles to Mr. S., who is the cause of them, and, like the lamb he really is (I'm truly awfully fond of him) he said, after my outburst, "Good, good—I'm *glad* you've said all that. Now we'll start to put things right." So to begin with, we put on our bonnets and a firm expression and went to interview a Lady at the Ministry of

Labour, who, after verifying that I *did* write in an earnest application for staff three months ago, and *didn't* have any reply, decided that perhaps we *did* qualify for a stenographer (ye gods! we want two stenogs, a reporter, a sub-editor and a whole posse of general jills-of-all-trade) and that she would "set things in motion." So *maybe, maybe,* within a year or so, we may acquire an extra help! If we don't, I shall be just a Tired Out Old Woman in no time!

Tonight, for the first time for ages, I took a share of a meal—some peas, half a marrow, and a damson pie—over to Thirza's, and, Thirza providing some soup, minced steak and potatoes, had a decent meal. Haven't had time to concoct one lately, and to get a decent meal necessarily implies "concoction" these days; catering is *very* difficult and trying. Half the time one goes—if not hungry, certainly never quite satisfied. I buy my rations fortnightly—because the amounts for a single person—1 oz. of cooking fat, 2 oz. of butter, 2 oz. of bacon, 1 $^1/_2$ oz. of cheese, and so on)—are too ludicrously small if bought weekly. I eat them all up in the first week, and in the second week live on vegetables and bread! Restaurant meals are hopeless—very unappetising, and very poor in food value. And very expensive, incidentally. A friend who is staying at the May Fair Hotel which, if not quite the level of the Ritz, Berkeley, or Claridge's, is certainly on just the rung below—complained to me yesterday that for dinner they'd given her *CORNED BEEF.* She looked surprised (she is home on leave from West Africa) when I told her that CORNED BEEF DAY was one of my FEAST DAYS! And milk—oh! Phylabe, what wouldn't I say to a glass of milk! Haven't had one for about 5 years! We get 2 $^1/_2$ or sometimes just 2 pints a week. And because of transport troubles it is *very* often (in London at any rate) sour within a few hours of delivery. Things are certainly worse now than they've been at any time before, and we are told the winter will be more difficult still. We realise, of course, that most of Europe is worse off still, and most of us are willing to give up some of our rations for starving Europe; but it has to be realised that we are going very short—of *necessities.* Luxuries are non-existent. And the *trouble* and *time* involved is a worse trial still. But I mustn't grumble any more. I will, though, about one other thing. *Everything* is "in short supply" and so has to be hunted for. We're used to that. But imagine the troubles involved when sanitary towels disappear from the market! It has been practically impossible to buy any in London (central or west, at any rate) for the past month! I took it upon myself to go to the Board of Trade and lodge a protest. I received a beautiful official explanation—shortage of cotton yarn for the gauze, decrease in labour force due to holidays and the fact that many of the married women had left industry because their husbands were coming home, and inability of distribution machinery to adjust itself quickly enough to the present movements (since the war ended) of population. They believe the position will be relieved by mid-October (another month hence!!) [.] Well, I ask you!

Must go to bed now. Good night.

Thursday morning

It's raining. Bother. I shall get my poor little pink legs splashed. Today is Pasting-Up Day—the day I like best in the whole month—when I sit with paste and scissors and snip up the proofs and stick 'em in the dummy. It's really a game, and I could play it for hours. There is going to be a problem today, however, for yesterday I had 1 $^2/_3$ pages stolen from me for advertising, which means I'll have to squeeze a quart into the pint pot. Never mind—I like such problems.

This is still a *lovely job*, but it has nearly killed me lately with overwork. It is going to be wonderful in the future, when we can get (and afford) staff. We're going to start various new mags. I shall have fun as Editor-in-Chief!!! Thirza and I both count on being Managing Directors within two-three days? Years? Decades!!?

November 4

Well, it's nearly 2 months since I wrote the foregoing, and during that period the "situation has gradually deteriorated." In fact, I've resigned. With much sorrow and after much thought; but it was the only possible solution, for Mr. Smedley and I just didn't fit in, and we were far too much on top of each other in our cramped little offices to agree to differ. But isn't it sad? A year ago I thought this wandering child had put down a root at last, but here I am again, rudderless as ever (to mix my metaphors a bit). Admittedly there's a certain charm about the situation—to have the world before you and no ties to hold you back; but it's beginning to develop some less charming characteristics for this middle-aged and rather tired experimenter. I could welcome a spot of security now! Last Tuesday (in Leeds) I

Edith Base and Mr. Smedley at *Corsetry and Underwear Journal* Exhibition in July 1946.

lunched with a very-dear-long-ago friend and we reminisced. We started off level some 20-odd years ago on the *Newcastle Journal.* He has gone bee-line along a policy of "getting on"—always changing his job for the better and never changing until the right minute; now he's just settling (after a notable war-job) into established Civil Service of a high grade with a sure salary and comfortable pension.[36] Me, I'm just back to scratch—"on the street." (Meaning, to us journalists, Fleet Street—not Leicester Square among the frail sisterhood!—I'd better explain!!) Reg reminded me that almost the last time he saw me I was considering an offer of a job on one of our solider provincial dailies—"then they mentioned a pension and you fled in terror." It is true—I had a mortal horror of tying myself up for life out of reach of variety and experience. That same time I took

36. Reginald Bacon, Cecil's brother, was later to hold the position of assistant director of the Economic Information Bureau at the Treasury; in 1951, he became personal public relations officer to Prime Minister Clement Attlee.

Edith Base and Reginald Bacon on Exhibition river trip in 1946; smartly dressed woman on right is an unidentified New Yorker and man behind on left is Mr. Smedley.

another job at less than half the salary, just because it was "romantic" and airy-fairy—that was the job on *The Countryman*, which advanced me nowhere professionally; but it brought me some of my most beloved friends. There are different sorts of moss for rolling stones to gather, and I regret nothing I've done. But—to be aged 42 and be still rootless and (financially) moss-less is beginning to strike me as a situation requiring some careful thought!

Meantime, I've just been enjoying a week's tour at the *Journal's* expense, gathering "copy" in Leeds, Glasgow, and Carlisle, and finishing up with a weekend at home. Now it's Sunday afternoon and I'm entrained for London again and Monday-morning-at-the-office. My resignation doesn't take effect until Dec. 31, so I've plenty of time to find me another job. . . .

Phylabe, *when* are you going to write to me? I know I'm a miserable correspondent, but, darling, I do believe you are worse! There's been no word from Bessie, either, for months. My sole channel for transatlantic news is via Virginia-Thirza, and I feel fearfully remote. Nobody loves me! Doesn't that move your tender heart to pity, my dove? I don't know what to write to you about— too out of touch! I can resort to "description"—that this blinking train has stuck in mid-England for no apparent reason, with nothing but a field of cows to see on one side and a field without cows on the other; that it's true November weather—thick, dank, grey, muggy; that it has poured rain on us all the week, but the route from Glasgow to Carlisle on Friday was radiant and aflame with red and copper leaves and rusty bracken; that I've just eaten a hunk of most excellent pie, made by Mother from a hoarded tin of American sausage meat of a richness and juiciness we'd forgotten were possible; that if this train doesn't move soon I'll scream; that nevertheless, travelling has improved immeasurably since V. J. Day— more trains, less crowded; nobody at all standing in the corridor on this journey; that I don't like the post-war world—do you?; that they've shunted us on to a side track, run a northbound train past us, and are now running *us* back towards the North from which we've just come!—hooray! that we're moving in the right direction at last. Mother and Chris spent a week with me in London and returned a fortnight ago; their normally 6-hour journey lasted 11 $1/2$ hours! Because the war-weary old engine broke down and apparently we haven't any spares these days. Oh Phylabe, Britain is in a mess. Why don't your people recognise it and admit that we got there because we put *everything we'd got* into holding the line, not just for ourselves, but for civilisation, including very largely the U.S.A. Reprints from some of your papers appear over here and move us to dismay and despair; some of us to disgust and some of us to anger and vituperation. It is a tragedy of unfriendliness. No doubt quotations from some of our more irresponsible journals arouse just as much fury and ill-feeling among Americans. My own feelings are entirely without national boundaries—I cannot think of mankind except as indivisible or of nations except as parts of the same family, and I am helpless and terrified against the floods of bitter and blind prejudice among the peoples. But in this country there is no doubt the people have stood so much and gone without so much that they are not in a mood to be long-suffering or patient, and certainly not magnanimous, anymore. It is no good denying that the sudden cessation of the lend-lease arrangement, which put this country economically into a ghastly hole, and hit the plain man literally in his stomach, was felt here to be a mean and almost treacherous blow from a country we had counted our closest friend—a country, moreover, that could not have retained its wealth but for our expenditure of "blood, toil, sweat." It did more to destroy Anglo-American friendship than anything else could have done. It sent a wave of contempt over this country for a nation that apparently cared only for its dollars. It will take all the work of all the statesmen to expunge that feeling, and I can give you no idea of the way those of us who love America, and feel that our two countries are the ones that hold the future in their hands, pray for wise and far-looking decisions from the various conferences at present in progress. Phylabe dear, if for no other reason than that by doing so we add a mite to the sum of international friendship, *do* let you and me remain loving friends! Do not let this letter offend you. Believe that I have written it quite dispassionately, trying to give at least one American an insight into the feeling of England, and that I care most urgently and deeply about the outcome of things between us.

November 6

I've been out to supper tonight and just come in at nearly 11 p.m., but I've had to make a tart in preparation for supper guests here tomorrow, so while it is baking I'll add a few lines to my letter.

Nancie Anderson, my Newcastle friend who is national organiser for BPW Clubs, has just become the tenant (temporarily while she is campaigning in the London area for a few months) of Thirza's spare room, and I've been over there for supper. Tomorrow it is Thirza and another N/C friend who will be my guests, and I've got a haggis to feed them on, brought from Scotland. Do you know what a haggis is? I'm sure there must be enough Scots in USA to have made their national dish well known—but in case you have never met one (haggis, I mean) I will just tell you that it is a fierce and awesome beasty. But both my guests come from North of the Border, and I'm next door to a Scot myself, so we shall tame it. . . .

I've started looking for a new job today and applied for three vacancies, all for editors for trade journals. But I don't really like trade journalism. I'd rather work on a news journal or periodical. But the thought of a racketing newspaper office makes me groan. I'd rather be on a country weekly. But the thought of leaving all my friends and starting off . . . in a new place makes me shiver . . . so what would you suggest I do?!! I feel too utterly lethargic and weary to do anything, and only wish I could find a new lease of energy and vigour somewhere. I'm ashamed of myself, but I just can't overcome this desire to get away from everything and think of nothing and sleep and sleep and sleep. I'm sure that all I need is a good holiday, but of course there's no possible way of getting one without a cessation of income, and as I'm not ill I can't bring myself to do that. But I *am* fed up with this state of being, in which every small effort, whether physical or mental, seems just more than I can face. The pace of life in London is wearying, too—the fight to get on buses, the queuing for everything, the noise, the crowds. Mostly I love its vitality, but often now I find it too exhausting and irritating. I keep dreaming of a little house with a big garden in a village. Wouldn't it be heaven? Come and share it with me!

The tart is well baked and I must get to bed. I'm very busy this week—have a lot of stuff to write for the December number and it should all be in by the 10th. So I'll say—Good night, Phylabe dear.

Oh—one word more. What do you suppose was waiting for me when I got home from Glasgow? A letter from Bessie! All about her new home and her second honeymoon and her garden and her Charlie—and brimful of happiness and activity. I was *so* glad to hear from her. Now for a letter from Phylabe!

Good night again, my dear. I'll finish off the letter here and post it tomorrow without further delay. It is high time you had a letter from me!

With all my love and loving wishes,
Ever your
Edith

✉ **30**
29 Stanley Gardens London W 11
November 26, 1945

Phylabe my love
Just at lunchtime I discovered with an awful shock that today is the last day for posting to U.S.A. and Canada for Christmas delivery,

so this is a most hasty little note and not at all the really Christmassy letter I should have liked to greet you with on Noel Day. I have been at a Rubber Control meeting all the afternoon, and had to interview some new staff when I returned, so now I am left with exactly half an hour before the last post to write to you, and to Bessie, and cards to Rose and Virginia. So you see it can be no more than a few lines. Also I fear the enclosures are entirely inadequate to express all the friendship I would like you to feel coming over the sea from Britain! Our shops are empty of all attractive goods, and it is difficult to buy presents at all. When the war time shortages are really over, then you shall have a REAL Christmas parcel, my dear.

Meantime, lots and lots of love to you, and a most merrily-mer-rily-goes-the-time Christmas. I wish I could send you a big box of English holly, bright with red berries! And come and sing a carol under your window at midnight! Maybe one day I will.

Love and love, aye,
from your
Edith

✉ **31**
Dec. 14. 1945

Phylabe my love

Just a wee pre-Christmas note! We live too temperamentally here! I resigned, was persuaded to stay on, was sacked, and won back, and today resigned again, AND was again persuaded to stay on! So *wearing!* Thirza nearly as bad (we were *all* sacked!—for 5 minutes—the boss has a hot temper!).

I'm sending you papers about the Loan,[37] which is making us all very anxious and sad. The article I've marked really expresses what most of us moderate people are feeling. This is a liberal paper—

---

37. President Truman had ordered suspension of all Lend-Lease operations and the cancellation of most contracts as early as August 21, 1945. The action caused a financial crisis in Great Britain, and Truman was later to admit privately that the move had been premature. After prolonged negotiations, the United States granted the United Kingdom $3.75 billion, but under conditions that caused bitter British criticism of the United States.

halfway between the Socialists and the Tories, and in the main a balanced, far-looking, statesmanlike paper. Some of the press is much more bitter, alas. The fruits of victory seem very meagre for Britain. Goods are shorter now than *ever*, and little prospect of improvement. You would be astonished, I think, if you came here, to find how austerely we live. But I hate to seem to grumble—I am only so *very* anxious that *one* American at least should understand. Quotations from your papers—I hope they're the worst ones!—seem so unfriendly. *Why* did Mr. Roosevelt have to die?!!!

Happy new year to you, my dearie. I'm in a great rush now!

Love always
Edith

◆

1946
January 14, 1946–December 29, 1946

✉ **32**

29 Stanley Gardens, London W 11
Jan 14 1946

Dearest Phylabe

Your Christmas Eve written-in-a-manger letter arrived half an hour ago and not another minute is going to pass before I start answering it. There is your previous one, which reached me just before Christmas, waiting to be answered too—waiting in spite of the fact that I've been *longing* to write ever since it arrived. I can only keep on apologizing to you and explaining that there is never *time*— but it is such a footling sort of excuse! Now I am in bed with near-bronchitis, or I shouldn't even be writing today. Don't know whether the typewriter-in-bed idea is going to work—I am getting on more slowly than if I were writing by hand and it is exhausting muscularly! But I am such a poor hand-writer, I hate writing by hand, usually it is so slow, and prolonged writing causes me to have fibrositis—so I'll continue to try to type at this curious angle for the present.

The bronchial attack is the *inevitable* consequence of our freez- ing office. Britain is very short of fuel, so there is a regulation that if you have one form of heating in your building, you may not intro- duce any other. Our three large office rooms have two hot-water radiators among them but from some fault in the circulating system they never get more than tepidly warm. We applied for permission to have wires brought from the electric system which operates in the corridor just outside the door. Permit refused because we have hot water radiators! This has been going on for months—since August, when I first started agitating for something to be done, because I knew it would take weeks to get anything achieved. Three weeks ago a big freeze started, and we really suffered in our office. We wore all possible extra clothing, and had hot drinks every now and then; but the cold got into our bones all the same. Last weekend it got warm again, and *then* we began to feel the results of the cold. Thirza was off with a chesty cold, my typist has gone down with Vincent's angina, Norman can hardly speak for a nasal catarrh, and yours truly has succumbed to one of her best bronchial do's. I feel *angry*. Being subject from birth to bronchitis, I take the *utmost* care to avoid an attack—wear warm clothes, pump myself full of preventive vitamins, treat every slight cold with the deference due to double pneumonia—and then am defeated by a blankety-blank piece of Governmental red tape! Don't you agree that it's infuriating? By dint of care I've not had a really serious do of bronchial trouble for 12 years. That particular one cost me four months in bed and left me with a permanent slight weakness of the heart, so you will see why I try hard to avoid more. I'd have taken to my bed a few days ago, only I was in the thick of preparing the February number of the *Journal.* Yesterday (Sunday) at home I finished last bit of "copy," Thirza collected it this morning and is putting it on the train (to go to the printer at Leicester), so I can now relax and be ill in comfort till the proofs come back. Then I'll have to paste-up! I have made up my bed in the sitting room, where I can have the benefit of the wireless, the pleasant sight of all my books, and more comfortable warmth and better light. My bedroom is never used for anything but *sleeping* in and all the amenities of the flat are concentrated in the sitting room. So here I am, not at all sorry for myself, nice and cosy, with all sense of responsibility shelved pro tem—and I am doing something I've been longing to do, write to my Phylabe.

My beloved Phylabe, how your last two letters have touched me! What you tell me of your struggles to make your land produce good crops, against difficulties that we in this country can scarcely imagine, fills me with sorrow and anger and pity. Admiration too—very, very great admiration. When I think of your Dad working away in loneliness at the ranch, and of you spending your Christmas nights in the barn with the sheep, I don't know what to think—except to feel ashamed of myself for ever having grumbled at anything in my own easy, comfortable life. Here we tend to think of America as a land of nothing but wealth and supremely high standard of living.

We are scarcely to be blamed, perhaps, for your films tell us very little else and the Americans who come here mostly give the same impression. But your letters bring home very close to me the understanding that America's wealth is of course based on the hard work of her people and that the lend-lease food by which we have lived was won from the soil of America by blood, tears and sweat as food has always had to be won by the sons of Adam. You told me these things at the right time, too, for, like most people in this country, I was being affected by the wave of bitterness against America that her attitude towards the loan to Britain caused. I still feel that America has *got* to be self-sacrificing, not just to help Britain but to ensure the economic stability of the world (on which her own prosperity depends); but at least you have entirely cured me of bitterness, my dear beloved Phylabe, and I love not only you more and more deeply, but your great country too, and am renewed in my most heartfelt belief that the world is one and indivisible and there must be no hatred or bitterness or meanness or jealousy between nations or individuals—and *can* be none if we will only substitute true friendship.

The sort of thing that happened to your fruit crop when your "patriotic" neighbours sabotaged it because the gardeners were Japanese will *surely* become less and less frequent as general education progresses. It is so *stupid* and *wrong*. Why does not God despair of man? It takes *me* all my time not to! The same sort of thing happens here, of course. Recently a large number of English residents of Hampstead, one of London's best known suburbs, started a powerful campaign to get rid of the many German and Austrian refugees who now live there. They were occupying houses while British citizens had no homes to live in, was the cry; send these beastly foreigners back to their own country. I am glad to say that the Hampstead Council flatly refused to turn the refugees out, and there was a terrific outcry in the more enlightened press, holding the "patriotic" Hampsteadians up to ridicule and scorn. But they have far too many supporters, among supposedly educated people who are not educated sufficiently, however, to see any further than the ends of their smug little curling noses. And the number of people who talk anti-Semitism is appalling, too. I am constantly involved in battles for Jews, Germans, Foreigners in General. And that reminds me to say Thank You for your battles for Britain. I am sorry you have to, but I can just picture you brandishing your sword over the man who brought your pay check and said your English friends must be getting fat. Bravo, Phylabe! You and I would make a good sparring team, I'm sure, for that is just the sort of remark that makes me want to fight too! Not only when applied to my own country, I mean, of course, but to anybody who seems to need a defender. For an earnest peace lover I sometimes think I'm remarkably bellicose!

Are you following the doings of UNO in London at present? I sent you two papers describing the first assemblies. Considering it is taking place within a stone's throw of my office, it's shameful that I've seen nothing of it, not even the flags around the hall. The reason is that in the last week of my magazine's month I don't have time even to take the ten-minute walk across the Park to Westminster. I did mean to go and stand outside St. James's Palace to see the delegates rolling up for the State Banquet; but it POURED with rain. If office affairs were different I'd certainly try to get into the hall for at least one session, but it is quite impossible. But I do pray for blessing on their deliberations for they certainly have a lot depending on them. Has America got over her panic at Britain's returning a Socialist Government? You've no idea how *safe* I feel now with this Govt. in power! Under the Conservatives I was always *terrified* of the things they might do, especially internationally. And Churchill I've never thought of as anything but a good filibuster, though he had the qualities to make him a good popular leader in war. Attlee is ten times the statesman—and my faith in the integrity and clear sighted idealism of my old pal Ernie Bevin is boundless! It is really rather comic that a good Socialist like me (I used to be no end of a Tory, by the way) should be editor of a journal owned by a really ramping Tory and supported by capitalist manufacturers! I am very tactful! But never dishonest! At the moment the dear old manufacturers are all dying to export—because prices are controlled at home but not overseas and they could make bigger profits by selling abroad. Of course they don't admit that—they say they want to help the country to buy back essential imports. The Govt. says textiles mustn't be exported freely yet because the people at home who have gone short for so long must be supplied first. I must say that seems sense to me, but you should hear the manufacturers! "The Govt's MAD. They say 'Export!' but when you want to, they tell you you can't. These ruddy Socialists haven't any SENSE. They don't know how to GOVERN a country. We shall lose all our markets while they dilly-dally." Talk about battles! The Govt ought to issue me a suit of plate armour. I'm *always* fighting for them. I must say the dear old manufacturers take it in good part, and so does the boss. We argue like stingo, but he always ends up, "Well, it's your job to direct the policy of the paper"—so in go my sturdy pro-Government leaders, which is really jolly decent of him.

I've not really told you the ins and outs of my recent career, have I? I must do so. . . . I've twice resigned from this job, but twice have been persuaded to stay on, and that's how it is at the moment. The trouble is really temperamental. Mr. Smedley and I just weren't built to get on together. It's such a pity, because in many ways I like him frightfully, and in many ways he likes me ditto. Chiefly he likes my work. But, in addition to politics, there are many other points of discord. I must say in my own defense that it's not only me he gets across—Thirza and Lawrie (our artist) and even patient gentle Norman (the production manager) and Doris, the advertisement manager, are always getting worked up into fury and declaring they won't stand it a moment longer. What chiefly got my goat was to find myself being treated as an undependable junior—being asked always to tell where I was going when I went out, being required to work fixed hours (which is impossible—if I conformed to his 48-hours a week I'd never get the *Journal* out; I have to work lots more, night after night at home at some periods); but he suspects I am doing him in the eye if I go five minutes late in the morning or leave early at night in the periods when I'm *not* so busy.)—and other things like having all my letters opened and read out to the morning conference before ever I see them. So many *little* things, but how they did mount up, infuriate me! Then he changes his mind so much—one day we're all set on some new development then the next it's all off again. Life became just too undependable. . . .

After a long period of constant exasperations, I decided to leave, though very sadly, for I like the *Journal* and love the work. I gave about 10 weeks notice so that a new editor could be engaged and I could break her in before I left. I looked round for another job, and there were several, including one as assistant editor of *Ideal Home,* a well established and high class monthly, which would have been a well paid and dignified post, though I didn't *particularly* yearn for it. The truth is that I like *life,* and *people,* and *news,* and describing vague theoretic ideal homes month by month seemed an arid occupation. My present job suits me because it concerns a live and important industry, it's *full* of news and people and growth, and

keeps me on my toes to follow trade and economic policies and ten-
dencies. Also, though Mr. Smedley is trying, I'd much rather be in a
small personal kind of concern than a cog in the mighty wheel of
Odham's Press (which owns *Ideal Home*). Well, to cut a long story
short, Mr. Smedley persuaded me to stay on, and furthermore
promised me an assistant, who began just before Christmas and is a
very nice girl, though disappointing as a journalist. . . . She is writing a novel and has written children's stories. But oh dear me, Phylabe, people who "write" are seldom good journalists!. . . . So now
I'm faced with the dilemma of having to tell her she's no good and
must leave, or of training her till she *is* a journalist. But I need *help*,
and urgently. There's far too much work for me. Then my secretary
is a ninny, who can't be trusted even to address an envelope cor-
rectly. I spend more time correcting her mistakes than she saves me
by her typing. Thirza, of course, is a tower of strength, and the soul
of efficiency, but unfortunately for me she's almost entirely engaged
on organising our summer exhibition.

Now it is MARCH 9

I really don't know what has happened to all the intervening weeks,
except that I've been working like a steam engine and not been very
well. I was away from the office for three weeks, and then went back
against doctor's advice because I couldn't leave the poor old mag.
any longer. It was "me nerves" as they say on Tyneside—nervous
exhaustion, with some anaemia, and general lassitude after the
bronchial influenza. Since then I've been attending a clinic three
evenings a week for treatment for the fibrositis in my arm, shoulder,
neck and head. I am beginning to feel more like myself again, but I
am still a bit lackadaisical and tired. I am trying to find a new job—
had a sad blow two or three weeks ago when I hoped to get a post as
assistant editor of *Good Housekeeping*. I didn't get it because I was *too
good*—*they* said so! for the job; and oh dear, *wasn't* I disappointed! I
wanted it *because* it was less responsible and I could have done it (I
think) with ease. My present job, which I do with practically *no* help
(haven't even a girl to type my letters at present), takes too much
out of me.
    Dear Phylabe, your wonderful parcel did me more good than all
the doctor's dope and advice! *How* it cheered me up! I lived in the
comfort of thoughts of your kindness for days. (In fact, I have in my

mouth at the moment a piece of your milk chocolate—I am at the hairdresser's—which I have been allotting to myself on a strict ration for days! We don't get *milk* chocolate—haven't for years; it is only for children.) And those Almond Crunch toffees!! Do you know, I had forgotten that sweets *could* taste like that—*really* taste of butter and sugar. Heaven knows what *our* sweets are made of, but they really often aren't nice at all and leave an unpleasant flavour behind. I was tickled to death at the S. T.'s [sanitary towels]—they are still a scarcity here, believe it or not—though I believe your country is sending us shiploads! The tin of corn I am going to open tonight, when Cecil is coming to supper—perhaps the sausages too, though that would be shockingly extravagant! You would laugh at our parsimony these days; we laugh at it ourselves! Our bacon ration of 3 ounces a week, for instance, we spin out by eating not more than 3 inches of a rasher at one time. I make one Shredded Wheat serve four breakfasts. When we had a few apples, we never ate more than half an apple at a time. Otherwise there are too many meals with nothing but bread! I don't think I will ever be extravagant again! Just as I feel I shall never be able to discard old clothes again till they fall to pieces. But we'll see! Meantime I'm just trying to explain why I still have some of your dear presents left because I'm too economical to bring myself to consume them!

The lipsticks were excitingly new in colour—*truly* a tonic to see oneself with a new mouth! And the pet of a brooch! What *delightful* things you find to give me. But now I must reply to that part of your letter in which you ask what more you can send me. Dearest Phylabe, *nothing*, please. It is most kind and loving and generous of you to want to, but please believe me when I say you will make me very unhappy if you spend your money (and your time) on gifts for me. I told you about our shortages because I think you will be interested and also because, in general terms, it seems right that America (a vast impersonal thing, not just my dear Phylabe) should know that we *do* go short, *very* short.

Now it is Easter Sunday, April 21st, and I'm at Whickham—

but I'll continue where I broke off. . . . I don't mean that I never want to have a Christmas present from you again! But that's different . . . it would be quite a different thing to feel you were denying yourself to send me food and clothing, though I do most thoroughly appreciate your loving kindness and am touched to the heart by it. We *do* go short—there's no sense in denying it. Our diet is plain and in many ways inadequate (two of my friends recently returned from visits to U.S.A.—one and Eire—the other—told me they suffered from acutely upset tummies as a result of the rich food they got in those countries!!)—but we are accustomed to it and although we lose a bit of pleasure (haven't tasted real cream for six years!) and a bit of weight (I was measured up last week and have lost 2 inches at my waist and 2 inches at my hips!!) and I never had much to spare!)—still we get along very nicely. The same about clothes. We go well patched and darned and rather shabby, but we can hold out now till the tide has turned . . . but *don't* think of us as starving or naked, because in this country, thank God, we aren't that way. We are only too conscious of our comparative wealth and ease when we look east and see the starving people of Europe. . . .

I wish you were with me at Whickham now. April is such a beautiful month in England—I expect it is in Colorado too. The hedgerows are the shiningest loveliest green, and the woods are breaking into leaf in a thousand different delicate hues, and the cherries and pears are "hung with snow along the bough." All the daffodils are a-blowing, and the primroses and violets are out, and the birds sing and sing and sing. I expect your springs are much the same.

Since writing the last paragraph Chrissie and I have been for a walk over Tinkler Fell, a dear favourite walk of mine whenever I'm at home, for it's wild and high and you can see right across Northumberland to the Cheviots in the north, and right across Durham County to the South. But oh dearie me, alack and alas, what do you think is happening? They are opencast mining for a seam of coal that runs 15 or 20 feet below the surface, and they have churned up the whole top of our fell and dredged great chasms across it to get at the coal. The rock they have dredged and blasted out is piled in miniature mountain ranges alongside the chasms, and the whole conformation of the land is changed. Alas, this coal runs almost to Durham County—all over Whickham and the farm lands around. If they go on mining it there will be no beauty left. Our county, which must have had great natural beauty at one time—and still has a great deal—has already been much despoiled as a result of the *underground* coal mining, for the custom has been to tip all the displaced slag etc. in great, ugly "heaps" at the pithead. They disfigure every valley and every village in the mining districts.

But this *opencast* mining is going to do much greater damage. Perhaps even your papers have carried stories about the fuss there has been over the opencast mining at Wentworth, a famous beauty spot in Yorkshire. The miners themselves petitioned the Minister of Fuel to leave the coal and spare the beautiful park and woodland. But their petition was rejected and we have just heard on the wireless today that over 5,000 tons of coal was carried from Wentworth in the first week. Imagine the holes they must have blasted to get so much! You had better hurry up and come to England soon or there'll be no beauty left! Industrialisation has made a mess of our lovely land! I've been reading, over the past few months, Professor Trevelyan's *Social History of England* (it was published in America first, about three years ago when there was no paper for such books here, so you may have read it). He is deeply nostalgic about England of the late Eighteenth and early Nineteenth Centuries and claims that no country was ever lovelier than England then, when the land was fully cultivated (in our distinctive meadows-and-hedge-rows-and-copses pattern) and not at all blemished by "dark satanic mills" and railway sidings and slag heaps and ribbon-building. Oh, it *must* have been lovely—there are still bits to see. All my beloved Cotswold country, for instance. But it is passing, and the war, of course, has dealt it many blows.

April 30

Last night I heard a broadcast about England in 1300—it must have been almost lovelier then!! I rather wish I wasn't a 20th centurian!! . . .

For a long time I have been neglecting my gramophone in favour of the wireless, but recently my goddaughter Dorothy, who is reading History at London University, has been visiting me a good deal and putting records on the gramophone. I have a good collection of Bach, Beethoven, Schumann, Tchaikowsky, Chopin, some Mozart and some moderns. I should like more and more Bach, and if I had to be narrowed down to one composer (which of course I haven't) would exclude every other but Bach. My tastes in all things grow more and more austere, I think—in music, literature, art, architecture, and personal living. Not that I entirely forswear the Tchaikowskys of any art, or fail to enjoy them! But they no longer carry me with them. Do you know the voice of Tiana Limnitz? Her name sounds like a Pole or Russian, but she sings so far as I know chiefly in Germany. I have some records of her which seem to me lovelier than any other vocal recordings I have ever heard, and yesterday I switched on the wireless and heard part of a recorded German performance of *The Magic Flute* in which she sang as Pamina. I have her records of two arias from Verdi's *Otello* (Desdemona's "Lied" and "Das Gebet") which make my heart beat faster every time I hear them; and two others from *Der Freishutz* which are nearly as wonderful. If her recordings are available in America (mine are His Master's Voice recordings), do bang sixpence some time on those songs from *Otello*.

My nicest indulgences lately have been to go to the Ballet at Covent Garden. You know of old that I'm a devotee of ballet, and now the English Ballet has risen to glory and a national home in Britain's largest (and only?) opera house. It's a great thrill to go there and see the prewar splendour of crimson velvet and dazzling crystal chandeliers revived, and feel the excitement of the audiences—five or six thousand strong and deeply enthusiastic. (The Opera House has been a dance hall for troops and their lassies during the war.) We have two very remarkable dancers in Robert Helpmann and Margot Fonteyn, and a good team behind them, fed by the Vic-Wells Ballet School. (Incidentally, my new so-called secretary—aged 17 and fresh from school—has a sister who has just been accepted this week in the Vic-Wells Junior Ballet. Great excitement on everybody's part!!) Now ballet is an art in which I *do* cling to Tchaikowsky! It wasn't meant to be an austere art—but it can't help reflecting the times and our new English Ballet was born and nurtured in war and sometimes—mostly—shows it. Two of Helpmann's new ballets, "Miracle in the Gorbals" and "Adam Zero," are social tracts first and works of art only second (though they *are* works of art too). The "Miracle" is based on the "beating up" of a man and the suicide of a girl in the vice ridden Glasgow slum, and "Adam," a history of the life of Man, includes a balletisation of a Buchenwald prison camp scene. Both ballets include jitter-bugging scenes. Well, I ask you!—No. Quite definitely I prefer my ballet to move in the lovely, romantic, unreal and thoroughly escapist world of "Swan Lake" and the "Sleeping Princess"! (The "Sleeping Princess" is, I must say, the main work performed in the current season.)

I'm sometimes shocked to think what a reactionary I am in the art world, always nostalgically harking back and frantically trying (against world forces!) to dam back music to the Contrapuntalists, church architecture to the Gothic, street architecture to the Eighteenth Century, poetry to the Victorian and ballet to Imperial Russia (painting I don't care enough about it—could do without it; it seems to me a needless art—but I would burn Picasso at the stake!). It's all wrong and it probably means I'm a coward in face of life and progress—but oh, God! the mess of jerrybuilding in modern towns, the ugliness of contemporary music, the horror of modern painting, the sordidness of so much present-day writing. *Surely* all this is a regression (to the dark backward and abysm!) and not progress!

I'm reminded, in writing this, of an argument I had some 15 years ago with a very delightful, clever and enterprising friend of mine who was expatiating on the marvels of modernity. She was so vivid and enthusiastic and sure of herself, so much so that, although I wasn't convinced by her arguments, I was rather ashamed of myself for being so unprogressive, and I remember saying sadly "I'm afraid I belong to the century before the last." "Oh, goodness," she exclaimed "I belong to the century after the next!" Well, it was a bold claim, and it quite crushed me at the time, but the moral of the tale is that my friend became the mistress of a very well known public man professing similar "modern" views, has been living with him in his own house (the country manor house where his ancient family have lived for generations) in the most blatant and shocking way (his wife and children also being there), and two years ago herself bore him a son. They all seem very pleased with themselves, and it may be that they are morally more honest and healthy than the people who smother down their natural affections and passions to maintain a standard which is, after all, artificial. But I don't *know*—. I wish I *did!* I envy them their *certainty*. Perhaps we *could* build a better world if we sloughed off all the encrustations of civilisation and started afresh from the bare soul. . . .

This is Saturday and I'm not at the office, but I have a heck of a day in front of me. Am spring-cleaning (have colour-washed my ceilings and painted the woodwork), and must do a hectic finish-up, hanging the curtains, *etc.*, in time for the arrival at 4 p.m. (I go to meet her at Paddington) of Anne Bartlett, one of my Cotswold ex-*Countryman* friends for a short weekend. She is the one who was private secretary to Sir Wilfrid Grenfell of Labrador for a time (till your country refused to have her earning dollars in New York with them any longer!), but she is something of a recluse these days, and hasn't been to London in years. It is a great achievement to have lured her out of her country retreat, so I must do her proud while she's here! Then I must do the miserable fortnightly shopping, which involves endless queuing for entirely unsatisfactory gains. Then with the proceeds (if forthcoming in the right kind) I must cook and bake.

Most important of all, I have to write an application for a job which, if it comes off, *WILL BRING ME TO AMERICA*. However, let's not count any chickens yet! There'll be formidable competition, I know. It's the Winifred Cullis Lectureship I'm after—somebody wanted to lecture to women's organisations in both countries in a way to improve Anglo-American relations (get at the women—the hand that rocks the cradle and wields the power behind the throne!). It seems very much up my street, except that I've never regarded myself as a professional speaker. But, as I say, there'll be a lot of competition!

I was lunching yesterday with a journalist friend who travelled to USA with G.I. brides on the *Queen Mary* and spent a month in New York. She, too, had her tummy completely laid low by the rich fats and sugar of N.Y. food! We're a lot of half-starved scarecrows over here, really! Incidentally, our rations are going down again this week.

I mean to send you some copies of my *Journal*. But they are so scarce that I would be awfully glad to have them back again if you don't mind! Sorry to ask you to take this trouble but we just have no spare copies at all.

I am really going to finish on this page. I enclose a snippet of the new dress I'm making from a hoarded pre-war piece of real silk; to go with a navy ditto coat when—if—I ever get time to do it.

Goodbye, my dear, and all my love to you. I hope I hear from you again soon and I hope you hear from me again soon!

Love and love
Edith

✉   **33**
29 Stanley Gardens
London W 11
October 30, 1946

Belovedest Phylabe
. . . My apologies for the bad writing . . . as usual I am writing on a train and it seems an unusually jerky one.

I've been away from London for nearly a fortnight and feel distinctly homesick, in spite of the fact that the first week of my absence was spent at Whickham. Since then I've been on a business trip to Leeds, Bradford, Manchester, and Congleton (Cheshire), visiting mills, factories and warehouses, and am now on the way back to London. It was lovely to be at home—I didn't want to leave, and so far as work is concerned don't want to go back to London at all! I am still editing the *C & U Journal,* have just finished off another *Export Annual,* and am just starting to prepare a *new* monthly, *Underwear and Stockings,* which will deal with the knitted (or hosiery) side of the underwear trade. The firm seethes with enterprise, and energy! It is really quite a remarkable, little firm and will probably have a progressive and prosperous future. But I have never been able to decide whether I wanted my personal future to be bound up with it—though I think my feeling is crystallising now against staying with the firm. I have thoroughly enjoyed getting to know the inside of an industry; it is a lively and attractive industry and I like the people in it; and there is always intense satisfaction for me in mastering a new subject. But I must say my spirit quails at the thought of doing it all over again for another industry—stockings—and I just don't feel attracted to it. I would rather use my energies on something else—though unfortunately I've no clear ideas as to *what* else, so I just go on taking the line of least resistance and staying on. Mr. Smedley—the boss—does everything to make me (and the others) *want* to stay. We are a very good team, and it seems he recognises the fact and is trying to bind us to him. He has offered to start numerous small new companies to promote new enterprises—the partners to be himself and one other. Thirza has accepted his proposition of a company of two, him and herself, to promote exhibitions (she is no longer—has not been for a year or more—my assistant on the editorial side; she organised the big exhibition we held last July, and is busy on plans for another next year). He has offered me carte blanche to start any sort of publication I like—a public journal, say, as a change from trade journals. But my instinct wars with my reason and I really long to escape before the organisation gets me too securely into its clutches! It's difficult to explain, except by saying I wasn't cut out by nature to be a big business woman, and such ambitious projects frighten me. My happiness is in doing fine, detailed work. I like to earn a comfortable income, but I don't yearn for great wealth and I *certainly* don't seek power and influence. I want a quiet life and more leisure for cultural pursuits, and I don't foresee either coming to me in the Smedley organisation. Maybe it's cowardice that makes me want to run away—but I have always had a strong faith in instinct as a guide through life and my present strongly instinctive feeling is that the longer I stay with Smedley, the farther I am getting away from my right path. So don't be surprised if I write soon to tell you I am starting out in a fresh place! . . .

I have recently become, jointly with Thirza and another girl, editor of the B & PW Federation magazine. But it is a hopeless job because, not having published before the war, we have no proper paper allocation. At the moment our main concern is to find a printer who can manage to let us have a small amount of paper—but that's more difficult than you in your country could imagine. I started off by preparing a number for publication on September 10, but the paper was not forthcoming and still, two months later, not a word has been published. It is the most frustrating and maddening task I've ever taken on. However, our national newspapers are still limited to 4 pages on 3 days of the week and 6 pages on the other three, so I suppose we can't grumble.

. . . We are getting things shipshape again though there is still much to be done. Houses are our main shortage, because of bomb destruction and the *complete* cessation of building for six years; and that makes hotel accommodation hard to find, too, though the remedy is simple there—just book well in advance. Food? Getting much better, except for bread, milk, and eggs, among essentials. Hotel allowance of bread for breakfast is one slice of toast. You may ask for a second piece if you require it, but I doubt whether anybody would venture to ask for a third. Bread is not served at other meals unless you count it as a *course* (we may only have 3 courses at a meal and if you have bread with your soup, the two together count as two courses and if you then have meat and vegetables you have had your whack and have to go without pudding). I never ate vast quantities of bread, so I manage just fine. But I *don't* manage fine on my milk ration of 2 pints per week. (Children and nursing mothers get more.) That worries me a lot, for I used to drink a lot of milk before the war. To *drink milk* these days is—for ordinary adults—unknown. I've not drunk a glass of milk, that I can remember, for six years. We've had lots more fruit this last year, but mostly peaches and grapes, (from Italy) which are expensive. Peaches (small ones) did get down to 6d. and 8d. each (large ones 1s.) for a time, and grapes are 4s. a pound at present—their lowest. But I consider them too dear even at that to buy except for special occasions. The home-grown apples are in season at present and that's heavenly! At Whickham I had some oranges—the first since last Christmas. We get about one shell egg per month, though it rose to two or even three a month in the summer. There isn't much meat, the bacon ration is 6 ounces per month, sausage is difficult to find and very poor anyway, but there's plenty of fish—a great boon, for we had almost none, except frozen cod, throughout the war. Our butter ration has recently gone down to 2 ounces a week, but margarine went up to 4 ounces (we formerly had 3 ounces of each) to balance it. The cheese and cooking fat rations are minute, and most other foods are on points so that only a very limited quantity can be bought. None of us goes hungry, but there is still nothing rich or delicious or more than a little tempting about our food. The most noticeable improvements are in the way of supplies of pots and pans, cutlery, household gadgets and so forth, production of which practically ceased during the war. There are increasing supplies of these goods now, and everybody is stocking up rapturously. Clothes are still a terrible problem. The rags people wear! Even the nicest people!! Our top clothes don't look too bad, but we don't put our washing out on the linc! Chrissie and I both have blouses which we've made out of old window curtains; Mother was making new window curtains out of the best parts of old sheets. We still have lots of pride, but we have no vanity.

All that won't make you want to come to Britain, though, except perhaps to gaze at the wild animals in the English zoo! But really life goes on very pleasantly and easily. Rail travel has much improved—this is an excellent, fast, comfortable and uncrowded train on which I am travelling. We could make you very happy here, and would adore to have the chance!

We are just about in to Euston, so I will end my letter, meagre though it be. If I don't finish it and post it tonight, it may be weeks before I get round to it again, for once back at the office I know I shall have no spare time. I'm still grossly overworked—still produce the magazine, plus extra Export numbers, Exhibition albums etc.—with no help but my junior shorthand typist (so-called). It is no easy job, believe me—I take mountains of work home and even on my (again so-called) week's holiday last week, I had to take home with me work which occupied *all* of 3 days. There'll be a horrible accumulation on my desk after this long absence, and I'll have to start right off on the Christmas number and work like a demon for the next fortnight to get it out. So this will be all for this time, but I *will* write again soon, for there's Christmas coming and you must certainly have a letter from me then.

Meantime, my dearest love to you, and my constant thoughts.

Ever
Edith

✉   **34**
As from 29 Stanley Gardens
London W 11
November 27, 1946

Darling,

I'm sitting in the lounge of the Grand Hotel, Bristol, waiting for a table in the restaurant, so I shan't wait until after dinner to start writing to you, as I'd planned. Your letter arrived yesterday morning . . . only 5 days . . . to reach me! It was almost as good as talking to you on the telephone! If this can get back to you as quickly—by air mail which I've never used yet—it will be marvelous. I was meaning to write your Christmas letter this week, but by air mail I can get a much later one to you by December 25! Isn't it lovely!

I'm posting this weekend, however, a small—very small—Christmas parcel to you. I hope it will arrive in time, and I hope it will fit you! I've assumed you are a little smaller than I in all directions! One day I must *see* you and find out for sure. It *could* be next spring, I almost believe. Mr. Smedley is half converted to the view that I ought to visit corset places in America. Thirza says it rests with me to persuade him the other half, so maybe I'll really try. It would probably be only a short visit—2 or 3 weeks; and mostly around New York, and perhaps Chicago. If you *could* come to N.Y. and meet me—or if I could come part of the way toward you (I'd joyfully come all the way, but doubt if it would be possible in the time), I should be the happiest she alive! I will keep you posted! Mr. Smedley is a *difficult* man—but at heart he's generous and progressively minded; and at the moment I believe he's full of good will towards me. Only yesterday we had a most curious heart-to-heart in which with tears in his eyes (I am not joking) he told me how much he liked me and wanted me to be happy and go on working with him. So perhaps he will bribe me with a trip to America—here's hoping! My friend Phyllis Hartnoll, who is chief reader for MacMillan's the publishers, is going to N.Y. on the *Queen Elizabeth* in January and offered me the spare berth in her cabin. But that's not a nice time to come, is it? Phyllis is editing a monumental history of the theatre (*world* theatre) for the Oxford University Press and has the very nice job of going all over the place to study the theatre on the spot.[38] Hence her visit to New York. Lucky girl. She has a delightful cottage in the Cotswolds—I must have mentioned her before after some of my visits. She writes a good deal of poetry (and publishes it in various periodicals)—she won the Newdigate Prize for poetry when she was at Oxford. But she doesn't look like a poet, or even the highly intellectual bookworm she is, being very fat and jolly and a great gardener, beekeeper, jam maker, Women's Institute President, and exquisite needlewoman. You'd like Phyllis.

(Incidentally, a friend of hers, a nurse in an Oxford hospital who writes novels in her spare time—Mary Renault—has just won M.G.M.'s £30,000 prize with her last novel!!)[39]

I am burbling! Partly the result of eating too much dinner on top of 3 teas and a super-good lunch. I was taken out to lunch in Bath and given—sherry; roast goose with stuffing, apple sauce, potatoes, peas and cauliflower; apple tart and custard; and coffee. Then I arrived in Bristol at 3:30 and had half an hour to spare so had tea and a bun; then the man I went to see (at his corset factory) gave me more tea, which I accepted out of politeness; then I came on to the hotel and saw they had some magnificent pink iced cake so—as it was dark and pouring rain and there was nothing else to do—I ordered more tea! Now for dinner I've had oxtail soup, some nameless fish "supreme" but cooked with onions, of all inappropriate things, with potatoes and (tinned) peas, and some fairly horrible trifle smothered in synthetic cream—very sickly. *Not* what I should call

38. *Oxford Companion to the Theater.* Phyllis Hartnoll was with MacMillan from 1934 to 1969. She was a lecturer at the Royal Academy of Dramatic Arts in London 1950–1954, and a visiting lecturer at Princeton, Yale, and Purdue Universities in the United States.
39. Mary Renault won the Metro-Goldwyn-Mayer Annual Novel Award ($125,000) for *Return to Night.*

a good meal—though it all *looked* very tempting. Poor chefs! They do their best with very odd materials these days. Anyway, now my belt feels tight and I'm distinctly sleepy—but that's this wretched romantic soft-light (there's also sweet(?) music) in the hotel "palm lounge." The nearest approach to a palm that I can see is some beastly pink paper chrysanthemums in a vase on the piano. And this is Bristol's Grand Hotel! However, there is perhaps some excuse for it all. Bristol was most terribly bombed. This is my first visit to this famous, old city, and I was horrified to see how much of it has been destroyed. I've not seen any place so bad. The centre of the city, where all the great shops and commercial premises were, just isn't there any more. The "streets" are just paths through acres of topless cellars and rubble. I had the greatest difficulty in finding my way to the hotel, and I was misled by a bus inspector who told me it wasn't worth-while taking a bus (it was rush hour and I expect he wanted to save all his seats for homegoing workers, not Grand Hotel pluto-crats(!) like me). I walked for 20 minutes across this almost trackless area of devastation so it must have been at least a mile (in the dusk and the rain!) [.] I would normally never stay indoors on a visit to a new place, but would be out sight-seeing, rain or fine; but what I saw of Bristol in that first 20 minutes took all the heart out of me. So per-haps I should not jeer at the pink paper flowers and the dreary lounge. The hotel is an island in a sea of bomb-prairie. Several of the other hotels in the town just disappeared in the blitz.

Bath is another city I have visited today for the first time. I was unfortunate in the weather—pouring rain and no views of the hills that must surround the city so beautifully—but the man I went to see drove me round a bit. . . . He himself has a most lovely house (mansion) in Lansdowne Crescent; one of the show-place Regency terraces. But there was blitz-damage everywhere; his house had been blasted and blasted again, but he is one of the lucky ones (or let us be honest—one of the wealthy ones who can afford to get things done) and he has got his house repaired. His furniture—all genuine pieces of the period, and of great value—had been blown into hundreds of pieces (by blast—not a direct hit) but they had raked over all the rubble, even out in the garden and down the street, and a skilled man has built up the furniture again so that the joins are scarcely to be seen. By the way, he was not allowed to keep his whole house for himself and family—he was allowed 4 rooms; the rest was requisitioned for evacuated Civil Servants, and those are still there. Four-fifths of his factory was also requisitioned by the Ministry of Food for storage space, and he has just got it back. But that was perhaps a good turn, for the Min. of Food did a lot of damage for which they are now paying handsomely, and my man is getting a beautifully done-up next-to-new factory! (The Government Departments don't mind paying damages. They simply take it out of the taxes which people like me pay!)

We're still in a frightfully penurious state nationally but more things are getting back into the shops. I bought a small vacuum hand-washer the other day—something I've longed for all through the war but couldn't get. One of our great London household stores had received a consignment of 4 (before the war they would have ordered in thousands), and I was lucky enough to get one. (In fact I bought 2—one to give away to somebody I know will rejoice to have it.) But it was simply the copper contraption—no handle. I had to get somebody else to put a bit of a broom shank in the slot to make it useable. A lot of our returning amenities are like that—incomplete; but one takes the bits that *are* available and is thankful!

I've been indulging in an orgy of spending. It's a sort of reflex action after years of doing without. I'm not normally an extravagant person, but I can't resist this urge to spend money, or to acquire things, which has been coming on me lately! I've bought dinner knives, forks (second hand pre-war stuff—there still isn't anything new worth buying), and 3 silver jugs (also old), and a copper kettle (old) and a mincing machine . . . and a couple of pictures, and three hats!!! (Hats aren't rationed.) It's a sort of kleptomania—you see something you've not seen for years and you'd die to possess it. I daren't think how much I've spent in the past six months. . . . But clothes aren't so easy to buy, especially good woolens, and shoes. (I shall *have* to come to America, to get some shoes!) I spent from July till the beginning of November haunting the shops for a twin set (sweater and cardigan), which Mother and Father said they would give me for my birthday, and finally I found one—*literally* one! At Harrods, biggest store of all. They had *one*, and I pounced on it, and by good luck it was a nice cherry colour that I can wear. Shoes I have not been able to find at all—one has to queue endlessly, and I just haven't time. I haven't got a pair of shoes to carry me dry, so if it rains I have to get wet feet or wear my snowboots (which I mostly do).

This letter is getting too big to travel by air. Well, I shall send it in separate envelopes. Once I start talking to you I don't like to stop. There's heaps I'd like to tell you yet. How I went to the opera on Monday to hear *The Barber of Seville,* and how I'm taking three youngsters to a thrilling-to-think-about production of the 17th-century masque, *The Faerie Queen* (by Purcell and Inigo Jones!!) at Covent Garden on Dec. 14. And, how I'm going to Christmas Parties at the Soroptimist Club (did I tell you I was on the Executive, also Press and Publicity offices?) and the BPW Club and the Women's Press Club (did I tell you I was Assistant Hon. Secretary?)—and how, in fact, I have a whale of a time, though I sometimes wonder if I wouldn't show more sense to stay at home and read a quiet book! My current life and your current life could hardly be more different, could they? I suppose I really love the speed and movement of London life, and I doubt if I could stand up to the rigours of your life at the ranch, but your life has a permanent and solid worth which mine lacks utterly, and I almost envy you the space and quiet in which you spend your days. All the same, I feel your life must be very hard and comfortless sometimes. You are a most brave and admirable person to live it so and yet keep a kind and loving heart towards such undeserving light-weights as I—and to keep, too, your fine ideals and your spirit of service to humanity. Your kindness towards me makes me ashamed. In all our busy-ness and responsi[bili]ties and cares you spare thought and effort to the idea of sending me gifts, and I feel a sort of guilt in letting you! . . .

We have just won (after a lot of agitation) permission to send food parcels to Germany. Unfortunately this is limited to rationed foods, and those are the things we can least well afford to give. But we can at least do without our sweets, and they are certainly going to the German children. Cecil and I are determined to save up a parcel somehow before Christmas. Apart from rationed food and soap, I learned the other night from a Soroptimist friend who has been in Germany recently that *BOOKS* are a desperately urgent need in Germany. She told of school classes of 30–40 children with only 2 or 3 books among them, and of student teachers without books at all. Well, that is one direction in which Cecil and I can help, for we have lots of books, including many in German, and we are going through our respective libraries and sending everything we can spare that's suitable. I'd like to send my whack to individuals, in the hope that the feeling of personal friendliness might better help to heal the bitterness of war; but I don't know anybody. However, there are organisations which will distribute parcels.

It is 10:30 p.m. and time I was in my bed. If I don't retire from this cup-chinking lounge soon, I'll be tempted to order more tea! Tomorrow I go on to Bridgewater in Somerset to visit the "Partos" brassiere factory—then home again to sleep in my own bed tomorrow night. I don't really like being away from the flat!

This is my last sheet of thin paper, so I will end here. I will write again before Christmas, Phylabe dear. Will you be with your Dad for Christmas, or bringing Christmas Eve lambs into the world again, as last year? I hope you have a *happy* Christmas, whichever way you spend it, dearest girl.

Goodnight now. I love you lots and long to hear from you again.

Ever your Edith

✉ **35**
29 Stanley Gardens London W 11
December 10, 1946

Dearest Phylabe

This shuttle-service post is most thrilling. This morning brought two letters from you, one post-marked in Colorado at 2:30 pm on the 7th and the other on the 6th. It's just too amazing to think of! . . . Yes, I'm all for air mail—more letters even if shorter ones. I did get rather a shock at the postage on mine, but that was because it was my first air mail letter and I didn't know about the weight. This one won't be nearly so expensive—and though it could be nearly as heavy, because I was just over the $1/2$ ounce weight, it won't be, because I haven't much time. . . .

I've been getting very tired of corsetry and underwear, and now that we are starting off on our new journal *Underwear and Stockings* (meaning Hosiery—knitted stuff), I feel more and more like throwing it up. We'll see what the New Year brings. . . . What I'd like to do would be a rather (but not too) highbrow cultural magazine for women. There's not one just like my idea of one, and though I haven't mentioned it to anybody yet I think I might suggest it to Mr. Smedley. He might be willing to back it, and of course I couldn't afford to do it without somebody with money behind me. . . . But I don't suppose Mr. Smedley has enough money to carry a new public journal in present conditions, so perhaps I will just keep my Cultural Women's to myself for the present. . . .

Last Saturday in a little antique shop in Notting Hill Gate (my London suburb, where I live) I saw some nice spoons and forks, thought they were very nice plate, and went in to price them. But they were Georgian silver, so I had to say No Thank You. I had thought they might cost £5 or so (6 table forks, 6 dessert forks, 6 dessert spoons), but I understood the man to say they would cost about £15. Later I was overcome by desire to own SILVER forks and spoons, and thought I would be extravagant and bang £15 on the set. Ever since then I've been enjoying the thought that I already practically owned a set of silver forks and spoons! Today at lunchtime I dashed on out to N.H.G. to buy them and—what do you think? The price was not £15 but £52. *Most* shattering. I suppose I ought to have known that silver (Georgian) sells at about 22s. per ounce, but having started out (and being still mainly stocked by) Woolworth's sixpence-a-piece cutlery my ideas of value are all wrong. But it's sad all the same.

Phylabe dear, you have made my mouth water with your mention of Mexican prints in a parcel for me! . . . Bother John L. Lewis if he holds it up (bother him anyway, as I imagine you'll agree). I'm so glad that dreadful strike is over, by the way. I hope your industry soon gets back to normal again. I will send you yesterday's *News Chronicle* with a leader on Lewis. I think the view expressed is the one fairly generally held here—that even if they have done good in the past, his methods are dangerous and wrong. . . .

To return to your most kind promise of parcels coming to me-wards, I am waiting all expectancy to discover what "formals" are! This is a new word to me! But as they will make me blouses (you say), they must be textiles of some sort, and as such I can assure you they will not only give me most enormous *pleasure*, but will fill a perilous gap in my needs as well. I have to warn you that you are going to receive Christmas presents of parachute cotton from the Base family this year! It was just too marvelous to be able to buy a whole parachute—26 square yards all told—Free of coupons! I passed some of it on to Chrissie, and the same sort of thoughts invaded her head as invaded mine! I started off valiantly to make Everybody presents of parachute cloth. . . .

The thought of the food parcels is entrancing too. It is most astonishing that you can order one to be sent me from Denmark!
. . .

Now it is ABSOLUTELY ESSENTIAL that I do some work! I "close" for "copy" for the January number today, and had a last whack of subbing to do, but I handed it to my new henchwoman to see what she could do with it. Hence my "holiday." Now I have only the leader to write, and a few paragraphs, and the Jan. number is done except for pasting up when the proofs come back next week. I'm planning to go home for Christmas, but the journey is going to be awful. I tried weeks ago to book sleeping berths there and back, but they had all gone; and today it suddenly occurred to me that I ought at least to try to book a seat (it has only recently become possible again to book seats on trains). Alas, all gone! So I shall either have to Q frantically for the few free seats, or put off my journey till Christmas Day, when the rush will be over. But I shouldn't reach home till 6 pm or so, and that would be just too disappointing. So I must join the free fight, I suppose, for the Christmas Eve trains. I feel very anxious to go home this year, for Mother is getting very frail, and in a letter this morning I hear she has been ill again. The cold is too much for her these days, I fear. She is very sweet and gentle, and I wish you could meet her. Father is a much more stalwart soul, though he has nothing on Mother for spirit. They're both rather marvelous, in fact!

So now—good night, my dearie. Another letter soon, I promise.

Ever your
Edith

✉ **36**
On the train—Sunday December 29, 1946

Belovedest
Christmas is over, and it's work tomorrow again, and "there is nothing left remarkable beneath the visiting moon." That's because Cecil and Theodore and I saw *Antony and Cleopatra* last Monday evening, with two of our most accomplished actors, Godfrey Tearle and Edith Evans in the name parts, and it was utterly magnificent. I never see a Shakespeare play without thinking there's no more satisfying entertainment, because it feeds the heart and the mind and—

so *richly*—the ear, and I go round in a state of word-intoxication for days after. My old editor, who brought me up journalistically right from the cradle, used to enjoin me to read daily, as he did, something of the Bible and something of Shakespeare. The result (in *him*), was that he wrote lovely flowing sonorous and poetic prose and saw all life as such stuff as dreams are made on. But of course, being a man and no Martha, *he* had no dishes to wash, shopping to do, potatoes to peel, clothes to mend, meals to plan. It irks me sorely, bitterly sometimes, that because of all the Martha-chores I (and most women) are set at such a disadvantage in the world of intellect which males inhabit so proudly. And the lordly males look down from their eminences and say pityingly that of course women haven't the mental capacity, or the creative ability, and all the masterpieces of the world have been created by men. How we could disenchant them, if we could get rid of our female consciences and reject the responsibilities of life as the average male does! And yet men like my Mr. Smedley have the impudence to suggest—assert—that women are poorer workers because they are always thinking about the shopping! They would pay us lower wages. But we ought to be paid *more* because we do so much more work in the world—whatever started me off on that? Oh yes. Just the irritation I sometimes feel because I (and other women) cannot buy narcissi to feed the soul because all their emotional and mental pence are used up on the dry bread of material maintenance—forgive me! It's not a Christmassy, New Yearly train of thought!

Have you had a happy Christmas, Phylabe dear? . . . Shall I tell you about my Christmas? I must start 'way back at last Saturday, Dec. 21st, when I spent the morning having my hair shampooed and set "on the top," "Edwardian" or "swept-up" (whichever description you prefer), and the late morning and afternoon queuing up at the shops, and the evening at the Soroptimist Club party. To go back to the shopping for a moment what do you think I bought? A (second-hand) mahogany chest, bow-fronted, of drawers! It is this awful urge to acquire! Can't resist it! But I do need more storage space, having only one small chest in my flat, so that clothes are aye higgledy piggledy. Then I went in my decent black frock and my new hair-do to the party, and had a lovely time, eating limitless supplies of creamy (synthetic but very good) cakes and playing games and winning two prizes . . . a packet of serviettes and a half pound of tea, which last was bread returning to one after being thrown upon the waters, for

I'd given all my spare tea towards a parcel for Germany, then been reminded it was tea week at the office so that I had to empty my caddy. Lucky, wasn't I?

On Sunday I had Cecil and Theodore to lunch and tea. Cecil is my fondest and truest and Theodore is his 19-year-old son, at present doing his war-service in forestry in Devon. I had collected their meat ration and promised to cook it for them, as Cecil (again no Martha!) cannot do more than boil a tea kettle in his bachelor flatlet. I was lucky enough to get a nice piece of lamb, which I roasted, along with potatoes and onions, and boiled sprouts; followed by apple charlotte (apples from Whickham garden) and coffee. Theodore brought me a tin of steak with the request that I'd make it into a pie for them to eat later in the week; so after lunch, while they listened-in (no Marthas) to a symphony-and-choral concert, I baked pastry and pies in the kitchenette. For tea—North Country variety, which is a meal, not just a refreshing snack—I gave them toasted dropped scones, mince pie, fruit cake, and jam tart. After tea, while we talked of Greek and Roman civilisation and letters (they talked, I listened) and music and the Labour Government, I sewed and sewed and sewed at my belated Christmas presents. They left at 9, and I went on sewing till 12:30 but was 1000 miles from finishing. Monday, of course, I spent at the office, meeting C & T at 6 pm for sandwiches and coffee before *Antony and Cleopatra*. After the theatre, we had supper at Cecil's—toast and margarine and tea and some funny Algerian(?) wine which may or may not have been the cause why we were so merry (like you, the Bases and most of their friends are non-drinkers and non-smokers, so this wine was in the nature of a joke). Most of our hilarity was occasioned by an unwittingly comic remark of mine—"why in the play, did they always talk of sexless Pompey?" Oh, oh! How Edith bowed her head in shame at not having known it was Sextus!! And how the tears rolled down all six cheeks with mirth! They took me home about midnight, and then I sat up till 3:45 a.m. [sewing] . . . and doing the ironing. Tuesday—office again, at least till lunchtime, when we . . . went out for a Christmas lunch. On the way Thirza and I did shopping—got TOMATOES, of all strange things at this time of the year. Heaven knows where they'd come from. And DATES IN SMART BOXES (ruination at 3s. and 2 points a box, but we couldn't resist 'em), and TANGERINES (also ruination at 3s. per pound, but so Christmassy). Then I went home and snatched 2 hours sleep before I packed, and at 10:30 Cecil arrived to escort me to the station. My 11:30 p.m. train didn't leave till 2 a.m.!! And didn't arrive at Newcastle till 9:30 instead of 6:30. But I got a taxi without any delay and was home to eat my Christmas breakfast (bacon and egg!!!) by 10 a.m. . . .

My stay at Whickham was largely filled with eating! My kind little Mother, who spares no effort to make her prodigal daughter's visits happy, believes that four square meals a day are a necessary ingredient of enjoyment. So we ate huge breakfasts at 9, large luncheons at 1, huge teas at 5 and huge suppers at 9. My willingness to please her by eating all she put before me only just lasted out the four days! I shall now fast for the rest of the week and get back to normal! But in my bag I have a fat 5 lb. chicken collected from Aunt Annie's farm on Friday! And my Christmas Cake from Mother. So it won't be a very good fast!

The weather has been glorious—sparkling frosty sunshine and air like champagne. Not so heady as your mountain air I'm sure, but heavenly after London's soft air. I've done a little bit of walking in it, along our lonnens and over our fell; but mostly I've been visiting . . . and last night Chrissie and I went to an informal and nearly all-women dance, and danced barn dances and schottisches and polkas till I, at any rate, could hop no more. Today I'm spending mostly in the train and most uncomfortably for it is crammed with people so that movement is virtually impossible. I have a sleeping baby's head on the forearm of my writing arm so I write from the wrist only like a bad pianist. 'Scuse bad writing, please. . . .

We ought to be in King's Cross in 10 minutes, though it's dark and I've no idea where we are or how late we are running; but I'm weak with heat and lack of oxygen in this sweltering squash of humanity and shall end here with the largest and loveliest possible wishes to you for everything that is good and happy in the coming year.

My love and loving thoughts, to you always
Edith

1947
January 20, 1947–September 2, 1947

29 Stanley Gardens
London W 11
Jan. 20, 1947

Dear love

I am a bad girl, thoroughly lazy and idle, no good, an artful dodger. By every law and canon I ought at this moment to be writing my leader for February. The printers are waiting for it; publication will be delayed if I don't do it. And I'm not going to do it till I've written a wee scrap at least to my Phylabe. I'm tired, I'm sick, I'm aching and dog-weary. Can't decide yet whether it's a duodenal ulcer or pleurisy. It may be something to do with the day of the week, which is Monday (Bluesday). Or it may just be that obscure malady which is apt to descend upon me at this last minute of each month, when all's done but the Leader and I feel like a cornered rat—and a thousand little devils all around me tempt me with reason after reason why I should do this, that and the other first and put off starting on the hated, dreaded, abominable and obnoxious Leading Article. My excuse at the moment for writing to you is that it will soften up my writing muscles for the Great Job—quite a good excuse, really! I certainly need some limbering up. I've just been home for lunch—and that was wicked of me, too, for it takes 2 hours, whereas I could have lunched in town within one hour and been back here and had the Leader written by this time! What it is to be born a prevaricator! It's not my FAULT, is it? Just my misfortune.

Anyway, darling, a letter is overdue from me to you, because TWO SIMPLY WONDERFUL PARCELS have arrived at 29 within the past few days. . . . Do you know what was in the parcels you had sent? I think you probably don't, so I shall tell you. Well, first to arrive was the Danish one. It contained—a 2-lb. tin of butter!!! (16 weeks ration! This is being kept for the present with a very special purpose in view), a 2-lb. tin of steak (this is going to help me to throw a party which I've been wanting to do very much but just didn't feel equal to on the commissariat side); a carton of sticky stuff called Sirolade, which doesn't fall into any known category but as it reminds me in consistency of the cod-liver-oil-and-malt I used to take as a child—though it doesn't taste of c.l.o.—I am eating with a spoon feeling perfectly sure it will do me good in one way or another. Then there was a carton of cheese of a superior kind such as we haven't had for years; and a tin of cream which I forthwith golloped up greedily and rapturously. So you see that was a really hunger-satisfying parcel, and I at once felt a great deal fatter for just having opened it out.

Then your American parcel came, and was much more FUN, as well as being full of solid food, because the contents were in lots of small packets, very thrilling to open out. This one contained—a packet of large raisins; 2 packets of small raisins; tin of sardines; tin of Party Loaf, packet of soap flakes, tin of lobster (ooh, delicious; can't ever buy it here because it's frightfully costly in points—would take all my month's ration for one small tin); tin of lemon juice (very, very precious, though I DID get a pound of lemons at Christmas—first ones for ages); then, to round everything off beautifully, a box of delicious sweeties. So you see how you have enriched me! . . . I can only say . . . Thank you, and leave you to imagine—as with your sensitive understanding I know you can—what delight and happiness you have brought me.

I can't extend this letter much longer—in view of that dratted Leader—but I will just answer your questions about duty on parcels. I don't remember that I have ever had to pay duty on any of yours—certainly not within the past few years; and I understand that for worn clothing none is ever required. Thirza had a parcel some time ago from Virginia and had to pay some duty (about £2) because it contained NEW clothing, but Thirza says it was well worth it. . . . Mr. Smedley and various other friends received gifts of stockings at Christmas without being required to pay duty, and no doubt small packets of that kind just slip through. I've not heard of anybody being required to give up coupons. Does that make things clearer?

I'm told the thing to do is to write "Unsolicited Gift" on the parcel in large letters.

Must stop, dear. . . .

Ever
Edith

✉ **38**
29 Stanley Gardens
London W. 11
Sept 2/47

Dearest and best of Phylabes—

The carpets are up, the curtains are down, the packing is half done and the flat is like a slum—I'm eating a vegetarian rissole presented by my kind next-flat neighbour—I have to get down to sewing my wedding frock (sadly behind hand) without delay—there's a bale of ironing waiting to be done—Cecil and I have a list of 73 jobs to see to before the end of the week—but I'm going to start a letter to you while I'm eating my supper, even though I know it will *never* become the letter I'd like it to be.

My very, very dear—your wedding gift to us has left us simply overwhelmed. Words *absolutely* fail to express all that we felt when we opened out your wedding card and found that most wonderful, most generous gift. How very, very kind you are. I just can't think what I've done to deserve such wonderful friends—but I haven't done anything at all and indeed don't deserve anything at all of such loving thought and help. I've been feeling recently almost too painfully much that "to him that hath shall be given"—having my beloved Cecil was more than I'd dared to hope from life, but, while I was still dazed with wonder and joy over that, more and more and more love kept pouring over me from friends I had hardly known *were* friends. I just didn't know people could be so kind. If I could tell you of *all* the eager offerings of little bags of sugar, of the delvings into treasure chests for prewar scraps of lace to trim undies, of our Bessie's delicious thought of sending me a "shower" all the way across from Victoria, B.C. (even the rice to throw at the wedding!!!)—you would dissolve into tears, as I have done more than once. Perhaps it's because I'm growing old, because I've known much sadness and learned to live with it—perhaps just

Mr. and Mrs. W. W. Base
request the pleasure of the company of

Miss Phylube Houston

at a Reception at 52 Reddons Road
Beckenham, Kent,
on Saturday, September 20th, 1947
at 3 o'clock
following the marriage of their daughter

Edith
to
Mr. Cecil B. Bacon
at the Office of the Registrar,
Royal Borough of Kensington

52 Reddons Road
Bekenham,
Kent.   R. S. V. P.

Invitation to wedding reception for Edith Base and Cecil Bacon.

because like Levin in *Anna Karenina,* like Nigel in *Portrait in a Mirror,* like all the lovers of all ages, my heart is super-full and my perception ties all hyper-charged—for some or all of these reasons I'm finding happiness almost too much to bear—and a sudden, unexpected, wonderful expression of love such as your letter and your gift brought, just makes me dissolve into tears. Don't mind if I shed a tear or two more this minute, will you, dearie? I do thank you from my heart, and Mr. Houston, too, of course, for piling so much more happiness onto the top of my soaring hill of rapture. Everything is marvelous. Most of all this wiping out of 5000 miles of distance between hearts—.

Breakfast time on Sept. 3. now. Got the sleeves pinned into my dress and the hem turned up last night, but need permission to go

Wedding photo, *front row:* Mrs. Base, Cecil Bacon, Edith and Mr. Base; *back row:* Edith Cullingworth, Miss Taylor (Edith's English teacher), Edith's Aunt Annie, Reginald Bacon, Edith's Aunt Alice, Theodore Bacon, and Chrissie Base.

and fit myself in front of my neighbour's long mirror (something I lack) before I can stitch 'em. Tonight I'm going to the annual meeting and dinner of the Corset Guild, so shall get nothing else done. Must go, though, to bid my farewell and introduce my successor (Margaret Kornitzer) to the folks. I leave Corsetry and U. the day after tomorrow—isn't it lovely! On Monday I "flit" (is that an American term too for a house removal?). From Monday my address will be:

    52 Reddons Road
    Beckenham,
    Kent
and from Sept. 20 my name will be
    Mrs. Cecil B. Bacon
Isn't it lovely?

Edith and Cecil Bacon, on
Oxford Street in London,
September 1949.

I'd love to tell you all about the house, but there isn't time this time. Ask Bessie to tell you as much as she knows. When I'm married I'm going to write you *real* letters—no more hurried, ill-written, incomplete, unsatisfactory snippets.

I'm thinking about you two girls and Charlie and your Dad, all together now as I write. Have a lovely holiday, my very dears,—how I do wish I could tele-see you (better still be with you, but that seems too fantastically impossible whereas after hearing your voice across the ocean it seems quite imaginable to *see* you.—By the way, Thirza and I are *horrified* to know how much that phone call finally cost you). . . .

Must fly now—9 a.m. and I'm due at office at 9:30 (30 minutes journey away and I'm still only part dressed, and I *must* go and buy some *bread!*).

My best and dearest love to you all, and again thank you, thank you, thank you, for your gift and all your friendship.

Ever your
Edith
P.S. I've not said Thank You for the veiling—I *do,* now!